THE WELLCOME ARCHAEOLOGICAL RESEARCH EXPEDITION
TO THE NEAR EAST PUBLICATIONS
VOLUME I

LACHISH I
(TELL ED DUWEIR)

THE LACHISH LETTERS

GENERAL VIEW OF TELL ED DUWEIR LOOKING EAST
showing road and gateway area extreme right of mound.
Photograph by R. Richmond Brown.

THE WELLCOME ARCHAEOLOGICAL RESEARCH EXPEDITION
TO THE NEAR EAST

LACHISH I

(TELL ED DUWEIR)

THE LACHISH LETTERS

BY

HARRY TORCZYNER
BIALIK PROFESSOR OF HEBREW IN THE UNIVERSITY OF JERUSALEM

LANKESTER HARDING

ALKIN LEWIS

J. L. STARKEY

PUBLISHED FOR

THE TRUSTEES OF THE LATE SIR HENRY WELLCOME

BY THE

OXFORD UNIVERSITY PRESS

LONDON   NEW YORK   TORONTO

1938

The contents of this book are copyright. Neither letterpress nor
illustrations may be reproduced without permission of the Trustees
of the late Sir Henry Wellcome.

Printed and bound in England for
the Trustees of the late Sir Henry Wellcome
at the University Press, Oxford.

THIS BOOK

THE FIRSTFRUIT OF EXCAVATION AT LACHISH

IS GRATEFULLY DEDICATED TO

Sɪʀ HENRY WELLCOME, LL.D., D.Sc., F.S.A., F.R.S.

WHOSE CONSTANT ENTHUSIASM FOR RESEARCH

INTO THE SCIENCE AND HISTORY OF MAN

LEADS ON TO DEEPER KNOWLEDGE

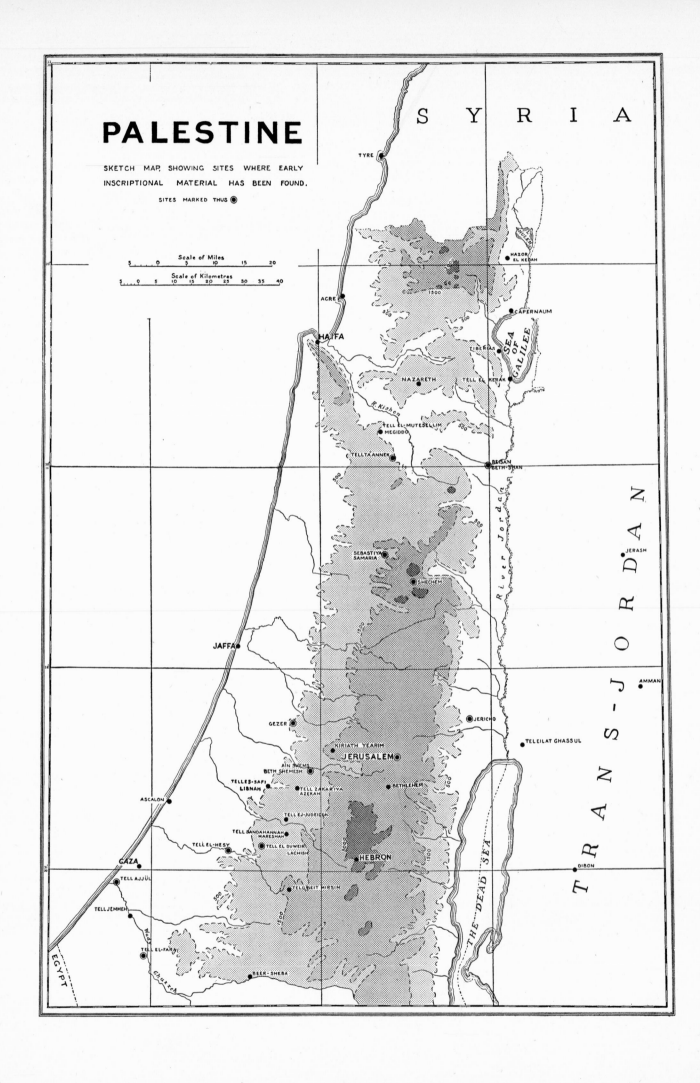

PALESTINE

SKETCH MAP, SHOWING SITES WHERE EARLY
INSCRIPTIONAL MATERIAL HAS BEEN FOUND.

SITES MARKED THUS ⊙

Scale of Miles

Scale of Kilometres

SYRIA

TRANS-JORDAN

EGYPT

TYRE

HAZOR
EL KEDAH

ACRE

CAPERNAUM

HAIFA

TIBERIAS

SEA
OF
GALILEE

NAZARETH

TELL EL KERAK

R. Kishon

TELL EL-MUTESELLIM
MEGIDDO

TELL TAANNEK

BEISAN
BETH-SHAN

River Jordan

JERASH

SEBASTIYA
SAMARIA

SHECHEM

JAFFA

AMMAN

GEZER

JERICHO

TELEILAT GHASSUL

KIRIATH YEARIM

JERUSALEM

AIN SHEMS
BETH SHEMESH

BETHLEHEM

TELL ES-SAFI
LIBNAH

TELL ZAKARIYA
AZEKAH

ASCALON

TELL EJ-JUDEIGEH

TELL SANDAHANNAH
MARESHAH

TELL EL-HESY

TELL EL DUWEIR
LACHISH

HEBRON

GAZA

DIBON

THE DEAD SEA

TELL AJJUL

TELL BEIT MIRSIM

TELL JEMMEH

Wadi Ghuzzeh

TELL EL-FARA

BEER-SHEBA

FOREWORD

THE Lachish Letters, found at Tell ed Duweir, the site of ancient Lachish, are given here in preliminary reading and explanation, as the result of my studies of the ostraca in Palestine, repeated examination in London at the Wellcome Research Institution, during June and July, 1935, with a final revision of readings and interpretations in Jerusalem in April, 1936.

In these studies I was considerably aided by the staff of the Expedition; I discussed with Mr. Starkey the many questions arising out of the documents, and his archaeological observations helped to bring the words of the old scribes to life; Mr. Richmond Brown's excellent photographs taught me to see more clearly what seemed almost invisible on the original sherds; and last, but not least, Mr. L. Harding, the assistant and draughtsman of the Expedition, checked with me all my readings, and his sharp eye and unbiased mind gave me a very helpful criticism of my experiments. Mr. Harding has added to this publication the hand copies, the comparative chart of alphabets with notes, and the description and measurements of the sherds. Mr. Starkey has contributed the historical report on the discovery of the letters and the archaeological facts concerning them.

For all this kindness I desire to express my profound gratitude to the Wellcome Archaeological Research Expedition who, through the Director and his staff, bestowed upon me the great privilege of being instrumental in restoring the Lachish Letters, this lost chapter of the Holy Scriptures, to the world.

My thanks are also due to Dr. E. Rosenthal, Dr. S. Rawidowicz and Mr. C. Rabin, who, during my sojourn in London, 1935, helped me to procure books and references needed for my rather hurried work.

The reading of the Lachish ostraca has been a very fascinating, but also a very difficult, task. During my studies the new facts arising have more than once changed my views on even main questions connected with the interpretation of our letters, and new facts may necessitate still further alterations. All these changes have only added to my belief in the great importance of these invaluable documents.

The reading of these ostraca should not be attempted on the basis of the photographs alone, good though they be; blemishes, pieces of grit in the body of the sherd, scratches, etc., cannot in many cases be distinguished from ink marks. On the other hand, many of the characters are actually clearer in the photographs than on the originals, and only a careful collation of the two can produce any satisfactory or reliable result.

H. T.

B

SKETCH OF LACHISH

showing double fortifications constructed by Rehoboam and maintained until the fort's final destruction, 588–587 B.C.
Note arrangement of outer and inner gates, flanked by towers, and position of palace-fort crowning the site.

Drawing by H. H. McWilliams from aerial photograph and plan of actual remains excavated.

CONTENTS

LIST OF ILLUSTRATIONS

THE DISCOVERY

THE Wellcome Archaeological Research Expedition to the Near East, under the auspices of the late Sir Henry Wellcome, Sir Charles Marston and Sir Robert Mond, excavated at Tell ed Duweir, for the third season, from November, 1934, to April, 1935.

In the New Year work was resumed on the bastion and gateways in continuation of the first campaign, when the Persian structures and roadway had been removed. The immediate problem was, therefore, to examine the earlier level; this work was done under Mr. John Richmond's supervision.

The Persian road was constructed on limestone and chalk rubble about two feet thick; immediately below was a well-preserved cobbled surface, covered with a thin film of ash and burnt debris. Only that part of the road surface which had been cut into by a drainage trench passing out from under the north jamb of the inner gate had been disturbed. This drain sweeps southward in a bold curve, passes under the outer gate, and continues below the descending outer roadway.

Three rooms against the south wall of the bastion open on to the road between the inner and outer gateways. Only the lower and foundation courses of these chambers remain, and those to the west, flanking the outer gate, are damaged by fire. The external wall to the south has naturally suffered most, and the roughly-hewn blocks of both "nari" and "mizzi" limestone are split by thermal fractures, or are partly calcined. The mud mortar was reduced to a pink-grey powder. A reference to *page* 223 shows the arrangement of these rooms within the bastion.

The first room to be examined was Fig. F. 18 c, underlying the foundation courses of a Persian structure, possibly a tower, which had not been affected by fire, and it was not until the last course was removed that any burnt debris became visible. At first this consisted of limestone flakes in pinky-yellow earth, derived from mud brickwork. At this point the top of a stone bench was exposed against the south wall; just below this the colour changed to grey, and the lower levels were quite black. The soil contained much carbonized vegetable matter; in the upper zone of this deposit, close under the east wall, fragments of 16 of the Lachish Letters were found.[1] These inscribed potsherds are only a small proportion of hundreds of jar fragments found in this room. As so many had been affected by fire, it is impossible to know how much correspondence may have been destroyed in this way. The black ash lay on the flat stones which paved the floor; their upper surface was blackened by fire, though the heat was not sufficient to cause thermal fractures. The outer wall was 85 cm. thick, and the eastern jamb of the outer gate was built against it; there was no north wall to the room. The masonry of this period is poor; where a stone wall is two courses thick, few, if any, headers are used to bond the two faces. This faulty system of construction is characteristic of provincial building in the hill country to-day, and much damage to houses during the earthquake of 1927 was due to it.

Under the paving was an earlier plastered floor to the chamber. It consisted of crushed "nari" limestone, and showed no traces of burning, as it had been sufficiently protected by the paving.

---

[1] The position is marked by a cross on the Plan, *page* 223.

To the north, the floor surface merged into the level of the roadway without any threshold. It is quite certain that the conflagration inside the room was directly connected with the firing of the bastion from without, and is contemporary with the final assault, as evidenced at so many points along the line of the city's outer defence wall. Huge bonfires had been maintained to breach it, though the south-west corner of the mound and the bastion probably bore the brunt of the attack.

Our first season's work on the defences indicated that this firing should be equated with the destruction of the city at the end of the Judaean kingdom, at the time of Nebuchadnezzar's campaign shortly before he destroyed Jerusalem in 586 B.C. (*See Palestine Exploration Fund, Quarterly Statement*, 1933, *page* 198.) The burnt olive stones found in the embers of the fire suggest the autumn as a seasonal date.

Professor Torczyner's researches reveal the homogeneous nature of the correspondence, and the fact that five letters once formed part of the same pot emphasizes the short intervals between the dispatch of at least some of them.

From its position between the two gateways and the open side to the road, the chamber might have served as a guard-room, and messages might well have been received there by the senior officer. The correspondence dealing with military and political matters passed through the hands of this man, although there is no clue to his rank. However, " lord Ya'ush" may have been Governor of the City, whose archives would probably have been housed in the region of the palace-fort or keep, or perhaps he was only the senior military officer.

The bastion, which protects the two city gates, would naturally form a key position; apart from controlling the gates, it connected the battlements of the outer or lower defence wall with the inner city wall. (*See* the sketch showing restorations of the city's defences and the position of the keep, *page* 8.) The evidence may imply that Ya'ush used the region of the bastion as his headquarters during the military preparations for the impending siege.

An alternative suggestion is, however, that this room, with its stone bench against the south wall, may have been used as a court-room. That the region of the gateway was a meeting-place for the city elders, where tribal law and custom was debated, is amply attested in the Old Testament. It may therefore be that the Lachish ostraca are documents which were relative to an inquiry dealt with at what may well have been the final sitting of the local tribunal.

Professor Torczyner, on the evidence of his readings, favours this view, and the absence of internal documents may be explained by the use of papyrus for the official Government side of the correspondence. Though such papyri may have been in the room, they would have been totally destroyed in the fire.

After the first inscribed sherd was found by us, on January 29th, 1935, all the pottery fragments from the floor deposit were taken down to the camp house, scrutinized that evening, and carefully washed in filtered water, the forefinger being used to remove any dirt that adhered to the surface. No brush or abrasive action was employed. On that memorable evening we saw many texts for the first time. Dr. Aage Schmidt, of Denmark, who was staying with us, was an enthusiastic witness of the discoveries.

The search for inscribed fragments was now extended under the supervision of Mr. C. H. Inge; all soil from the Persian roadway was passed through quarter-inch mesh sieves, so that the smallest fragments should not evade us. The dump-head, where soil had been thrown before the discovery of the ostraca, was also sieved. This did not amount to much, as only three truck-loads

12

had been taken away. One fragment rewarded our efforts, No. XVII, and another, No. XVI, was picked up about a foot below the surface of the Persian road in the ballast used for its construction. This fragment is perhaps the most tantalizing of all, in view of Professor Torczyner's suggestion that it formed part of a letter which probably contained the name of the prophet (*see page* 173).

All potsherds, large and small, were subjected to the most careful examination by Mr. Harding and Miss Tufnell. This work, which occupied some weeks, resulted in the discovery of many missing fragments, and three or four new letters. All these were in a very poor state, and some had been overlooked in our initial search.

At first I feared the inscriptions were but ordinary business accounts, or magical charms, and I sought the earliest opportunity to visit our greatest authority on Palestinian Archaeology and Semitic Philology, Père Vincent, of the École Biblique et Archéologique Française, who immediately allayed my fears. On reading the greetings in Letters II and III he recognized that they were documents of a literary nature, with the exception of one, which he saw was a list of private names.

The following day Père Vincent gave me further information, and handed me a complete translation of the list of names in Letter I. He pointed out that Letter II had been addressed to my "lord Ya'ush", and read in line 14 of Letter III the title "sar ha-ṣaba'", commander of the army.

The similarity between our writing and the Samaria ostraca at first suggested to him an eighth-century date, in accordance with Dr. Reisner's suggested dating.[1] However, after the list of names had been read, such an early date seemed improbable, and he then suggested the seventh century. These deductions were made in complete ignorance of the archaeological context, which I intentionally withheld. This evidence undoubtedly pointed to an early sixth-century B.C. date. His impartial dating on palaeographic grounds is of no little significance when we see the slight evidence available for the date of the Samaria material; a study of the comparative chart facing *page* 220, drawn by Mr. Harding from the photographs of the ostraca, emphasizes the striking similarity of the script.

As a result of Professor Torczyner's readings our "archaeological" date is upheld, and it seems impossible that nearly two centuries separate the letters from the Samaria ostraca. That an almost cursive script, found in towns so widely separated as Lachish in Judah, and Samaria in Israel, should remain static for that period is also unlikely. It is fortunate, therefore, that the Lachish Letters can be so closely dated. Mr. S. Yeivin, with Dr. H. L. Ginsberg and Dr. B. Maisler, examined the ostraca in camp; in the limited time at their disposal they made an independent preliminary reading of Letters I, II and III, and told us something of the first six lines of Letter IV. It was left to Professor Torczyner to discover the full significance of the text on the reverse of this letter, where the forts of Lachish and Azeqah are mentioned.

In the second week of February, Professor Harry Torczyner, Bialik Professor of Hebrew in the University, Jerusalem, very kindly consented to examine our find, and from that time till his departure from London, where he spent some five weeks in intensive study, he has ungrudgingly devoted all his energies and scholarship to our problem.

---

[1] *Harvard Excavations at Samaria*, I, *page* 227, and *see page* 31 of this volume.

The difficult business of photographing the ostraca was undertaken by the Expedition's photographer, Mr. R. Richmond Brown. His initial experiments resulted in a series of photographs which were invaluable in preliminary decipherment. Mr. L. Harding set himself the task of preparing hand copies of the letters, twice actual size; he appends an account of his methods, and details of the potsherds which bear the inscriptions. The improved results of later photographic experiments were a valuable aid to the decipherment of the letters, and considerably more was visible of Nos. III, V and VI in the full-scale photographs than could be read by the aid of a lens. In all cases the best definition was obtained from full-scale pictures.

Mr. Harding's excellent hand copies, made independently of any readings of the text, have materially assisted these researches, as Professor Torczyner points out in his Preface.

Since the ostraca have been in London, thanks to the generous permission of Mr. E. T. Richmond, Director of the Department of Antiquities, Jerusalem, the Lachish Letters have been submitted to further photographic experiment. Professor Laurie has examined them under infra-red and ultra-violet light; Mr. Rhys-Jones, of the Courtauld Institute, kindly photographed one or two with his new apparatus; Colonel Mansfield also undertook similar experiments; and Sir Robert Robertson, of the Government Laboratory, London, made various photographic experiments and examined the composition of the ink. We are deeply indebted to all these gentlemen for the great interest they have shown, and for their part in the solution of these problems.

However, Mr. Richmond Brown's photographs remained the best available, until Mr. Alkin Lewis, of King's College, London, introduced us to Mr. Olaf Bloch of Messrs. Ilford Ltd., who, by using half-tone panchromatic plates with a tri-colour red filter, obtained the best pictures we had seen of Nos. III, IV and VI (August 16, 1935). Mr. Richmond Brown's photographs had been made on Ilford panchromatic film, with a red filter.

Mr. Alkin Lewis offered to continue investigations on the composition of the ink used in the letters, and made further suggestions for intensifying it. The results of his many lines of inquiry are given in his accompanying report. Dr. C. M. Wenyon, of The Wellcome Research Institution, kindly gave Mr. Lewis all the necessary laboratory facilities.

Finally, the Expedition tenders grateful thanks to all those who have read the proofs.

J. L. S.

INTRODUCTION TO THE TEXTS

THE Lachish Letters are the first real personal documents in pre-exilic Hebrew writing found in Palestine. Very few written documents had previously been found in the country of the Bible, only the well-known Siloam inscription, a few names of months on the Gezer calendar, nearly 70 legible ostraca from the Samaria excavations, repeating such words as "a jar of wine (or oil) from a certain place to N.N.", one almost illegible short ostracon from Ophel, Jerusalem, and a great number of names inscribed on seals, weights and jar stamps. How poor this material was can be judged from the fact that in all these inscriptions not even the full alphabet was preserved; the ṭ being very doubtful in the Gezer calendar, and—outside ancient Israel—in an equally doubtful example from the Mesha' stone and in a clumsy development upon jar stamps.

This material will now be considerably augmented by the 18 ostraca from Lachish with nearly 90 fully readable and some fragmentary lines of clear writing, beautiful language and highly important contents.

The script of Lachish makes us realize for the first time that the Phoenician-Hebrew alphabet, known until now mostly from Phoenician inscriptions upon stone, is not really a writing intended for engraving, but a script invented, and used particularly, for writing in ink upon papyrus, hide (parchment) and potsherds. We now realize that the ancient Jews could write quickly and boldly, in an artistic flowing hand, with the loving penmanship of those who enjoy writing. The Lachish Letters, not sent from Jerusalem, but (with one exception) from a smaller place (as suggested later, probably from Qiryat-Ye'arim) are written by different scribes, as proved by the different forms of the signs used in the letters. Thus, writing was almost common knowledge, and not a secret art known only to a very few; it certainly was practised by many officials in the king's service.

This writing took many centuries to develop, and proves to have been in use, not only in the last years of Judah's kingdom, but for many generations before. In their general features the alphabets of Lachish strongly resemble the writing of the Ophel ostracon and to a lesser degree, but still closely enough, that of the ostraca of Samaria, though these documents do not equal the artistic penmanship of our letters. The writing itself, even to the feature of the dividing dots between the words, reminds us of the Samaritan writing, the last living development of the ancient Hebrew script. Jews in general use the square characters developed from the "Assyrian" script, a branch of the Aramaic offshoot of the Canaanite alphabet. A comparison of the writing of the scribes of Lachish with that of the Samaritan priests, particularly in their copies of the Pentateuch, shows not only the near relationship between the ancient and the late script, but also the decadence of this almost extinct sect, which has yet, as we now see, faithfully preserved its traditions.

We now know how the ancient books of Kings and Prophets were written, according to the script, the division between the words, their splitting at the end of the lines, and their spelling; knowledge of these facts will from now on be the basis for any work on textual criticism of the Bible. There certainly were later stages of different writing and spelling in the history of textual tradition of the Bible, which should not be overlooked, but any work upon the text will have to start from the original conditions as shown in the Lachish Letters. At least in his mind the scholar must visualize the Biblical text re-copied in this original form.

Since the letters are originals (*see later*) we find no examples of faulty readings in them; but as rather hastily written messages, they are not free from mistakes of the scribe, who wrote *e.g.* עבך instead of עבדך, Letter III, 21, or corrected his writing in VI, 8 by putting a forgotten letter on top of the word. Sometimes he puts a letter only once, which should be written twice, belonging to two words, as ויכאמר for וכי יאמר, III, 8; or חיהוה for חי יהוה, III, 9 (*see also* the notes on these passages). Such cases of haplography, however, may not always be mistakes, but an actual rendering of the popular pronunciation of these words, exactly as we abbreviate in writing and in pronunciation word-compositions like "don't" for "do not" and so on. Often the scribe omits to put the dividing dot between two words, and in Letters VI and XVIII the dots seem to be almost entirely missing. Nowhere is an abbreviation of a word found; also the name יהוה is written in full; twice, however, as in Elephantine and in proper names, only יהו seems to be written instead.

The material upon which our letters are written is the baked clay of potsherds. But there can be no doubt that the more usual and certainly frequently used material was papyrus, as I tried to prove in my article *Bibeltext* in *Encyclopaedia Judaica*, vol. VII, *pages 522 sqq.* The Bible throughout speaks of *rolls* of writing, which would be written on expensive animal hide only in exceptional cases, but usually on papyrus.[1] In other instances, where the Bible refers to writing, tying up and sealing of documents, the methods described are those practised when using papyrus (*cf.* Job XIV, 17): "Sealed upon the ties is my transgression and thou smearest over (with sealing clay) upon my sin" חָתֻם בִּצְרוֹר פִּשְׁעִי וַתִּטְפֹּל עַל־עֲוֹנִי. Also the misunderstood passage in Isaiah VIII, 16, צוֹר תְּעוּדָה חֲתוֹם תּוֹרָה בְּלִמֻּדָי does not mean "Bind up the testimony, seal the law among my disciples", but simply "Bind up the testimony, seal the instruction (given here) *upon the ties*!" לִמֻּדִים is a well-known word for "ties" in the Mishnah.[2] Thus, where no publicly exhibited inscription is intended, the Bible clearly describes writing on papyrus. It has long been known from Egyptian sources, that by the end of the second millennium B.C. papyrus was being exported from Egypt to Phoenicia (Gebal-Byblos), and this trade must have been very important, since the name of this city became the regular word for a book, and for the Bible. Aramaean scribes are depicted on Assyrian reliefs of Tiglath-Pileser III (Olmstead, *History of Assyria, page* 179), and on the stela of Bar Rekub, Tiglath-Pileser's vassal, King of Sham'al in Syria, a eunuch and scribe are seen: "The papyrus roll under the scribe's arm and an Egyptian pen-box in his hand illustrate the progress of the new method of writing in the East".

The seal impression of "Gedalyahu who is over the house", found in the excavations at Lachish (he was probably none other than the son of Aḥiqam, last governor of Judah, *see P.E.F. Quarterly*), shows, like other seal impressions from Palestine, the distinct impress of papyrus, and in one of our letters (IV, 3), writing on a sheet (of papyrus) is particularly mentioned: "I have written on the sheet according to whatever my Lord has said". Writing on potsherds was resorted to, it seems, as a substitute for papyrus, which material would certainly be scarce in wartime, particularly when the Babylonian army made trade with Egypt, whence papyrus was brought, increasingly difficult. Papyrus was still the material used where sealed official

---

[1] In Isaiah VIII, 1, no writing of an actual document is meant. As shown in my book *Die Bundeslade und die Anfänge der Religion Israels*, 2nd edition, *pages* 35 *sqq.* גִּלָּיוֹן and חֶרֶט are not "sheet (of parchment or papyrus)" and "slate pencil" (they did not scratch on slates) but as וְהַחֲרִיטִים הַגִּלְיֹנִים Isaiah III, 22–23, names of garments. Isaiah writes on a garment of a man not a report—but the name of its future possessor: "(belonging) to Maher-shalal-hash-baz", his son, whose birth he is announcing.

[2] *Cf.* l.c., *Preface and pages* 33–35. Nothing is to be learned from the word ספר book, letter, this being an old loan-word from Accadic *shipru* "sending, writing".

messages had to be sent; for less private despatches, as in other countries, potsherds were used.

As interesting as the calligraphy is the language in which our letters are couched: pure Biblical Hebrew, bearing a striking resemblance to the language of the books of Kings and Jeremiah. However, the spelling is different. Often, as in other inscriptions, words are written defectively, while some words, as עיר "city", are more than once given in full spelling. Of importance for the phonetics of Biblical Hebrew is the spelling of the names compounded with יהו; *see* the remarks on Letter I. As the God-name Yhwh, mostly given in full form (יהוה), but apparently twice spelt יהו, thus the pron. suff. 3. p. sg. masc. is always written with ה, as in the Meshaʿ inscription and sometimes in the Bible (*cf.* the remarks on II, 5). For the verb in 1. p. sg. perfect, we find in our letters twice, as it seems, in emphatic expression the spelling ידעתה, etc. Some rare Biblical forms reappear here, such as נחנו for אנחנו (IV, 10, 11), or מנהו instead of ממנו (III, 12), and particularly, if the reading is correct, the energetic imperfect ידענך (V, 7 and IX, 7). For the syntax it seems important to find the short construction ידע קרא "to know (to) read" side by side with נסה לקרא "he tried to read" in III, 8–9, the anticipation of the object in ואת הודויהו שלח לקחת "Hodawyahu (acc.) he sent to take" instead of "to take Hodawyahu he sent", III, 17–18; or in a different way in וסמכיהו לקחה שמעיהו "and Semakhyahu—him has taken Shemaʿyahu" (IV, 6); or the abbreviated relative clause וספר נדביה···הבא "and the letter (which) Nedabyahu… had brought" (III, 19). That our letters were hurriedly written despatches is obvious from the fact that they sometimes show an elision of self-understood words, as in VI, 6, דברי ה[נבא] לא טבם לרפת ··· ידים "the words of the (prophet) are not good (and liable) to loosen the hands . . ."; IV, 12–13, "we do not see Azeqah" for . . . "the signals of Azeqah", etc.

For the lexicography, some new words found are of particular importance, as תסבה "the turning"; בית הרפד "the sleepinghouse, sleepingroom"; the new use of the words הפקח "the open-eyed" for "the prophet", or of לנצח "forever" for the past. New to us also is the expression השקט ידים "to make the hands rest or sink" as a synonym for רפּת ידים "to loosen the hands", and particularly עת כים (=עַתָּה כַּיֹּם) "even now" used frequently in greeting formulae, a phrase which now can be found in the Bible, where the Massoretic tradition had not recognized it, and thus the character of כים as a misunderstood enforcing particle in Biblical Hebrew may be properly established. Another interesting phrase may be "to curse the seed of somebody", used apparently in the form יָאֹר זֶרַע לַמֶּלֶךְ "he curses (the) seed to the King" (V, 10), reminding us of a similar wording in Malachi II, 2–3, and of the Arabic curse: "May Allah destroy thy house".

Rarely used Biblical words are also of interest, such as דלת for the "papyrus-sheet"; רום "to hint at", or "to refer to"; נכד "the grandson or grand-nephew"; and a word known in its proper use only from the Mishnah, משאת "fire beacons, signal stations".

The letters themselves are given in the following chapters in transliteration and translation, followed by a philological commentary and general remarks about their contents. Each letter has been examined independently and the commentary also tries to show how the understanding of these very difficult documents was reached. A final chapter gives in connected form a summary of the results concerning the contents of our letters and the historical background. Here only this may be said: Our Lachish Letters represent certain documents out of one correspondence, between Hoshaʿyahu, the commander of a small outpost to the north of Lachish, probably Qiryat-Yeʿarim, and Yaʾush, the military governor of Lachish, and commander of other fortresses along the Philistine border. There is probably one military order of Ya'ush to Hosha'yahu and at least 14 (of the other documents almost nothing is legible) letters of Hosha'yahu to Ya'ush. All these letters of Hosha'yahu are exculpating letters, and thus it is highly probable that in the documents found in the open room at the gate of Lachish we have the dossier of Hosha'yahu, the commander of Qiryat-Ye'arim, examined before the military court at the gate of Lachish, after that smaller fortress—perhaps through its commander's fault—fell into enemy hands. This dossier may have been brought to the court from the archives during the last days of the city, and left there to become scattered in the fire, which would also have destroyed all documents written on papyrus, sparing only these messages on potsherds as evidence of the last military trial held at the gate of Lachish.

The documents forming this "dossier", and brought to the court, possibly cover a period of a few years. Some of them, as Letter IV, telling that Azeqah, the great sister-fortress of Lachish, no longer sends signals, can date only a few weeks before the fall of Lachish, while other messages were written probably months or years before this time. Letter IV also brings definite proof that Tell ed Duweir is the site of ancient Lachish.

Of extraordinary interest are Letters II, III, VI, XII and XVI, dealing—as perhaps are other ostraca—with the part Hosha'yahu is accused of having played in the tragic fate of the prophet Uriyahu, the son of Shema'yahu from Qiryat-Ye'arim, these being perhaps some of the actual documents on which the report about this prophet in Jeremiah is based.

The Lachish Letters are the first personal documents found, reflecting the mind, the struggles, sorrows and feelings of ancient Judah in the last days of the kingdom, within the typical form of ancient letter writing.

In these letters we have the most valuable discovery yet made in the Biblical archaeology of Palestine and the most intimate corroboration of the Bible to this day. Whilst in other important finds the enemy of Israel speaks about his wars and sieges, or assimilated half-Jews in Babylonia or in Egypt record their life and doings, here for the first time we have authentic and intimate contemporary reports from Jews, faithfully following their God, about their inner political and religious struggles, as told in the book of Jeremiah. The Wellcome Archaeological Research Expedition to the Near East was very fortunate indeed to add these letters as a most sacred chapter to our Holy Bible.

H. T.

18

LETTER I

Photo: R. Richmond Brown

20

LETTER I

TRANSLITERATION

1. גמריהו · בן הצליהו
2. · יאזניהו · בן טבשלם
3. חגב · בן · יאזניהו
4. מבטחיהו בן ירמיהו
5. מתניהו · בן · נריהו

TRANSLATION

1. Gemaryahu son of Hiṣṣilyahu
2. Ya'zanyahu son of Ṭobshillem
3. Ḥagab son of Ya'zanyahu
4. Mibṭaḥyahu son of Yirmeyahu
5. Mattanyahu son of Neriyahu

NOTES

LINE 1. *Gemaryahu* "Yhwh has fulfilled". The same name occurs in Jeremiah XXXVI, 10, 11, 12, 25, as the name of a high official under the king Yehoyaqim (Jehoiakim). He is the son of Shaphan and the father of Mikhayehu (Michaiah) and therefore not our Gemaryahu. The same name in abbreviated pronunciation is Gemaryah (Gemariah), Jeremiah XXIX, 3; this Gemaryah is the son of Ḥilqiyah (Hilkiah), who was sent by Zedekiah, king of Judah, to Nebuchadnezzar, king of Babylon, with El'asah (Elasah), a son of Shaphan, the father of the first-mentioned Gemaryahu. The name Gemaryahu also occurs as Gemaryama in Babylonian records from Nippur of the 10th year of Darius (*cf.* Schrader, *Keilinschriften und Altes Testament*, 3rd edition, *page* 467), and as גמריה in Elephantine. While Gemaryahu and many other similarly composed names are given in the Bible almost as often in their abbreviated form as in full, the full form alone is used in the Lachish Letters. Even from the facts previously known one could have inferred that the shorter form represents only a later pronunciation under Aramaic influence. Thus the abbreviated spelling is more frequent in Ezra, Nehemiah and Chronicles than in other Biblical Books, and a name such as Nehemiah נחמיה, not occurring in Israel's earlier history, is mentioned in this abbreviated form alone. Thus the post-exilic prophet זכריה, Zechariah, appears only in this form, while other Zechariahs of pre-exilic times are mentioned also in the fuller form. Likewise in the Aramaic papyri of Elephantine we find a great number of proper names, such as ידניה, יאזניה, חלקיה, זכריה, זבדיה, הושעיה, הודויה, דליה, גמריה, גדליה, (ברכיא) ברכיה, אמריה, אזניה, אושעיה, אוריה, צפליה, פנוליה, פלליה, פלטייה, ענניה, עבדיה, נריה, מלכיה, מיכיה, מחסיה, (מפטחיה) מבטחיה, ישעיה, ישביה, יוניה, (ידניא) שפטיה, שמעיה, שלמיה, רעויה, צפניה, while the fuller form is represented only by עבדיהו (81, 22 f.; 43; 82, 2), and the God-name ענתיהו (44, 3) combining, not a verb or a descriptive attribute, but the name of another deity with the name Yhw(h).

Additional confirmation is given, on the other hand, by the names found up till now only in ancient Hebrew inscriptions on stone, seals, jar stamps, etc. (*cf.* Diringer, *Le Iscrizione Antico-Ebraiche Palestinesi*). There we find many names, mostly Biblical, the reading of which is certain, such as מיכיהו, ישעיהו, ירמיהו, יקמיהו, יחליהו, יאזניהו, חנניהו, חלקיהו, (י)חזקיהו, זמריהו, זכריהו, גדליהו, אביהו, נחמיהו, even שמעיהו, שכניהו, (דמליהו or) רמליהו, צפניהו, פדיהו, עשיהו, עמדיהו, עוריהו, עזיהו, עבדיהו, נתניהו, נריהו, מעשיהו, etc.[1] Against this there is not one really certain instance of an abbreviated name. In the very few cases where a seal actually seems to show the shorter form, יה stands at the end of the line (as in Diringer, tav. XIX, No. 21), where the ו could be overlooked. Only once (Diringer, *page* 182, tav. XIX, No. 23), a name חנניה occurs in the middle of an inscription of otherwise doubtful reading and uncertain origin (Assyria?), and even here ה may be misread for the compound letter הו.

The name of Ḥizqiyah(u) (Hiskiah), king of Judah, mentioned in the Hebrew Bible seven times as חזקיה, twice as יחזקיה, 66 times as חזקיהו, and 38 times as יחזקיהו, is usually given in Sennacherib's Assyrian inscriptions as (*a*) Ḫa-za-qi-a-a-u; (*b*) Ḫa-za-qi-a-u; (*c*) Ḫa-za-qi-ú, and only exceptionally in the shorter form Ḫa-za-qi-ya(-a) (*cf.* Tallqvist, *Assyrian Personal Names*, page 88 and Luckenbill, *Annals of Sennacherib*, 31, 76; 32, 18; 33, 17; 69, 23; 70, 27, 30; 77, 21, and 86, 15). This form may be regarded here as "Assyrianised" by the scribe who may have seen in the ending "u" the (superfluous) vowel of the then obsolete Accadian (Assyro-Babylonian) nominative. But, in any case, the number of the Hebrew references in itself (104 against 9) is sufficient to show that

---

[1] Add also the name שלמיהו from unpublished seals in the private collection of Dr. Reifenberg, Jerusalem, and now (1937) also עזריהו and שפטיהו from seals recently found at Tell ed Duweir, the last name showing also a clear ט.

the longer form is the correct spelling. For the Hebrew עזריהו and עזריה the Assyrian transliteration Az-ri-ya-u—if the same name is intended[1]—seems as one would expect it to be in Assyrian. Thus, I-li-ya-u for Hebrew אליה(ו) occurs in Assyrian legal documents (*cf.* Gesenius-Buhl, *page* 25 a, 41 b). Against it Uriya (*cf.* Schrader, l.c., *page* 467) for Hebrew אוריה(ו) may be a later "Aramaized" or "Assyrianized" spelling. Thus, a name occurring in an Assyrian tablet found at Gezer is correctly spelt, Na-tan-ia-u (*Macalister, Excavations at Gezer*, 1, 28). The Judaean נדביהו is given correctly as Nadbiyau in Assyrian transcription (Schrader, l.c., *page* 488), but after the exile the Aramaic-speaking Jews in Babylonia, as in Elephantine, pronounced this name as Nadbiya (Clay, *Babylonian Expedition of the University of Pennsylvania*, IX, 27, 65). *See also* Assyrian Yauḥazi (*i.e.*, יהואחז) for the Biblical אחז as the name of the Judaean king. From the evidence of our ostraca we may now conclude definitely that the full form גמריהו had alone been in use, at least in Judah, before the Exile, while the shorter גמריה is due to Aramaic influence.

The ostraca of Samaria, while they also give the unabbreviated form of the God-name in compound proper names, show a different spelling based on different pronunciation בדיו, אביו, שמריו, עגליו, עבדיו, מרניו, ידעיו, גדיו, apparently because the Samarians had no clear pronunciation of the ה. This regional[2] difference is shown also in a few names, such as שבניו, קניו, עזיו, אביו on seals, which may come from the Samaria region rather than from Judah. The spelling used at Lachish indicates a clear pronunciation of the ה, and this same distinct pronunciation is shown in the above-mentioned Assyrian transliteration of Judaean names such as Ḫa-za-qi-a-a-u, A-ḫi-ya-u, I-li-ya-u. On the other hand, the transcription of Jewish post-exilic names in Babylonia as Aḫiyama, Banayama, Gamaryama, *i.e.* Aḫiyawa(a), Banayaw(a), Gamaryaw(a), would therefore represent rather the "northern" pronunciation, גמריו, אחיו, thus showing that the Judaeans, too, had lost their pronunciation of the consonant ה under the influence of the Babylonian language. The name Aḫiami, if representing אחיו Aḫiaw, also occurs in this form in the Babylonian letter found at Ta'annek, showing this North-Palestinian pronunciation in use by the second millennium B.C.[3] *Cf. also* אחיו as a name of Babylonian Jews after the Exile, I Chronicles VIII, 31; IX, 37. The same name וְעֻזָּא וְאַחְיוֹ בְּנֵי אֲבִינָדָב II Samuel VI, 3; I Chronicles XIII, 7, may rather be taken with Wellhausen as an appellative noun: "and Uzza and his brethren" וְאֶחָיו (better than וְאַחְיוֹ "and his brother"). Thus, also, in I Chronicles VIII, 14 וְאַחְיוֹ is usually considered as misread for וַאֲחֵיהֶם "and their brethren" or וְאֶחָיו "and his brethren".

Hiṣṣilyahu. This pronunciation of the verb in the perfect tense seems certainly the most likely one, although the perfect may here have the sense of the present-future: Yhwh saves, Yhwh may save! The name Hiṣṣilyahu occurs here for the first time; *cf.* in Elephantine הצול, spelt by Cowley, Haẓul, *i.e.* Haṣul. פדיה Pedayah, II Kings XXIII, 36, father-in-law of Josiah, king of Judah; I Chronicles III, 18 f., son of Jeconiah and father of Zerubbabel, has the same meaning. Jeremiah XXXV, 3 mentions a Rekhabite in Jeremiah's time with the unexplained name Ḥabaṣṣinyah חבצניה (Habaziniah); is it possible that this name is misread for הצליה(ו)? With

---

[1] *Cf.* the literature mentioned in Gesenius-Buhl, *Handwörterbuch*, 17th edition, *page* 579 b.

[2] *Cf.* Diringer, l.c., *page* 40 and the literature mentioned there.

[3] From this we may infer that as the spelling of the Judaean names in the Bible has been partly altered according to later development under Aramaic influence, so some north-Israelite names are given in the Judaean Bible in changed spelling; *e.g.*,

the Israelite king's name אחזיה(ו) (Aḥaziah) may originally have been pronounced אחזיו (Aḥaziaw); but for this question careful investigation of names *beginning* with יהו also would be necessary. Jehu יֵהוּא, the name of the king of northern Israel, transcribed in Assyrian inscriptions *Ya-u-a*, may have no connexion with the God-name Yhwh.

more reason we may perhaps compare the name הצליהו with אֲצַלְיָהוּ II Kings XXII, 3; II Chronicles XXXIV, 8. This Aṣalyahu is the father of Shaphan, one of the officers employed by Josiah in 623 B.C. H. Ranke (*Early Babylonian Personal Names from the published tablets of the so-called Hammurabi Dynasty, page* 30) finds the same name in Babylonian A-za-(sa-)li-a, LT. II, 50, line 8.

LINE 2. *Ya'zanyahu* "Yhwh listens" (*cf. also* line 3). Another Ya'zanyahu occurs in II Kings XXV, 23 as officer under Gedalyahu (Gedaliah), the Babylonian governor after 586 B.C. His father is called the Ma'akhatite. In Jeremiah XL, 8, the same man's name is spelt Yezanyahu (יזניהו). In Jeremiah XLII, 1, Yezanyahu, son of Hosha'yah יזניהו בן הושעיה, appears in the same position, but in LXX, and in the Massoretic Hebrew text in XLIII, 2, 'Azaryah (עזריה) is given instead of Yezanyahu, and in LXX his father's name in both instances is Ma'aseyah (מעשיה), instead of Hosha'yah. Ya'zanyah (Jaazaniah) is also the name of the son of Yirmeyahu, grandfather of Ḥabaṣṣinyah (*see above*), the Rekhabite, Jeremiah XXXV, 3. Finally another Ya'zanyahu, son of Shaphan, about 592–591 B.C., is mentioned as an official in Jerusalem (Ezekiel VIII, 11) and a Ya'zanyahu, son of 'Azur in Ezekiel XI, 1 (LXX Cod. Vat. gives in both instances—erroneously—'Ιεχονίας—Jeconiah). For the name Ya'zanyahu in Hebrew seal inscriptions, *cf.* Diringer, *pages* 181 and 229. The name Ya'zanyah occurs also in Elephantine (Cowley, 52, 14, 17); *cf.* 'Azanyah אזניה in Elephantine (one 'Azanyah, Cowley, 12, 8; 18, 6 is father of יאוש) and Nehemiah X, 10.

Ṭobshillem "Good he has repaid". This seems to be the most probable reading of this hitherto unknown name. There are, it is true, in the Hebrew Bible, names such as Ṭobiyah(u) (טוביה(ו)) "Yhw is good" and (Aramaic) Ṭab'al (for Ṭab-el) "God is good", and thus one might perhaps expect the name of a deity in שלם: "Shlm is good" or take שלם as שָׁלוֹם: "Peace is good". However, there are no real facts to support the first explanation, particularly as no other Israelitic or Judaean Biblical name really shows שלם as a theophorous element (in אַבְשָׁלֹם or שְׁלֻמִיאֵל the elements אב or אל, not שלם represent the deity) and as nowhere in our letters any deity other than Yhwh occurs in proper names or otherwise.[1] The second interpretation of the name "Peace is good", although it could be the abbreviation of "Yhwh's peace is good" (*cf.* Assyrian names as Ṭāb-ashab-Marduk, "Good is the dwelling of Marduk"; Ṭāb-eṭer-Ashur, "Good is the protection of Ashur") would only be a tautology, as the Hebrew שָׁלוֹם does not particularly mean "peace" in opposition to "war", but "well-being" in general, and thus שלום and טוב are synonymous in the Bible and in our ostraca (*cf.* II, 2 f. and IV, 2). Thus even when Shlm is taken as a deity, "The Well-being is good" would remain a tautology proper. On the other hand, שָׁלֵם טוֹב or שִׁלֵּם טוֹבָה "to repay good" (as שִׁלֵּם רָעָה "to repay evil") is a usual phrase; *cf.* וְאֶת־צַדִּיקִים יְשַׁלֶּם טוֹב "but to the righteous good he shall repay", Proverbs XIII, 21; ויהוה יְשַׁלֶּמְךָ טוֹבָה תַּחַת הַיּוֹם הַזֶּה "and Yhwh reward thee good for this day" I Samuel XXIV, 20. Thus Ṭobshillem (-Yhwh) would be a most appropriate name for a new-born child: "(Yhwh) has good repaid"; and the name שִׁלֵּם "He has paid" (*cf.* III, 20) may originally be the same as our fuller expression. The defective spelling of טב for Biblical טוב (fem. טֹבָה for טוֹבָה, cstr. טֹבַת for טוֹבַת, pl. masc. טֹבִים and טוֹבִים, fem. טֹבוֹת and טוֹבוֹת) was to be expected. The pronunciation טוּב, used according to the Massoretic tradition for "the good" in *status constructus*, and in כָּל־טוּב "all the good" alone, is less likely.

LINE 3. *Ḥagab* "Locust", a name found in the Bible only once, in a document of a later time (Ezra II, 46), is there the name of a pre-exilic family, "the children of Ḥagab". *Ya'zanyahu*, perhaps the same as in line 2.

---

[1] *See* remarks on the name Elnatan, *pages* 30 *and* 58.

LINE 4. *Mibṭaḥyahu* "Trust is Yhwh". The same name occurs as Mibṭaḥyah or Miphṭaḥyah for two women, one the daughter of Gemaryah and one the daughter of Maḥseyah, in the Elephantine documents, among the names of perhaps the descendants of those Jews who, after the fall of the Judaean kingdom, went down to Egypt, taking with them the prophet Jeremiah, after the death of Gedalyah(u) (Jeremiah XLIII, 5–7.) Our Mibṭaḥyahu is the son of *Yirmeyahu* (Jeremiah), and in line 5 we have *Mattanyahu*, the son of *Neriyahu* (Neriah). There is certainly no sufficient reason to identify these men with Jeremiah, the prophet, and Neriah, the father of his scribe, although the possibility of their identity cannot be absolutely refuted. The name Yirmeyahu ("Yhwh shoots"?) is also the name of other men in Jeremiah's time. *Cf. above* to Ya'zanyah, son of Yirmeyahu, Jeremiah XXXV, 3; another Yirmeyahu is father-in-law of king Josiah (II Kings XXIII, 31; XXIV, 18; and Jeremiah LII, 1) and the same name occurs both earlier and later. Yirmeyahu on a seal is given in Diringer, *page* 214. A Yirmeyahu seems to be mentioned also in ostracon XVII, 3. Neriyahu "My light is Yhwh" is in the Bible not only the name of the father of Baruch the scribe; according to Jeremiah LI, 59 ff. it appears that the same Neriyahu, son of Maḥseyah, is the father of Serayah, to whom also, as to Baruch, Jeremiah dictates his words.[1] In the Bible no other Neriyahu is mentioned, but the name occurs in ancient Hebrew seal inscriptions (*cf.* Diringer, *pages* 178 ff., 208 ff., 213 ff.). In Elephantine the name Neriyah occurs as well as Maḥseyah, as Neriyah's father is called in Jeremiah LI, 59 ff. The New-Babylonian personal name Niriyama (Tallqvist, *Neubabyl. Namenbuch, page* 168) seems to be the same name.

LINE 5. *Mattanyahu* "Gift of Yhwh". This was also the name of King Zedekiah (Ṣidqiyahu) before it was changed into this latter form (II Kings XXIV, 17). The same name, spelt מתניה, occurs later (*cf.* Ezra X, 26; Nehemiah XI, 17, etc.). In Elephantine the shorter name מתן alone occurs, but in Babylonia we find Mattanyama, *i.e.* Mattanyaw(a) (*cf.* Clay, l.c., X, 55, *University of Pennsylvania, The Museum, Publ. of the Bab. Section*, II, 1, 28). On seals only Netanyahu, נתניהו is known (Diringer, l.c., *pages* 191, 192); but נ and מ being very similar in some inscriptions, the same name could perhaps be intended in the case of Diringer's seal 31, *page* 191. Many other forms of similar names are known (מתתיה(ו), מתני, etc.). For Neriyahu, *see above*.

GENERAL REMARKS

Ostracon I is a list of names similar to the lists found among the Aramaic papyri of Elephantine (*cf.* Cowley, *Aramaic Papyri*, No. 12, and Cowley's *Notes, page* 35 f.) and at other places. At Elephantine some of them are connected with accounts, while the purpose of others is not apparent. In our case this list—not a letter in itself—was found with the other ostraca, which certainly are letters written during a short period and sent to Lachish (*see later*). So this list, too, may not have been written at Lachish itself, but sent there in connexion with a question or a message. For a suggestion about this compare the notes on Letters III, VI and VIII. In this sense Ostracon I is also a letter.

The persons in the list may have no relation to any one mentioned in the Bible, although most of them have Biblical names. But the names themselves point definitely to a certain time, the period of the prophet Jeremiah, shortly before the destruction of Lachish and the Kingdom of Judah, a date confirmed by the other letters and by the archaeological facts as pointed out by

---

[1] *See* the note on Letter IV, line 3.

Mr. Starkey. Of the nine names mentioned in the list, seven are Biblical, and not less than six occur in the time of Jeremiah; the seventh name Ḥagab "Locust" being a "timeless" name, mentioned only once in the Bible at a later period, but even here as the name of an originally pre-exilic family. Three names, Gemaryahu, Mattanyahu and Neriyahu, appear again later in Babylonia, brought thither by the Jews who went into exile with Jeconiah and Zedekiah. No fewer than four names (Gemaryahu, Ya'zanyahu, Mibṭaḥyahu and Neriyahu) occur again in Elephantine, whither Jews went after the death of Gedalyahu, taking with them the prophet Jeremiah himself (cf. the list of names on page 198).

The names in this list—like those mentioned in the other letters—are very illuminating in another direction. Most of them—seven out of nine!—are compounded with the name Yhw(h)—and in the eighth, Ṭobshillem, it may be implied: "(Yhwh) has repaid good". In all these personal names the name Yhwh follows the verb as a strict rule. From these facts we can infer that at this period such was the usual form of compound names; therefore also the form יְכָנְיָהוּ Yekhonyahu (Jeremiah XXIV, 1; cf. כניהו, Jeremiah XXII, 24, 28; XXXVII, 1; יכניה, Jeremiah XXVIII, 4; XXIX, 2; Esther II, 6; I Chronicles III, 16 f.; יכוניה Jeremiah XXVII, 20) is the correct and idiomatic spelling of the name of the king who first went into Babylonian exile in Jeremiah's time, and not יהויכין, Yehoyakhin, as given in II Kings XXIV, 6 ff.; Jeremiah LII, 31; II Chronicles XXXVI, 8 f. This cannot be strictly proved, but as the form used exclusively in the names of the Lachish Letters, wherein the God-name follows the verb, occurs in the Bible more often than the reversed form, there is every reason to believe the first to be the correct rendering.

There certainly were also reversed names such as יהונדב (Jeremiah XXXV, 8, 14 ff.); יהונתן, (Jeremiah XXXVII, 15, 20, XXXVIII, 26) and even the name of the king יהויקים Jehoiakim,[1] in Jeremiah's time, but still, in our Lachish Letters not less than 15–16 names out of the 22 (21) of the form Gemaryahu occur, while no name of the form Yehoyaqim is to be found, pointing to a certain rule, a definite idea, according to which such compound names had been formed.

This certainly cannot be explained as mere chance, but must have been a rule strictly followed through a longer period. It has been mentioned how closely the names in our letters resemble those used a century later by the Jews in Elephantine, the descendants of the Judaeans who went down to Egypt with Jeremiah. But here again we find the same phenomenon; although these Jews turned to foreign cults and worshipped heathen deities besides Yhwh, still among the many names referring to Israel's God, there is, as in the ostraca of Lachish, no name compounded with אל instead of יהו(ה), and where the name יהו is used it is usually (in 33 names for even a larger number of people) put at the end of the name—in the abbreviated, Aramaized form אושעיה, אוריה, etc.[2]—while the form יהוחן, etc., is used almost exclusively for women.[3]

This leads to another point. It is astounding that the Judaeans of this period, mentioned in our letters, carefully avoid the name of any other deity, even such as אל, in their personal names, when compared with all the recriminations of the prophets in general, and of Jeremiah in particular, against Israel's and Judah's treachery "that they are gone far from me and have walked after vanity" (Jeremiah II, 5). Cf. the many "heathen" names in the Samaria ostraca

---

[1] See page 29.

[2] See the names mentioned above; among them, e.g. אושעיה is the name of at least five men.

[3] יהוחן for three different women, יהוטל and יהועלי for one

woman each, יהושמע for five different women; of men with such names only three (יונתן) יהונתן and (?) יהוישמע; יהואור (once); are to be found; יהוחנן is the name of the high priest in Jerusalem, not in Elephantine.

28

עגמש, מרבעל, יהועלי, חנאב, בעלמעני, בעלזמר, בעלזכר, בעלא, אלמתן, אלישע, אלבא, אחנעם, אלבא, אחמלך, אחמא, אבבעל as and even a "Yahwistic" name as עגליהו "The calf is Yhwh".

This in itself shows that something must have happened to lead Judah back to Yhwh exclusively, and an expression of this new spirit is to be seen in all these names built according to the same rule: Yhwh helps, עזריהו, הושעיהו; Yhwh saves, הצליהו, פדיהו; Yhwh hears (the prayer), שמעיהו (IV, 6), יאזניהו, etc., and we may not be far wrong in identifying here the act of general reformation inaugurated by king Josiah (Yoshiyahu) in the eighteenth year of his reign, as told in II Kings XXII and XXIII. Thus the most striking feature of this list of names seems to confirm a highly important point of Judah's religious history. This religious reformation of 622 B.C. must have set the rule for the names given henceforth to children at their birth, and must also have caused the names of grown-up men to be changed. Thus the alteration of the name of Eliakim (born about 635) to Jehoiakim (Yehoyaqim), ascribed, as it seems, in the Bible to Pharaoh Necho (II Kings XXIII, 34),[1] is certainly a token of a changed inner Judaean relationship to Yhwh and may be attributed to the same spirit as shown in Josiah's reformation. There was perhaps no need to transform this name entirely into יקמיהו, according to the type used as a rule for new names. However, as the name of king Jeconiah appears in both the unorthodox type Yehoyakhim and in the more correct form Yekhonyahu, the orthodox name of king Jehoiakim may have been יקמיהו, pronounced perhaps Yeqamyahu (for the name Yeqamyah, see I Chronicles II, 41; III, 18). Thus the name of the general, Kebaryahu or Yikhbaryahu, son of Elnatan (III, 15) shows that the general's *father*—the general himself being, according to his rank, already advanced in age—still had a name compounded with El instead of Yhwh apparently before the reformation (see also Letter III, general remarks), while his own name followed the Yahwistic rule.

This practice is in some way parallel to what the Bible implies about the first reformation by Moses. Here, too, as pointed out in my book on the Ark and the beginning of Israel's religion,[2] religious reformation caused a change of names, since Exodus VI, 3 gives Yhwh as a yet unknown name instead of El Shaddai (usually translated "God Almighty") as known by the patriarchs: "And I appeared unto Abraham, unto Isaac, and unto Jacob by (the name of) El Shaddai, but by my name Yhwh was I not known to them". According to this, Moses appears in Psalms XC–XCI,[3] the Psalm called XC, 1, "Prayer of Moses, the man of God", as a reformer, appealing to the believers in El Elyon = El Shaddai, to trust in Yhwh, who actually is the same God but prefers to be called by this, his true name:

"Thou that dwelleth in the secret place of the most High (Elyon) and abideth under the shadow of Shaddai (usually: the Almighty), I would say to *Yhwh*: He is my refuge and my fortress, my God, in him I trust.

For *He* shall deliver thee from the snare of the fowler . . ." (Psalms XCI, 1–3).

"For thee![4] Yhwh (who is) my refuge, (He is) the most High (Elyon) thou hast made thy habitation" (Psalms XCI, 9).

---

[1] But even the translation "and he (Eliakim) turned his name to Yehoiakim" is not impossible. Also II Kings XXIV, 17 may mean: "And he (Mattaniah) changed his name (when he became king) to Zedekiah".

[2] *Die Bundeslade und die Anfänge der Religion Israels*, 2nd edition, Berlin, 1930, *page* 66 f.

[3] *See* l.c., *page* 72 f. Psalms XC and XCI are only one "Psalm", just as Psalms XLII–XLIII.

[4] This is the correct translation of the Hebrew text.

The Pentateuch does not mention any name after Moses' work of reformation at Mount Sinai, compounded with (El) Elyon or (El) Shaddai; but among the contemporaries of Moses are three persons whose *fathers'* names still include the old God-name: Eliṣur, the son of *Shede'ur* (Numbers I, 5); Shelumiel, the son of *Ṣurishaddai* (*v.* 6); Aḥiezer the son of *'Ammishaddai* (*v.* 12).

Thus in the Lachish Letters the difference in the names of fathers and sons reflects the religious reformation that caused the change, except that the reformation in Josiah's time seems, while it lasted, even to have abhorred the name El, אל, and adhered exclusively to the name Yhwh.

However, in the time of Jeremiah there are a few names mentioned in the Bible compounded with other god-names besides Yhwh: Elnatan, the son of Achbor (Jeremiah XXVI, 22; XXXVI, 12, 25);[1] Elnatan, father-in-law of king Jehoiakim (II Kings XXIV, 8), possibly the same man; Elasah, אלעשה, the son of Shaphan (Jeremiah XXIX, 3); Elishama, אלישמע, the scribe (Jeremiah XXXVI, 12, 20, 21); Ḥanamel, חנמאל, the nephew of Jeremiah (Jeremiah XXXII, 7–9, 12); Yeraḥmeel ירחמאל, the son of the king (Jeremiah XXXVI, 26); Ishmael, ישמעאל, the son of Nethaniah (Jeremiah XL, 8); Abdeel, עבדאל, father of Shelemiah and Azriel, עזריאל, the father of Seraiah (Jeremiah XXXVI, 26).[2] However, we must bear in mind the following points: (1) Not all the persons named belong to the time after the reform of Josiah; thus Elnatan, the father-in-law of Jehoiakim, may be given by his name previous to 623 B.C. The names of the fathers of Shelemiah and Seraiah may also belong to the same earlier period, when even the king Jehoiakim was still called Eliakim. The names of these persons in this earlier period may have been carried on in the books whilst they had actually been changed. They may have been mentioned in the old sources on earlier occasions and the book kept the names used throughout history. (2) All the names, except Elasah, mentioned here, are names of unbelievers, opposed to the prophet and aiding in the king's endeavour to put him to death, men who certainly were opposed to the entire spirit of Josiah's reformation, while those men whose names occur in our Lachish Letters belong, as the study of the other ostraca will show, to a party strictly adhering to Yhwh and his prophets. The name Ḥanamel in particular can hardly be explained as compounded with El and may even be a mis-spelling for חֲנָמֵל Ḥanamal, "hail". As to Elnatan, *see also* notes on Letter III.

In connexion with this interpretation of the names, as showing the influence of the king Josiah's religious reformation, Mr. Starkey calls attention to the pedestal of a "heathen" altar (?) discovered at Tell ed Duweir just below the 588 B.C. road-level to the left of the city gate, which, it appears, had been destroyed, possibly by king Josiah's orders; *see* II Kings XXIII, 8: "And he brought all the priests out of the cities of Judah, and defiled the high places" (literally: the sanctuaries),[3] "where the priests had burned incense, from Geba to Beer-sheba, and brake down the high places of the gates that were in the entering in of the gate of Joshua the governor of the city, which were on a man's left hand at the gate of the City".

PALAEOGRAPHY AND ORTHOGRAPHY. The writing of Letter I differs from that of the other Lachish ostraca, except VIII, and shows a different hand from that of the other letters. Apparently

---

[1] Here the father's name is not mentioned.

[2] Of particular interest is the name of the prophet and priest Ezekiel (יחזקאל), living in Babylonia. But in view of the facts as seen from Lachish and Elephantine, there must be some explanation also in this case.

[3] Hebrew בָּמוֹת "bamot". In the *Bulletin of the Jewish Palestine Exploration Society*, vol. II (1934), *pages 9–16*, I have tried to show

that "bamot" are not "high places", but sacred *buildings* erected, both on high as in low places. In other cases the word is used in the meaning of "body", particularly "dead body". Thus the "bamot" may originally have been *grave sanctuaries*. The Biblical phrase "to ride on the *body* (במותי) of the clouds", etc., has now its parallel in Ras Shamra, where the goddess 'THRT is put on the במת (=body, back) of a donkey (*cf.* H. L. Ginsberg, *The Ugarit Texts, page* 27).

of all the ostraca only Letter VIII may have accompanied the list of names (Letter I). In the form of the signs used Letter I resembles the alphabet of the "Samaria Ostraca" more than our other documents; *cf.* the broad and angular ב, the tail of the י, the upturning lower stroke of the ל, the very broad and angular מ and נ with the right downstroke turning to the left, the narrow ש with its three parallel vertical strokes. This difference might suggest an earlier date for Letter I than for the other letters, but the archaeological facts are decidedly against such an assumption. The writing of the other letters is not uniform, or even consistent in itself, the scribes use the older "classic" forms (as seen in seal inscriptions) even in the same letter with the more cursive later development.

Note further the oblong, and at the ends, rather pointed form of the ט in lines 2 and 4, occurring here for the first time, since the ט known in its Canaanite type from Phoenician inscriptions had not been found before with certainty in ancient Hebrew inscriptions on stone, seals, weights, or pottery, except for a very poor development on jar stamps (*cf.* Diringer, tav. XXIX–XXX). In the ת in מתניהו, line 5, the thin strokes right and left from the main downward stroke are not on the level; note finally the ligature of מ and ר, ה and ו, to what looks like one single letter. The word dividing dot, or small stroke, is not always visible, but is certainly to be understood after each word.

For the orthography note the defective spelling of הצליהו, line 1, טבשלם, line 2.

LETTER II

Photo: S. W. Michieli

34

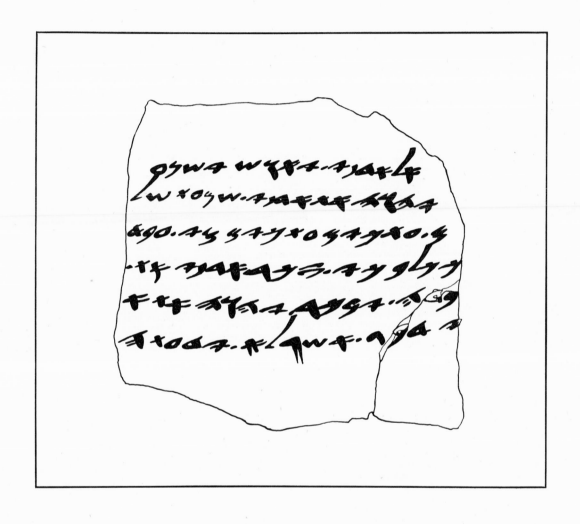

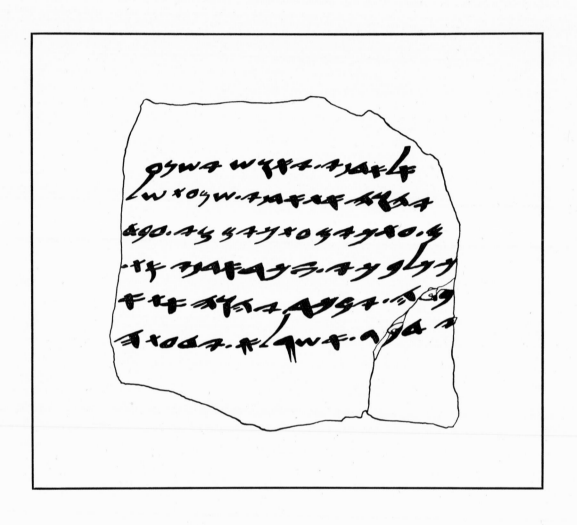

LETTER II

TRANSLITERATION

1. אל אדני· יאוש ישמע
2. יהוה את אדני· שמעת של
3. ם· עת כים עת כים מי· עבד
4. ך כלב כי· זכר אדני את·
5.]ע[בדה· יבכר· יהוה את א
6.]–‏–[י דבר· אשר לא· ידעתה

TRANSLATION

1. **To my Lord Ya'ush: May Yhwh let hear**
2. **my Lord tidings of peace (well-being)**
3. **even now, even now. Who is thy slave**
4. **a dog, that my lord remembered his**
5. **[sl]ave ? May Yhwh investigate (and punish)**
6. **my [saying] something which I did not (even) know !**

NOTES

LINE 1. *Ya'ush* (*cf. also* III, 2; VI, 1; XII, 1); the same name occurs in Elephantine (*cf.* Cowley, *Aram. Pap.* 22, 89; 34, 4; [40, 5]), and shows again how the Hebrew proper names of this period were kept by the Jews who went to Egypt with Jeremiah. Cowley gives (*page* 72) the "Aramaic" pronunciation Yeosh, but the name certainly represents the Hebrew verb יָאוּשׁ (*ya'ush*) as יָקוּם (*yaqum*) "he stands". The name has correctly been connected with the fuller form יֹאשִׁיָהוּ, Yoshiyahu, Josiah (*cf.* Gesenius-Buhl, 17th edition, *page* 280 b) and with its inverted form יְהוֹאָשׁ or יוֹאָשׁ Yehoash, Yoash (Jehoash, Joash), which name has been explained already by Nöldeke, *ZDMG.*, XL (1886), *page* 740, by reference to South-Arabic names containing the verb *'ws* (אוש); *cf. also* Noth, *Die israelitischen Personennamen im Rahmen der gemeinsemitischen Namengebung, page* 213. But it is also possible to connect these names with the Hebrew word אִישׁ "man", originally, as its synonym גֶּבֶר, "(the) strong (one)" (*cf.* Gesenius-Buhl, 17th edition, *s.v.* אִישׁ, *page* 32 b), where also the Accadic *ushu* "strength" is compared. Then the meaning would be "(Yhwh) is strong"; *cf.* the spelling יאושיהו, Jeremiah XXVII, 1. As Letter II, so also III, VI and XII at least are addressed expressly to Ya'ush, and as Mr. Starkey first pointed out, II, VII, VIII and XVIII are actually pieces of the same pot as VI. And as other letters also seem to deal with the same matters as III and VI, it is a fair and, as the examination of the letters proves, correct assumption that all these ostraca formed part of a correspondence addressed to the same man. One was also at first inclined to assume that these letters found scattered in the open room overlooking the gate of Lachish were the remains of the last letters which came to this room and its occupant, covering a very short period, during the last days before the conquest of Lachish. However, this assumption now appears impossible. Already from our letter, where a man outside Lachish calls himself his lord's "slave and dog", we may infer that the receiver was a man of high position and more than a local authority. (*See* notes on Letters III, IV, V and VI.)

ישמע has to be understood as a jussive form of the causative conjugation: יַשְׁמַע "may he let hear".

LINE 2. שְׁמְעֹת שָׁלֹם "tidings of peace"; there is also the possible reading שְׁמְעַת שָׁלֹם as a singular "a tiding of peace", applied in this case to the news following in this letter itself; but the variants of the greetings in other letters prove it to be meant in a general way. Thus also the meaning of שלם "peace" as "well-being" and, approximately, of עֵת כִּים as "even now" is clearly established. *Cf.*

LETTER	II	ישמע יהוה את אדני שמעת שלם עת כים עת כים
„	IV	ישמע יהוה את אדני עת כים שמעת טב
„	VIII	ישמע יהוה את אדני שמעת טב עת כים
„	IX	ישמע יהוה את אדני שמעת שלם

Letter VI shows a different formula for the greeting, which is fully discussed in its place. There also the form and exact meaning of עת כים is properly analysed, and it is also shown that this expression, so far unknown from other sources, occurs at least twice in the Hebrew Bible, where it has not been recognized by the Massoretic tradition.

The term שְׁמְעֹת טב or שְׁמְעֹת שָׁלֹם does not occur in Biblical Hebrew, but *cf.* שְׁמוּעָה טוֹבָה "good news" (Proverbs XV, 30; XXV, 25), מַשְׁמִיעַ שָׁלוֹם מְבַשֵּׂר טוֹב (Isaiah LII, 7) "he that publisheth (lets hear) peace, that bringeth tidings of good". The name יהוה occurs here for the first time in full, and is used in the same full spelling both in these blessings and in the formula of the oath: חי יהוה VI, 12;

XII, 3, or חיהוה III, 9. It is characteristic and important for textual criticism, that, although our letters may have been written very hurriedly, and the writer even forgets a letter here and there (*see* III, 9, 21), the God-name is usually written in full.[1] However, in two instances the shorter form יהו, as in the proper names, and as exclusively used in Elephantine, seems to be given (*cf.* the notes on V, 10 and IX, 7).

In Line 3 f. the writer (*i.e.* the sender, who is perhaps not the scribe) of the letter calls himself the slave and dog of his lord. This self-humiliating comparison is well known from the Babylonian Amarna letters, and from the Bible itself. In Amarna, *ardu kalbu*, "the slave, the dog", is a frequent combination, used not only in a humiliating reference to others as, *e.g.*, 71, 16 f.; 75, 42 f.; 85, 64 in Knudtzon's edition, but also about the writer himself, his lord's "obedient servant"; *a-na-ku arad sharri ù kalbu sha bi-ti-shu*; "I am the king's slave and the dog of his house" (60, 6 f.): *ardu-ka u ṭi-it shēpē-ka kalbu sha bīt sharri*; "thy slave and the mud of thy feet, the dog of the king's house" (61, 2 ff.), etc. The form of a question as used in our letter refers to others as well as to the writer himself: *mi-nu ab-di-a-shi-ir-ta ardu kalbu ù yi-il-ku māt sharri a-na sha-a-shu*; "who is Abdi-ashirta the slave, the dog, that he takes the king's land for himself?" (71, 16 ff.); or *u mi-ia-mi a-na-ku kalbu 1ᵉⁿ u la-a il-la-ku*; "and who am I, a single dog, that I should not go?" (202, 12 ff.), etc. In the Bible the following instances are known:—

I Samuel XXIV, 15 (14): אַחֲרֵי מִי יָצָא מֶלֶךְ יִשְׂרָאֵל אַחֲרֵי מִי אַתָּה רֹדֵף אַחֲרֵי כֶּלֶב מֵת אַחֲרֵי פַּרְעֹשׁ אֶחָד

"After whom is the king of Israel come out? After whom dost thou pursue? After a dead dog, after a single flea?"

II Samuel IX, 8: וַיִּשְׁתַּחוּ וַיֹּאמֶר מֶה עַבְדֶּךָ כִּי פָנִיתָ אֶל־הַכֶּלֶב הַמֵּת אֲשֶׁר כָּמוֹנִי

"And he bowed himself, and said, What is thy servant (slave) that thou shouldest look upon such a dead dog as I am?"

II Samuel XVI, 9: לָמָּה יְקַלֵּל הַכֶּלֶב הַמֵּת הַזֶּה אֶת־אֲדֹנִי הַמֶּלֶךְ

"Why should this dead dog curse my lord the king?"

and particularly II Kings VIII, 13: וַיֹּאמֶר חֲזָהאֵל כִּי מָה עַבְדְּךָ הַכֶּלֶב כִּי יַעֲשֶׂה הַדָּבָר הַגָּדוֹל הַזֶּה.

"And Hazael said, But what is thy servant, the dog, that he should do this great thing?"
(*Cf. also* II Samuel III, 8, and D. H. Müller, *Semitica I,* 6.) As I have pointed out in *Festschrift für Karl Marti* (1925), *page* 275, the same formula is used in the Bible in man's relation to God. According to II Samuel VII, 21, David says in his prayer to God: בַּעֲבוּר דְּבָרְךָ וּכְלִבְּךָ עָשִׂיתָ אֵת כָּל־ הַגְּדוּלָּה הַזֹּאת "For thy word's sake, and according to thy heart, hast thou done all this greatness". But "for thy word's sake and according to thy heart" is a very improbable combination, and "according to thy heart" itself does not make any real sense. However, I Chronicles, where the whole prayer is repeated, gives a variant of the text (I Chronicles XVII, 19): בַּעֲבוּר עַבְדְּךָ וּכְלִבְּךָ עָשִׂיתָ אֵת כָּל הַגְּדוּלָּה הַזֹּאת "For thy servant's sake, and according to thy heart, hast thou done all this greatness", still following in the vocalization the text of II Samuel. But no further proof is needed to show that the original text, preserved correctly in the consonants of I Chronicles, meant: בַּעֲבוּר עַבְדְּךָ וְכַלְבְּךָ "For the sake of thy slave and dog hast thou done all this greatness".

In the Lachish Letters the formula מי עבדך כלב כי occurs also in V, 3 f.; VI, 2 and possibly in IX, 2 f. Different from the Biblical formula עבדך וכלבך "thy slave and thy dog" (I Chronicles XVII, 19)

---

[1] As to the original form and meaning of the name Yhwh, *see also* my book, *Die Bundeslade und die Anfänge der Religion Israels,* pages 73–78.

or עבדך הכלב "thy slave the dog" (II Kings VIII, 13), our letters have עבדך כלב, which could be explained as "thy slave a dog", and would thus remind us of the phrase "one single dog" in Amarna (*see above*), or "a single flea", in I Samuel XXIV, 15 (14). But there is also a possibility that מי עבדך כלב כי stands for מי עבדך כלבך כי "who is thy slave, thy dog, that . . ." writing the double כ of כלבך כי only once, as in III, 9 חיהוה for חי יהוה, וכ יאמר III, 8 instead of וכי יאמר (*cf.* the note on these passages). In this case the haplography would show that כלבך was not pronounced כַּלְבְּךָ, thus separating its last consonant "k" from the "k" of the following כי by a vowel, but rather as כַּלְבָּךְ as used *in pausa* and generally in Mishnaic Hebrew.

The pronoun in [ע]בדה "his slave" in line 4, is written with ה and not with ו as is usual in the Bible, and in רעו "his comrade" (thrice) in the Siloam inscription. On the other hand the spelling with ה is used throughout in the Moabite stone (*cf.*, *e.g.* 1, 4–5 כי יאנף כמש בארצה ויחלפה בנה "for Kemosh was angry with his land, and him followed his son"), and occurs sometimes in the Bible as in אָהֳלֹה (Genesis IX, 21); עירה . . . סותה (Genesis XLIX, 11) (*cf.* Gesenius-Kautzsch-Cowley, *Hebrew Grammar*, 91 e), where it had not always been recognized by the Massoretic vocalization.[1]

It may be asked whether the different spelling of the pronoun with ה instead of the regular Massoretic ו is merely of orthographic character or whether it here implies a different pronunciation, such as the Aramaic ה in עַבְדֵּהּ, since also in Phoenician inscriptions the spelling with י instead of the Hebrew ו proves a similar pronunciation (*see* the notes on Letter III, line 8).

The last sentence, lines 5–6, presents great difficulties; the second sign in the verb after עבדה and the two last letters of דבר line 5 became clear only after the final cleaning of the ostracon, thus disproving any other previously considered reading. That which first suggests itself is—in accordance with "that my lord has *remembered* (זכר) thy slave"—"may Yhwh *remember* (יזכר) my lord"; but the sign is decidedly not ו (*cf.* the almost horizontal broad ו in line 4). And how should "may Yhwh remember my lord" be followed by "something which thou dost (or: I do) not know?" יזכר could also be interpreted as a causative form יַזְכֵּר "may Yhwh remind my [lord of] something which thou dost not know"; but הזכיר is not used in this way in Biblical Hebrew. The passages Isaiah XLIII, 26 הַזְכִּירֵנִי נִשָּׁפְטָה יָחַד, LXII, 6, הַמַּזְכִּרִים אֶת־יְהוָֹה אַל־דֳּמִי לָכֶם quoted by Gesenius-Buhl, 17th edition, *page* 198 b, have by no means this sense,[2] and such an explanation would distort the whole meaning of the letter. The writer expresses his thanks to Ya'ush "who had remembered his slave", *i.e.* who had thought him worthy of consideration and had bestowed upon him a favour or an honour; therefore he may wish to express in his blessings, that thus Yhwh may remember his lord and give him favour and honour—but certainly not that Yhwh may strengthen his lord's memory and make him remember something he may have forgotten and thus does not know. This would be irony, and does not fit in with the humble attitude of the letters. There is also no need to strengthen the lord's memory, who had remembered even his slave. However, the

---

[1] Thus in Proverbs XXVI, 6 the Massoretic vocalization מְקַצֶּה רַגְלַיִם חָמָס שֹׁתֶה שֹׁלֵחַ דְּבָרִים בְּיַד־כְּסִיל "He cutteth off the feet and drinketh damage that sendeth a message by the hand of a fool" gives no real sense. But as shown in *ZDMG*. lxxii (1918), *page* 165 the adage really meant . . . מְקֻצֶּה רַגְלַיִם חֹמֵם שֹׁתֶה "like the man whose feet are cut off and he uncovers his buttocks (thus showing his bodily defect to everybody) is he that sendeth a message by the hand of a fool", the fool will show to everybody his weakness. (For חמס "to uncover" *see* Jeremiah XIII,

22 נִגְלוּ שׁוּלַיִךְ נֶחְמְסוּ עֲקֵבָיִךְ "are thy skirts discovered, thy heels made bare", Job XV, 33 : יַחְמֹס כַּגֶּפֶן בִּסְרוֹ "He shall shake off his unripe grape as the vine"; Lamentations II, 6 וַיַּחְמֹס כַּגַּן שֻׂכּוֹ "and he has thrown off as a garden his twigs".) The correctness of this interpretation is confirmed by the continuation, Proverbs XXVI, 7: דַּלְיוּ שֹׁקַיִם מִפִּסֵּחַ וּמָשָׁל בְּפִי כְסִילִים "(As when) the legs of the lame are lifted (to dance) thus is a parable in the mouth of fools".

[2] *See also* immediately.

letter following the ‎י‎ in ‎ י־כר ‎ is certainly not ‎ ז‎, and it seems that no other letter than ‎ ב ‎ is graphically and linguistically possible; this is also the opinion of Mr. Harding who checked my readings with me. On this basis I tried the following interpretation:[1]

‎ בַּכֵּר ‎ (‎ יַבְכֵּר ‎ seems to be unlikely) is used in the Bible to show the preference given to a son by recognizing him as the firstborn (‎ בְּכֹר ‎; *cf.* Deuteronomy XXI, 15–16). Therefore the verb ‎ בַּכֵּר ‎ has developed in later Hebrew the general meaning: "to prefer, to privilege". Further, the now clear reading of the word in line 6 proved definitely that ‎ א ‎ at the end of line 5 and ‎ י ‎ the first letter on line 6, belong to a separate word, not to be joined with the following ‎ דבר ‎. This shows that two letters are missing, a small piece being broken off the sherd, on which were the right corner of the ‎ כ ‎ in line 4, the ‎ ע ‎ of ‎ עבדך ‎ line 5, and two letters of ‎ א[. .]י ‎ lines 5–6. For this word ‎ א[דנ]י ‎ "my lord" seemed the most probable reading, this being apparently the only noun which the writer compounds with the pronominal suffix of the first person (*but see page* 42). The difficulty of connecting "May Yhwh privilege my lord" with the following "something which thou dost not know", seemed to be relieved by the fact that our ostraca sometimes use abbreviated sentences (*cf.* the notes to IV, line 7; VI, line 5 *sqq.*). Thus our sentence could be understood as "May Yhwh privilege my lord (telling thee) something which thou dost not know", or even "I do not know".

Ya'ush has honoured the writer by sending him a letter to ask him about something. But what Ya'ush has asked he cannot answer; so instead of disappointing his lord by a negative answer he says in typically Oriental fashion: "May Yhwh privilege my lord telling him the thing which I do not know!" *Cf.* the similar attitude of Joseph, Genesis XLI, 16, and Daniel II, 27, whose courteous refusal was not meant as definite,[2] though it could be taken as such, but for the wish of the kings, who do not want to accept it.

The peculiar ‎ ידעתה ‎ can, as III, line 8 shows, be meant for "*I* do not know *it*" or even "I do not know" (*see* the notes on this passage). However, taken in itself this interpretation would not necessitate such a rendering. We could accept for it the translation: "May Yhwh privilege my lord, telling him something, which *thou* dost not know", adding as self-understood: "and which also I whom thou hast asked, do not know".

Now, is there another more likely interpretation? H. L. Ginsberg, in *Bulletin of the Jewish Palestine Exploration Society*, vol. III, *page* 80, offers a different solution. According to him we should have to accept the reading ‎ יַזְכֵּר ‎; the doubtful letter, he holds, is at least more like a ‎ ז ‎ than a ‎ ב ‎, particularly resembling the ‎ ז ‎ in Letter V, while differing from the sign used in line 4 of our letter. And although nowhere in the Bible ‎ הִזְכֵּר אֶת־אִישׁ דָּבָר ‎ is used for "to remind somebody of something", he takes it only as mere chance that this "idea" does not occur in the Bible. And "something which thou dost not know" he understands as "which thou hast not had in mind", thus reaching the following interpretation: Ya'ush has done one favour to his slave, but another one he has not granted. And thus the Letter says: "May Yhwh remind my lord also of the other favour which thou has not kept in mind".

However, this interpretation offers too many difficulties to be accepted even as possible. As a renewed careful examination proved again, the doubtful letter, as it stands, if not miswritten for a quite different sign, can by no means be ‎ ז ‎. It does not in the least resemble any form of this sign, neither in our letter nor in Letter V, line 10; there is not one single stroke suitable in size,

---

[1] Given here only in outline, as later on another, now more probable, explanation is offered.
[2] The same could be the case in our letter.

place and direction for any forms of the ז, the ⌐ of our letter, or the ⌐ of V, or any other form occurring in our ostraca. On the other hand, all the strokes visible of our sign can be parts of a rather big ב; the other letters of this word are also rather large. The phrasing יַזְכֵּר יהוה אֶת־אֲדֹנִי דָּבָר "May Yhwh remind my lord of something" is not only foreign to Biblical Hebrew, but in contradiction to it. הזכר when meaning "to mention" and thus connected with "something", which is mentioned, refers to the person "to whom" the mention is made by אל "to, unto", as וְהִזְכַּרְתַּנִי אֶל־פַּרְעֹה Genesis XL, 14 "and make mention of me *unto* Pharaoh"; כֹּל אֲשֶׁר יַזְכִּיר אֹתָהּ אֵלָיו Isaiah XIX, 17, "every one that maketh mention thereof *unto* it (*i.e.* unto Egypt)", and by ל "to" as Psalms LXXXVII, 4, אַזְכִּיר רַהַב וּבָבֶל לְיֹדְעָי "I will make mention of Rahab and Babylon *to* them that know me". Thus the idea "to mention something (or somebody) *to* somebody, to remind somebody of something", is certainly not unusual in the Bible, in its proper and correct wording, but as הזכר originally means "to mention" and therefore "to utter", "to invoke", and not "to remind", it is just as impossible to say in Biblical Hebrew יזכר יהוה את אדני דבר as in English "may Yhwh mention my lord something" instead of: "(un)to my lord". Furthermore, ידע "to know" may in some instances (as Jeremiah I, 5; II, 19; V, 1 "to see and know") be understood as "to keep in mind", particularly in the imperative: "And see now, and know" (V, 1). But even here the prophet, in order to strengthen the force of his words, insinuates that he who hears his words really does not know; he wants him not "to keep in mind" what he already knows, but to see, and only then he will know. However, the negative "something, which thou dost (or do) not know" can certainly not mean "a favour, which thou hast forgotten to bestow upon me".

It is also not in accordance with the humble attitude of the "slave" and "dog" in our letter to tell his lord plainly: "One favour thou hast done to me; but I am still waiting for another favour, which thou hast forgotten and of which God may remind thee!" And finally the words "Who is thy slave, a dog, that my lord has remembered his slave" indeed do not refer to any other favour than—as suggested above—the fact that *he had sent letters to him*. This is definitely proved by Letter V, lines 3–5: "Who is thy slave, a dog (that) thou (hast) sent to thy slave the [le]tter[s . . .]" and Letter VI, lines 2–4: "who is thy slave, a dog, that my lord has sent the letter of the king with the letters of the officers . . ." and so on. This formula is, as it seems, only the typical acknowledgement of letters received, not of special favours done (*see also* the notes on Letters V, IX and VII). Where Ya'ush has sent letters of the king, the writer says: "Who is thy slave . . ., that my lord has sent the king's letter". Where Ya'ush himself has sent his own letter he acknowledges receipt, saying: "Who is thy slave . . . that my lord has remembered his slave!" Nothing more than this is meant.

And therefore the remaining sentence independently must stand for the answer. And if no real answer is given, but reference made to Yhwh, who "may . . . my [lord?] something which I do not (or: thou dost not) know," the first interpretation would be mainly true: May Yhwh tell thee something which I do not know.[1] Though in particulars, as in the explanation of the difficult יבכר, it would remain partly doubtful.

However, there everything depends on the two missing letters at the beginning of line 6. If we really have to read אַ[דֹנ]י "my lord" at the end of line 5 and the beginning of line 6, there really may be no other explanation than that offered above. But as שלחך "thy sending", III, 7, and other examples now show, there is the chance of another word, at least an infinitive with the

---

[1] There is no need to mention other suggestions offered by different scholars, based upon the incorrect readings, יעכר/יזכר.

42

pronomen suffixum, standing here, and thus other possibilities open up. So we could think in connexion with דבר "a word" about a *verbum dicendi* as אָמְרִי "my saying (a word)".

And now a different, and more satisfying interpretation of Letter II would be possible if this ostracon is to be connected essentially with Letter III[1]—and likewise with VI and XII, dealing with the same matters as III. And as Letter II is written upon a piece of the same pot as Letter VI, there is every reason to assume that it is sent by the same man, approximately at the same time, and dealing with the same subject, as Letters III and VI.

In Letter III, the writer, Hosha'yahu, who, as it seems, is accused of telling secrets learned from confidential letters, declares on oath that he did not know anything of the contents of any letter passing through his hands. This solemn statement is repeated again and again, at least in Letters VI and XII. Thus it is not only possible, but most probable, that Letter II also is sent by the same man Hosha'yahu and gives the same declaration (for the question why this statement is repeated in more than one letter *see also* the notes on Letter V) as the oath in III, VI and XII in one short sentence, which, too, is an oath: "May Yhwh investigate (and punish!) my telling (אָמְרִי) something which I did not even know!" "My saying" is, as shown above, certainly a very plausible reading.

There remains only the difficulty of finding the fitting verb for the letters יבכר. This I am now inclined to understand as a different writing (perhaps also under the influence of יזכר in line 4) of יְבַקֵּר "may he investigate!". *Cf.* the same change of ק and כ, when near to ר, in בכר־בקר (Arabic بكر) in the meaning "early, morning", etc.; for בַּקֵּר "to investigate, to inspect", *see also* IV, 9,[2] and *cf.* the similar use of דרש "to seek, to investigate" for God's punishment in passages as Deuteronomy XVIII, 19 "whoever will not hearken unto my words . . . I will require it of him" (אָנֹכִי אֶדְרֹשׁ מֵעִמּוֹ), and often. For ידעתה, which then must mean "I do (or: did) not know (it)", *see* notes on Letter III, 8.[3]

Although this interpretation is not quite definitely established in particulars, the main idea can be taken as highly probable.

Letter II, according to this new explanation, is written by Hosha'yahu, the sender of Letter III, and gives the same statement: "I never have known the thing I am accused of telling" (*see* Letters V and VI).

The writing of Letter II differs in many points from that of Letter I, and is, in its excellent preservation, the best example of the bold, flowing and even artistic handwriting of ancient Judah. In the straight lines upon the curved surface, in the energetic features of the God-name in lines 2 and 5, one sees how the "ready scribe" both enjoys and loves to write. This single letter, coming from a place smaller than Lachish,[4] is in itself sufficient proof of highly-developed penmanship in ancient Judah.

Note particularly the rounded, more cursive, form of the ב, the broad ז and ש, the one-stroke ג, the long down-stroke of the sharp-pointed ר in contrast to the forms in Letter I. Note also the broad כ with its two distinct left-hand strokes as characteristic for the scribe of Letter II.

---

[1] As a matter of course I was looking for such a connexion between the לא ידעתה of Letter II and Letter III from the very beginning. However, a chance question of Sir Charles Marston made me look more thoroughly for the missing link. But only after recognizing the fact, that also in Letter III Hosha'yahu denies having *said*, what he in fact, did not know, the otherwise cryptic "my saying something, which I do not know" received sense and proper meaning.

[2] *Cf. also* the similar use of בקר in Biblical Aramaic, as in Ezra VI, 1: וּבַקַּרוּ בְּבֵית סְפְרַיָּא "and search was made in the house of the rolls".

[3] Accepting the reading proposed above one could perhaps translate "May Yhwh investigate my saying a word (about) which thou dost not know". But then (דַּבְּרִי (דָּבָר, "my speaking a word", not אָמְרִי, "saying, telling", would be expected.

[4] *See* the notes on Letter IV.

LETTER III

Photo: Messrs. Ilford Ltd.

46

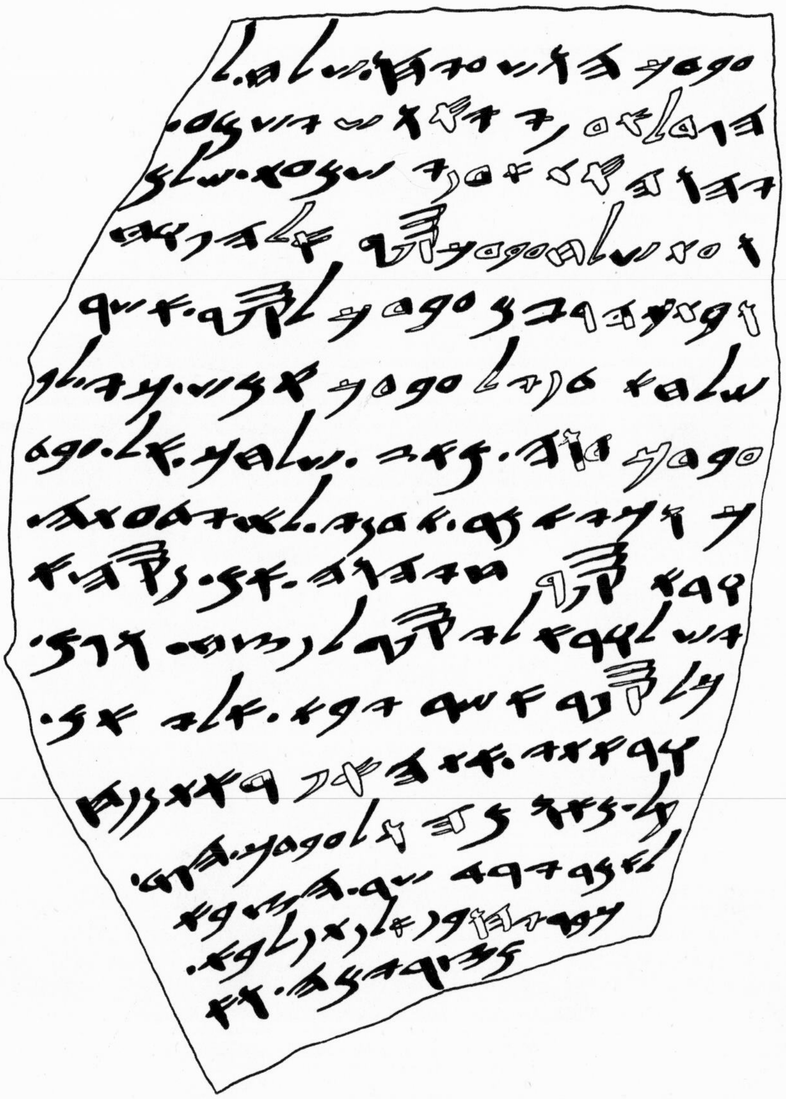

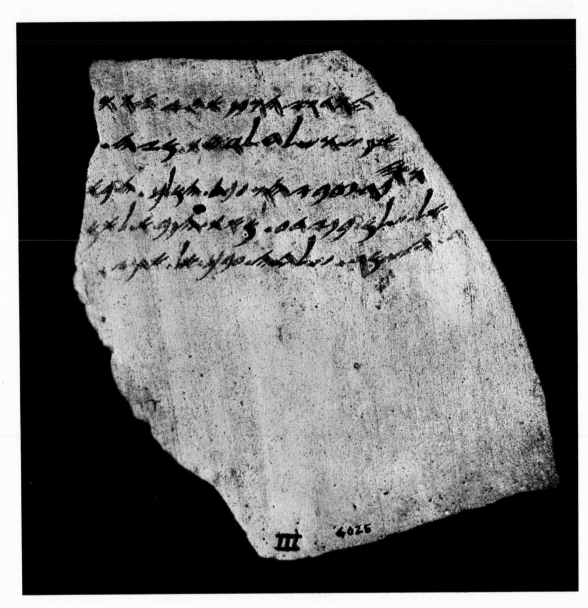

Photo: Messrs. Ilford Ltd.

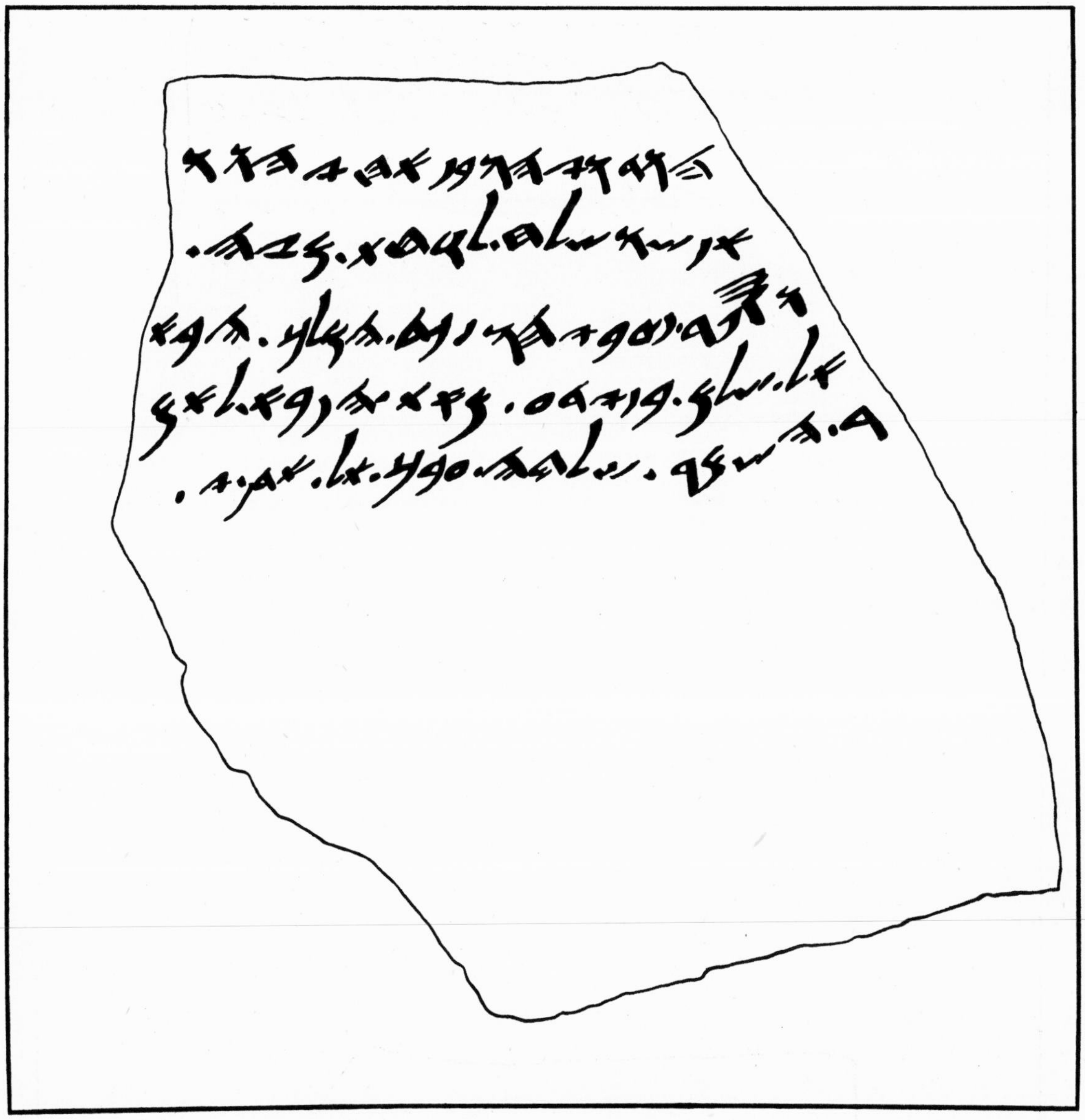

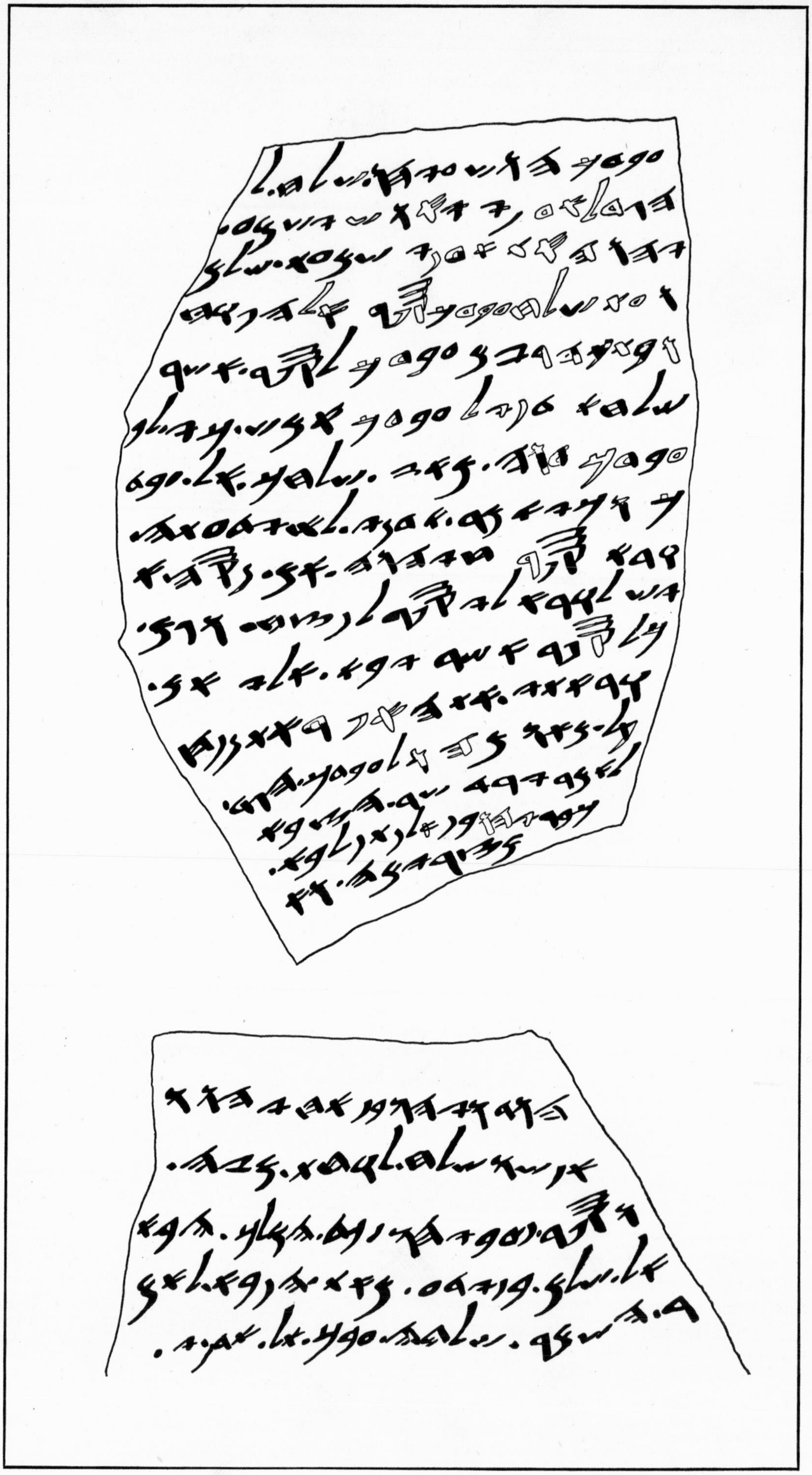

LETTER III

TRANSLITERATION [1]

OBVERSE

1. עבדך הושעיהו · שלח · ל
2. הג[ד] לאדני יאו[ש] ישמע ·
3. יהוה [את] אדני שמעת · שלם
4. [ועת] שלח עבדך ס[פ]ר אל הפקח ·
5. [ו]ב[נת]כה רזם עבדך לספר · אשר
6. שלח · אדני לעבדך אמש · כי · לב
7. [ע[בד]ך] דוה · מאז · שלחך · אל · עבד
8. ך · וכיאמר · אדני · לא · ידעתה ·
9. קרא ספר חיהוה · אם · נסה · א
10. יש לקרא לי ספר לנצח · וגם ·
11. כל ספר אשר יבא · אלי אם ·
12. קראתי · אתה [אפ] ראת מנהו
13. כל · מאומ[ה] ולעבדך · הגד ·
14. לאמר ירד שר · הצבא
15. [י]כבריהו בן אלנתן לבא ·
16. מצרימה · ואת

REVERSE

17. הודויהו בן אחיהו ו
18. אנשו שלח · לקחת · מזה ·
19. וספר · נדביהו נכד · המלך · הבא
20. אל · שלם · בן ידע · מאת · הנבא · לאמ
21. ר · השמר · שלחה · עבך · אל · אדני ·

TRANSLATION

1. Thy slave Hoshaʿyahu has sent to
2. tell my lord Yaʾush: May
3. Yhwh let hear my lord tidings of peace.
4. [And now:] Thy slave has sent a letter to the open-eyed
5. [and in it] referred thy slave to the letter which
6. my lord had sent to thy slave yesterday (and said), that
7. thy slave's heart is sick, since thou hast sent to thy slave
8. and that he says: My lord I do not know
9. to read a letter. Yhwh lives (to punish me) if anybody has tried
10. to read to me a letter for ever! And also
11. whatever letter came to me, I
12. have not read it and even not seen of it
13. anything. And to thy slave it has been told
14. saying: Down went the commander of the army
15. [Yi]khbaryahu the son of Elnatan to come
16. to Egypt. And

17. Hodawyahu (acc.) the son of Aḥiyahu and
18. his men he sent (= ordered) to take (= bring)[2] from here.
19. And a letter, which Nedabyahu the "nepos" of the king had brought
20. to Shallum the son of Yadduaʿ from the prophet saying:
21. Beware! has thy slave sent to my lord.

---

[1] No diacritical signs are used to indicate graphically doubtful letters, since all this can be seen more clearly from the hand copies and the photographs, and all points of doubt are fully discussed in the following notes.

[2] i.e. "he sent (= ordered) to bring Hodawyahu and his men from here".

NOTES

LINE 1. הושעיהו Hosha'yahu is a name found in the abbreviated form הושעיה Hosha'yah (Hoshaiah) in the Bible, after the exile (Nehemiah XII, 32) and in Jeremiah's time (Jeremiah XLII, 1; XLIII, 2, *see* notes on Ya'zanyahu I, 2), and also in Elephantine (Cowley, 22, 7; 25, 2; 40, 5; 52, 13). Many similar names are known. שלח "to send" usually means in our ostraca "to send a message", and mostly with or without the complement ספר "to send (sometimes = 'to write') a letter" (*cf.* lines 5–6, אדני. שלח· אשר· לספר "to the letter which my lord had sent"). In the same way it is often used in the Bible (*cf.* שלח ספר II Kings V, 5; שלח דברים Proverbs XXVI, 6; שלח without an object in the same sense, Numbers XXII, 10: "Balak the son of Zippor, king of Moab, hath sent (שלח) unto me (saying): Behold, there is a people"; שלח לאמר Genesis XXXVIII, 25, etc.) and in Aramaic. Used in this sense שלח seems to be the translation of the Accadic *shaparu* "to send, to write" occurring frequently in the Amarna letters. *See also* the note on שלח לקחת line 18.

The formula "N.N. has sent to tell" (שָׁלַח לְהַגִּד) gives the name of the sender of the message; there is no such introductory sentence in our other letters, which start immediately with the greeting, not mentioning the sender's name; also, while here Letter III adds an unusual introduction before the greeting, this in itself is rather abbreviated: "May Yhwh let hear my lord tidings of peace", while most of the other letters (but *cf.* Letter IX) add, at least once, the words "even now" or a similar expression. The introduction is reminiscent of the usual Babylonian formula: "To N.N. speaks thus N.N."

For the phrasing: שָׁלַח לְהַגִּד "he has sent to tell" *cf. also* II Samuel XI, 22: וַיֵּלֶךְ הַמַּלְאָךְ וַיָּבֹא וַיַּגֵּד לְדָוִד אֵת כָּל־אֲשֶׁר שְׁלָחוֹ יוֹאָב "So the messenger went and told David all that Joab had sent him for".

LINE 2. יאוש. The first three letters can be recognized and make the reading of the name reliable. For the greeting, *cf.* the note to Letter II, line 1 and VI, 1–2.

The reading of the lines 4–5 presented great difficulties. The ס, with the remains of a ר following soon afterwards, cannot belong to any other word than ספר, "a letter". Preceding this word the traces of עבדך were visible and then the completion of "thy slave a letter" into "thy slave sent a letter to" suggested itself and the traces fitted well with this reading. ועת "and now" as in IV, 2, is, although the most likely word in this place,[1] only conjectural, and any other word like הנה "behold" may have stood in its place, but the general meaning is not altered by this. The apparent down-stroke at the beginning of the line is not a letter, but a flaw on the surface of the potsherd.

After "a letter had thy slave sent to" the following word at the end of line 4 must have denoted a person to whom the letter was sent. For these signs I was at first inclined to read הן קח, though unable to make any real sense. Without some knowledge of the contents, the word הפקח seemed inexplicable. However, the reading הפקח is now quite clear; the ה stands next to the following sign without a word divider, and therefore belongs to this same word; the second sign is not נ with the following word-dividing dot (the dot is written quite differently and is a point, not a clear stroke as in this case), but a clear פ, the נ being written in these lines in a distinctly different form, *cf.* the angular נ in אדני, line 8. The signs קח are very distinct and so is the dot after the ח, showing that here the word is ended.

---

[1] Where in Biblical letters, as in Ezra IV, 17, no greeting precedes the word(s) "and now", which there seem(s) to stand at the beginning of the letter, certainly not the whole letter, but only the relevant part of it is quoted.

However, הפקח is certainly nothing else but the well-known Hebrew adjective פִּקֵחַ "open-eyed" (*cf.* the frequent פקח עינים "to open the eyes" in Biblical Hebrew), "seeing", the only nominal form known of this "root" in ancient Hebrew, with the article. *Cf.* Exodus IV, 11, "who hath made man's mouth? or who maketh the dumb, or deaf, or the seeing (פִּקֵחַ), or the blind? have not I the Lord?"; XXIII, 8, "and thou shalt take no gift: for the gift blindeth the seeing (פִּקְחִים) and perverteth the words of the righteous". There is no other linguistical explanation of הפקח. "To open the eyes" (*cf.* also the Arabic فَقَح "to open one's eyes") is the only meaning of פקח in Biblical Hebrew, occurring frequently as the basic meaning of the word also in post-Biblical language. Thus *e.g.* God alone is called (in later times) the פּוֹקֵחַ עִוְרִים "the one who opens the eyes of the blind and makes them see". Not until many centuries after the latest writings recorded in the Bible, we find a verb פִּקֵחַ עַל for "to take care of", which may be an elliptic development of "to keep (the eyes) open upon", but may also be of Aramaic origin (*cf.* the Syriac ܦܩܚ "better, right", ܦܩܚܐܝܬ "rightly", wherefrom a verb meaning "to put right, to take care of", could easily develop). However, there is not the least possibility of finding a Hebrew noun like פַּקָח or פֶּקַח for "caretaker" in Jeremiah's time. It is also not possible, as one might be inclined to do, to take הפקח "the open-eyed" in a contrary sense for "the blind one", according to the euphemistic use of the Aramaic סגי נהור "the one who has much light" for "blind", because this expression is entirely based upon a late misunderstanding of the proverb (Gen. Rabba 30): "In the street of the blind they call the *one-eyed* (עויךא, here as Arabic أَعْوَر, not the blind) rich in light (סגי־נהור)". There was no such euphemistic expression for "blind" in earlier Talmudic times, much less in Biblical Hebrew.[1] The special significance of פִּקֵחַ "the open-eyed" in our letter will be seen later. ספר "letter", as far as I can see, is the only certain Babylonian loan-word (a very old one) in the otherwise pure Hebrew of Lachish.[2]

In line 5 עבדך לספר אשר was easily readable. But to what could לַסֵּפֶר "*to* the letter" refer? That ספר meant "letter" and not perhaps סַפֵּר "to tell" was clear from the following "which my lord has (or had) sent". It is characteristic that in the Bible the combination לספר "*to* the letter (or book)" does not occur at all, while בספר, על (ה)ספר, הספר "the book (or letter), on a (the) book, in a book" are used very frequently, since the usual ways to mention a letter are "to write, send, read a letter, to write upon a letter, to read in a letter". But at last I recognized in the signs preceding the word עבדך the letters רזם, the Biblical form for the Aramaic (and therefore later Hebrew) רמז "to hint at, to wink at, to *refer* to". *Cf.* Job XV, 12 וּמַה־יִּרְזְמוּן עֵינֶיךָ "and what do thy eyes wink at?". And even this passage in Job XV, 12, we can now interpret more correctly: "and what do thy eyes refer to, (13) that . . . thou lettest such words go out of thy mouth?"

Thus in Job, as in our letter רזם stands for "referring to words"[3] said or written. And now the sentence can be easily reconstructed as: "and in it (*i.e.* in this letter; Hebrew וּבָתֹכֹה) referred (hinted, alluded) thy slave to the letter, which my lord had sent to thy slave yesterday".[4]

---

[1] *Cf.* my note in the Hebrew review *Dvir*, vol. II (Berlin, 1924), *page* 63.

[2] But perhaps also דלת "door" is to be considered as a loan-word from Accadic *daltu* to *edelu* "to shut", while ידל is not used in Hebrew.

[3] *See also* my German commentary on Job (*Das Buch Hiob, eine kritische Analyse des überlieferten Hiobtextes*, Vienna 1920) on this passage. A new, revised edition has been prepared.

[4] There is no room for the more correct fuller spelling ובתוכה (but *cf.* even in the Bible the defective בְּתֹכְכֶם Genesis XXXV, 2; Numbers XXXII, 30; בְּתֹכָם Job II, 1). Cassuto, l.c., *page* 170 *sqq.*, while following the main idea of the interpretation, in order to avoid the apparent difficulty, that Hosha'yahu, the sender of the letter "pretends", that he does not know to read a letter, prefers a negative sense: "ma in essa *non*—Hebrew: (ובה לא)—ha accennato il tuo servo alla lettera . . ." However, as shown further on, the

The correct reading of the following sentence, line 7–8, did not occur to me till January, 1936. Wrongly taking the faint three letters after ‏[ע]בדך‎ in line 8 as ‏אתה אחֹה‎, or ‏אַֽתֹה‎) "that thy slave ... (with) him", I had to look for a verb, and therefore, while realising that the last incomplete sign of line 7 could also be ‏ב‎ instead of ‏כ‎,[1] I erroneously accepted for the last signs of line 7 the reading ‏כילך‎ which I interpreted "that thy slave should go (‏= כִּי יֵלֵךְ‎) with him". Thus I found no way to connect the words ‏מאז שלחך‎ with the following sentence, or with the preceding words either, if taken in the more frequent relative sense ‏מֵאָז שְׁלָחֲךָ‎ "since thou hast written"[2] and tried to explain them as "then (= long ago) he already had sent thus".

However, as Ch. Yalon, in the *Bulletin of the Jewish Palestine Exploration Society*, vol. III, *page* 88, has pointed out, the letter is rather ‏ב‎ and not ‏כ‎. And as ‏לֵב‎, "the heart (of the slave)" is a substantive, it must be accepted not as the predicate but as the subject of the sentence. Now, Yalon's interpretation, "and in it hinted thy slave to tell (‏לְסַפֵּר‎) instead of ‏לְסֵפֶר‎), that (‏אשר!‎) my lord has written ... that the heart of thy servant is with him (‏כִּי · לֵב · עַבְדְּךָ אִתֹּה‎) since thou hast written to thy slave" is unacceptable,[3] mainly because friendship of the heart is no proper result of the lord's letter. This letter, which farther on makes the slave exculpate himself in an impressive oath, certainly did not make his heart friendly towards somebody, but rather *ache* under the accusation expressed in it, and it is this which causes his apologies. Looking for such a word, I found that what I at first was inclined to read as ‏אתה‎, was really ‏דָּוֶה‎ sick: "*that thy slave's heart is sick since thou hast sent to thy slave*". *Cf.* the Biblical phrases: Lamentations V, 17 ‏עַל־זֶה הָיָה דָוֶה לִבֵּנוּ עַל־אֵלֶּה חָשְׁכוּ עֵינֵינוּ‎ "For this our heart is faint (sick); for these things our eyes are dim"; Isaiah I, 5 ‏כָּל־רֹאשׁ לָחֳלִי וְכָל־לֵבָב דַּוָּי‎ "The whole head is sick, and the whole heart faint"; Jeremiah VIII, 18 ‏עָלַי לִבִּי דַוָּי‎ "My heart is faint in me"; Lamentations I, 22, ‏כִּי־רַבּוֹת אַנְחֹתַי וְלִבִּי דַוָּי‎ "For my sighs are many, and my heart is faint". This reading gives a new basis for the understanding of the facts to which our letter alludes. It is Ya'ush who, in his preceding message, informed Hosha'yahu that in some way he had aroused the Piqqeaḥ's and his own indignation. How this has been done depends on the interpretation of the following oath. However, his lord has not only informed him of the facts, but certainly also ordered him, to seek the Piqqeaḥ's forgiveness.

The following ‏וכיאמר‎ now clearly stands for ‏וכי · יאמר‎,[4] the Yodh being written only once for both words. We thus have here the same kind of haplography as, possibly, in ‏כלבך כי‎ for ‏כי · כלבך‎, II, 4, and certainly in ‏חיהוה‎ for ‏חי · יהוה‎ in the following line 9. Such cases of haplography are not unusual in the Massoretic text of the Bible; many instances of it have already been shown by S. D. Luzzato, Graetz, B. Epstein, Frd. Delitzsch and F. Perles;[5] *cf. e.g.* Jeremiah XV, 1, ‏שַׁלַּח מֵעַל‎ ‏פָּנַי וְיֵצֵאוּ‎ for ‏שַׁלְּחֵם מֵעַל פָּנַי וְיֵצֵאוּ‎ "Cast them out of my sight and let them go forth" and *see also* Lidzbarski's *Ephemeris*, II, 209 for similar cases in *Aramaic Endorsements on Babylonian Cuneiform Tablets*, as ‏בנשיא‎ for Ba-na-na-sha-a, etc.; *cf. also* notes on ‏לקרא · לי‎ in line 10.

As shown above, Hosha'yahu, in lines 4–7, says: "I have sent a letter to the Piqqeaḥ, referring in it to the letter received from thee yesterday, and declaring, that my heart is sick, since I received thy letter, informing me of some accusation directed against me".

---

difficulty leading to this rather forced explanation is to be solved in a quite simple way, and Hosha'yahu, in his letter to the Piqqeaḥ, actually refers to Ya'ush's message, saying, that his heart was sick, since he received it.

[1] My first copies note both possibilities.

[2] From my original manuscript, written in London, July, 1935.

[3] So is Albright's (l.c., *page* 13) "thy servant hath been mindful of it" following the same reading.

[4] For the meaning see *pages* 55–57.

[5] *Cf.* the literature mentioned in the latter's *Analekten zur Textkritik des Alten Testaments, Neue Folge, page* 24 *sqq.*

However, is this all that Hosha'yahu has to tell about the contents of his letter to the Piqqeaḥ? This depends upon the interpretation of line 8 *sqq.* The most natural way is to take the following as a continuation of lines 6–7 "(that thy slave's heart is sick) and [*that he says: My lord,*] I do not know (it) to read a letter. Yhwh liveth (and may punish me) if anybody attempted to read to me a letter . . ."

Another possibility has been suggested by U. Cassuto and W. F. Albright. The latter (l.c., *page* 73)[1] takes the following as: "*And if my lord* says: 'Thou dost not know it?—read (my) letter!'" (וְכִ · יֹאמַר · אֲדֹנִי · לֹא · יְדַעְתָּ[ה]וּ · קְרָא · סְפְּר[ִי]) as Yhwh liveth . . ."

However, there is no need to assume a quite unconnected "Thou dost not know *it*?" What is "it"? How could Hosha'yahu understand such a question? There also is no necessity to read סְפְּר[ִי] or [ידעתה]וּ and even to take קרא as an imperative. One could reach the same sense by simply translating: "And if my lord says 'Dost thou not know (לֹא · יְדַעְתָּה) to read a letter?' Yhwh lives (to punish me) if ever anybody tried to read a letter to me!" This translation, which is, indeed, suggested by Cassuto (*page* 172), may linguistically offer no insuperable difficulties.[2] However, there are other objections against it. First, it seems impossible to start with "*and if* my lord says*", naming, apparently, another point out of Ya'ush's refutable accusations, while nothing at all has up till now been quoted,[3] and while, when reference is made to Ya'ush's message, this is accepted as read and *obeyed*; further, the question: "dost thou not know?" should have been expressed by הֲלֹא instead of the misleading לֹא (*cf.* Letter VI, lines 8–9 הלא תכתב "dost thou not write?"). Then the answer to the question "dost thou not know to read a letter?" (or even to an imperative: "read my letter!") should be: "No, I certainly do not know it", not: "nobody has ever tried to read to me a letter". This can only be said continuing and amplifying the necessary statement: "I do not know to read a letter". And is it at all likely that Ya'ush should ask somebody who, as it turns out, does not, in fact, know to read: "Dost thou not know to read a letter?" It is certainly not a matter of course that everybody then knew how to read and write. Or would he even order such a person to "read the letter!" Only in addressing a man knowing how to read, and only in a rhetorical sense could one expect such a question as "Dost thou not know to read a letter?" or an imperative "Read my letter!" meaning: "Read the letter properly!" But then the answer must be quite different, *e.g.* "I certainly shall do this" or similarly, but not: "Nobody ever read to me a letter!"

And finally, it is very difficult to explain Hosha'yahu's words as apologies for such carelessness, if he says that nobody even has ever tried to read a letter to him. The letters came to him, this he does not deny; was it not his duty to *ask* somebody to read to him the letters which came to him, according to this explanation, from his mighty lord? No! Hosha'yahu's alleged misdeed seems to be rather that he has read a letter or letters which he should not have read, and perhaps spoken about their contents to unauthorized persons! And therefore he solemnly denies any possibility of having had knowledge of the contents of any letter coming to him.

---

[1] Partly following a suggestion of Mr. A. Sachs.

[2] Thus יְדַעְתָּה instead of יָדַעְתָּ in these inscriptions, although peculiar, may not be definitely excluded. However, "and *if my* lord says" where one would expect: "thou hast thus written" is very difficult. כי יאמר "If he will say" (Deuteronomy XV, 16) or כי תאמר "If thou wilt say" (Deuteronomy VII, 17; XVIII, 21; Isaiah XXXVI, 7, etc.) is used thus in the Bible only for an imaginary objection: "If it should come into one's mind to say"; but here one

could accept for "And when my lord has said" the perfect tense וכי אמר אדני (*cf.* IV, 4–5 וכי שלח אדני).

[3] Note, that in Letter IV, 4–5 "*And when* my lord has sent (שלח) about . . ." is said in proper continuation of lines 2–4: "According to whatever my lord has sent (שלח) thus has thy slave done. I have written on the page according to whatever my lord has sent (שלח) to me."

This conclusion, reached by examination of Letter III alone, seems now to receive further proof from Letter II (*see page* 43) where apparently the same man denies having said something, which—not knowing how to read—he did not even know! Thus he actually was accused of reading letters and telling their contents, and not of not reading them. For further definite proof of this explanation, *see* the remarks on lines 11–13.

For all these reasons we must prefer the other interpretation, taking וכ[ן] יאמר as the continuation of כִּי לֵב עַבְדְּךָ דָוֶה in lines 6–7: "that thy slave's heart is sick . . . and that he says: My lord, I do not know it, to read a letter. Yhwh lives (to punish me) if ever anybody tried to read to me a letter . . ."

There is only one difficulty connected with this interpretation, if we have to take ידעתה in line 8 as "I do not know it"[1] (to read a letter), that according to Biblical Hebrew one would expect ידעתי(ו)הו[2] or rather simply ידעתי "I do not know". However, even in the Bible ידעת without the Yodh occurs twice, Psalms CXL, 13, and Job XLII, 2 (*Qerē*), for ידעתי; furthermore it is not impossible, though unlikely, that at the end of the line הו had been written originally instead of ה.[3] There is also the further possibility that ה (cf. Letter II, line 3) even for the third person singular (עבדה, etc.) does not stand for "ō" as in the Massoretic vocalization, but rather as in Aramaic and Phoenician, for "ē".[4] *See page* 40.

However, in our passage as well as in II, 6 (*see above*) the simple "I know" would be the most satisfying reading, and thus ידעתה could perhaps stand here and in II, 6, simply for an emphatically pronounced יָדַעְתָּה "I know!".

We have to bear in mind that here, as in II, 6, לא ידעתה stands in an oath, where the verb could be spoken in an emphatic way, ending the vowel with "h", and this may even be the most likely explanation: "I certainly do not know!"

For the construction ידע קרא cf. Isaiah VIII, 4 כִּי בְּטֶרֶם יֵדַע הַנַּעַר קְרֹא אָבִי וְאִמִּי "For before the child shall have knowledge to cry my father and my mother". For the meaning cf. also Isaiah XXIX, 12: וְאָמַר לֹא יָדַעְתִּי סֵפֶר, which certainly is abridged for וְאָמַר לֹא יָדַעְתִּי [קְרֹא] סֵפֶר "and he saith, I do not know [to read] a book".

LINE 9. About חיהוה for חי יהוה *see note on* וכיאמר line 8. In VI, 12 and XII, 3 the formula is written in full: חי יהוה. The original meaning of the formula is not "as Yhwh liveth", but "Yhwh, the Judge of all our doings, liveth, and he may punish me, if (אם) I have done this or that"; cf. my article on חי יהוה in the Hebrew review *Leshonenu*, VI (1934), 127–137.

LINE 10. לקרא לי ספר literally "to read me a letter". The phrasing is unusual; cf. the Biblical קרא לִפְנֵי "to read before (somebody)" II Kings XXII, 10; II Chronicles XXXIV, 18: קרא בְּאָזְנֵי "to read in the ears of" Exodus XXIV, 7; Jeremiah XXXVI, 6, 10, 13–15: קרא נֶגֶד "to read in front of" Nehemiah VIII, 3. However, there may be a difference, not only in the more popular style of our letters, but also because here more than "reading before somebody" may be intended. The letters would have had to be read for him and to him to make him grasp their contents accurately. According to the writing of חיהוה, line 9, for חי יהוה the words לקרא לי could also stand for לקרא אלי "to read to me".—לָנֶצַח "(for) ever" is used here for the past, while in the Bible it stands in this sense only for the future. But, as I have pointed out in an article on לַמְנַצֵּחַ in

---

[1] With anticipation of the following object in the pronoun.

[2] As ה is always fully expressed in our ostraca, the spelling ידעתו is not to be expected.

[3] Thus Albright, l.c., for his different reading.

[4] In spite of this possibility, I have for practical reasons kept the Massoretic vocalization עֲבָדָה, etc., throughout this publication.

Leshonenu, VI, 120–126, the original meaning of נצח is "(to be) strong"; the verb נָצַח has thus also the meaning "to be victorious" (as גָּבַר); נִצֵּח in Pi'el means originally "to strengthen (the voice), to raise (the voice)" as הִגְבִּיר, and is used particularly for "accompanying a singer by strengthening music". This, "to accompany with music" is the meaning of the verb also in those cases where it has been misinterpreted as "to supervise". לָנֶצַח thus means in its strictest sense "with force, with vigour, absolutely", and only from such phrases as לֹא אֶעֱשֶׂה זֹאת לָנֶצַח "I shall not do this absolutely", or יֹאבַד לָנֶצַח "he perishes absolutely", the word received the meaning "forever". In our passage the original sense is still preserved, as also perhaps in certain Biblical passages; *see* Proverbs XXI, 28, לָנֶצַח יְדַבֵּר "he speaks with force"; Job XIV, 20, תִּתְקְפֵהוּ לָנֶצַח "thou attackest him with force"; XXIII, 7, וַאֲפַלְּטָה לָנֶצַח מִשְׁפָּטִי (read מִשְׁפָּטִי) "so should I deliver victoriously my right"; Habakkuk I, 4, וְלֹא־יֵצֵא לָנֶצַח מִשְׁפָּט "and judgement doth not go forth victoriously".

LINE 11. כל ספר אשר יבא אלי The imperfect יָבֹא does not stand here for future or present, but to express an action which continued for a longer or shorter period (Gesenius-Kautzsch-Cowley, § 107, b): "whatever letter came to me".

LINE 12. Here the word אף "also" is only conjectural, but may be correct, according to the traces left. Also אוֹ "or" (Cassuto) is possible. ראת (=רָאֹת, hardly רְאֹת) is written here in abbreviated spelling; but *cf.* ידעתה, line 8. The writer may have been influenced by the lack of space in this line;[1] *cf.* also VI, 15. Most interesting is the form מֶנְהוּ for מִמֶּנּוּ found in the Bible only in Job IV, 12 (but *cf.* the same expression written as two words מִן־הוּא Isaiah XVIII, 2 and 7).

LINE 13–15. כָּל־מְאוּמָה as in Genesis XXXIX, 23, and in II Samuel III, 35, there also in an oath: אִם לִפְנֵי בוֹא הַשֶּׁמֶשׁ אֶטְעַם־לֶחֶם אוֹ כָל־מְאוּמָה "(so do God to me, and more also,) if I taste bread or aught else, till the sun be down".

Here the question must be asked: Why is it that letters come to Hosha'yahu, if he does not read them and shows no interest in them? This can be understood only in this way, that the letters coming to him *are not intended for him*; he is only an intermediary, who has to forward the letters coming from other parts to Ya'ush or to the Piqqeaḥ, as well as Ya'ush's letters to his correspondents. Thus we find in XVIII, the immediately adjoining piece of the same pot as Letter VI (and II), the short notice that the writer forwarded a letter to Jerusalem; also according to line 21 he sends the prophet's letter to his lord. Furthermore, we are now at last able to understand Hosha'yahu's oath properly. If he solemnly declares that no letter coming to him has been read to him by anybody, he knows that his lord will understand that he refers to such letters only, which are not intended for him. *These* letters he does not read. But letters sent to him personally he certainly showed to somebody who knew how to read and who told him of their contents.

Thus what he wants to prove by his oath is this: How could I have spoken of the contents of the letters intended for others which came through my hands? I myself do not know how to read (this statement is absolutely necessary), and, as I swear, and as you may be able to investigate, nobody has read any of these letters to me. Thus there is no contradiction between his writing and receiving letters, and his oath, that he never reads or read any letter coming to him!

Now the person of Hosha'yahu becomes clearer to us. He is—as Letter III most clearly shows —one of Ya'ush's trusted subordinates in some place between Lachish and—as XVIII shows—Jerusalem. Not only Letter III, but also VI, and probably the other ostraca fragments of the same pot and dealing with the same topic, are sent by the same man—Hosha'yahu.

---

[1] It is not possible to read לראת "to see" instead of אף ראת (or אוֹ) as Cassuto also considers.

Hosha'yahu is accused of having read and spoken about letters connected in some way with the Piqqeaḥ, and against these accusations he defends himself in his letters to the Piqqeaḥ and to Ya'ush. This will become still clearer in the following; is it necessary to add that this definitely proves that לא ידעתה . קרא ספר, in lines 8–9, cannot possibly be a question: "Dost thou not know to read a letter?" or "Dost thou not know it? Read my letter!"? Nobody wants Hosha'yahu to read the confidential letters not meant for him!

The following sentence ולעבדך . הגד . לאמר can be read and translated either in active form: "and to thy slave he told (הִגֵּד), saying", or as a passive sentence: "and to thy slave it has been told, (הֻגַּד) saying". The latter impersonal rendering is certainly the correct one. The letters כבר of the name of the commander of the army in line 15 are distinctly visible, also some traces of other letters between this and the following בן, which can hardly be anything but יהו. Before כבר there is more space left than at the beginning of other lines, thus leaving the possibility, or even probability, that יכבריהו had been originally written although no traces of י are actually visible. Kebaryahu, or rather Yikhbaryahu, would mean "Yhwh is mighty".[1] One אלנתן, Elnatan (Elnathan), appears in the Bible as the father-in-law of King Jeconiah (II Kings XXIV, 8),[2] perhaps the same man as Elnatan, the son of Akhbor (Achbor), a high officer mentioned in Jeremiah XXVI, 22; XXXVI, 12 (25), though this is unlikely (*see* general remarks). The same name occurs later in Ezra VIII, 16, in Assyrian legal documents as Ili-natan, and in New Babylonian records as El-natannu (*cf.* Gesenius-Buhl, *page* 43 b). *See* the notes to Letter I and to Letter XI, 3.

LINE 16 *sqq.* In line 16, the last letter is not very distinct. The small word, beginning with וא and followed by one other letter, must be the preposition connecting the commander of the army with Hodawyahu (or Hodūyahu) and his men, mentioned in line 17. However, I am now inclined to read this word not וְאֶל "and *unto* Hodawyahu . . . he sent to take (them) from here", but, as seems palaeographically more satisfactory, וְאֶת, taking ואת הודויהו . . . שלח לקחת, literally "and Hodawyahu (accusative) . . . he sent to take", as standing for: "and to take (bring) Hodawyahu . . . he sent (message or order)" — thus avoiding the difficulty, that no object seemed to be mentioned expressly for לקחת "to take".[3] As a matter of fact, "Hodawyahu . . . and his men" is the grammatical object of לקחת and not of שלח "he sent". Or in other words: שָׁלַח לָקַחַת is rather one single compound verb: "*he let take*". For this construction "and Hodawyahu . . . he sent to take" instead of "to take Hodawyahu . . . he sent", here also caused by the intention of laying stress upon the person mentioned, *cf.* even such usual Biblical phrases as "the thing (or: the commandments) which Yhwh has commanded to do (הַדָּבָר אֲשֶׁר־צִוָּה יהוה לַעֲשֹׂות)" instead of the logical: "to do which Yhwh has commanded" (Leviticus VIII, 5) or with שלח: "all the signs and the wonders, which Yhwh sent him to do" (אֲשֶׁר שְׁלָחֹו יהוה לַעֲשֹׂות) instead of "to do which Yhwh sent him" (Deuteronomy XXXIV, 11).

For this phrasing compare, among the many passages where לקח in the Bible is used for "taking" somebody from one place to another, Genesis II, 15; XI, 31; XII, 5, particularly such sentences as Genesis XX, 2 וַיִּשְׁלַח אֲבִימֶלֶךְ מֶלֶךְ גְּרָר וַיִּקַּח אֶת־שָׂרָה "And Abimelech, king of Gerar, *sent and took* (= sent to take) Sarah" or I Samuel XIX, 14: וַיִּשְׁלַח שָׁאוּל מַלְאָכִים לָקַחַת אֶת־דָּוִד "And Saul sent messengers to take David".

---

[1] *Cf.* the interchange of the names כָּנְיָהוּ and יְכָנְיָהוּ with יְחִזְקִיָּהוּ and חִזְקִיָּהוּ.

[2] Called here Elnatan "of Jerusalem", which makes it unlikely that his father's name was known as Akhbor.

[3] Thus לקחת . מזה in line 18 does not stand for מזה . לקחתם as I assumed before.

For "to take men *from here*" (מִזֶּה) compare Jeremiah XXXVIII, 10: "Then the king commanded Ebedmelech, the Ethiopian, saying, Take from hence thirty men with thee (קַח בְּיָדְךָ מִזֶּה שְׁלֹשִׁים אֲנָשִׁים)". מִזֶּה "from here, from hence" occurs also in Letter XVIII, 2, and is very frequent in Biblical Hebrew; *cf.* Genesis XLII, 15; L, 25; Exodus XI, 1; XIII, 3, 19, and in אֵי־מִזֶּה "wherefrom?" Genesis XVI, 8; Judges XIII, 6; I Samuel XXV, 11.

LINE 17 *sqq.* הודויהו The name occurs in the same form in I Chronicles III, 24 (*Qerē*, the *Kethībh* being הודיוהו) for a post-exilic offspring of Jeconiah, and in the abbreviated form הודויה for other post-exilic Jews in the Bible and in Elephantine. The Massoretic vocalization is הוֹדַוְיָהוּ which, however, does not appear to make good sense, while the LXX ('Ωδουία) seems to approach the reading הוֹדוּיָהוּ which would mean "Acknowledge Yhwh, do homage to Yhwh", and might be preferable, although even here הוֹדוּלְיָהוּ alone would be correct. אֲחִיָהוּ is also a very well-known name, occurring, both in the full and in the abbreviated form אֲחִיָה, in the Bible for persons before Jeremiah's time and later, on the Ophel ostracon (*cf.* Diringer, *Le Iscrizioni Antico-Ebraiche Palestinesi, page* 74); as Aḫi'au in Assyrian legal records, as Aḫiyami in Ta'annek Nr. 2, Aḫiyama in New Babylonian records, and, in North Palestine pronunciation, as אחיו in Elephantine; *cf.* above to I, 1. Cassuto also mentions the possibility to read אָחִיהוּ "(the son of) his brother", which linguistically is correct, but otherwise unlikely.

LINES 19–21. In lines 19–21 a new item is introduced: "And the letter which Nedabyahu had brought from ... to ... has Hosha'yahu sent to Ya'ush his lord". Here the simple translation of lines 19–21 as two main sentences may be possible: "And a letter has Nedabyahu ... brought ...; thy slave has sent it to my lord". The anticipating of object and subject before the predicate וְסֵפֶר נְדַבְיָהוּ ... הֵבָא "and a letter Nedabyahu has brought" instead of וְסֵפֶר הֵבָא נְדַבְיָהוּ "and a letter has Nedabyahu brought" is certainly unusual, but might be in keeping with the wording of the preceding sentence: "And Hodawyahu ... he sent to take" instead of: "And to take Hodawyahu ... he sent". Here as there, Hosha'yahu in his colloquial "illiterate" speech places first, contrary to the rules of correct literary language, what is first in importance and uppermost in his mind, Hodawyahu and his men, or the fact of the letter and the name of its bringer, before telling what has been done about them. However, the syntactically more satisfactory alternative is to take נְדַבְיָהוּ הֵבָא as a relative clause depending on the main sentence in line 21: "And (as for) the letter (which) Nedabyahu ... had brought, thy slave has sent it to my lord". There is certainly no reason to accept such a far-fetched explanation as "And the *Sofer* (ספר scribe or officer) of Nedabyahu ... has brought word" (Ginsberg), nor is a purely oral message here possible. The following "thy slave has *sent it*" must refer to the letter (ספר) Hosha'yahu has mentioned. The "it" of שְׁלָחֹה cannot be explained—as I myself thought before—in an abstract way "Thy slave has sent (written) this". Hosha'yahu actually sends and forwards the letters he receives to his lord. Nor can הבא be read with Cassuto and Albright (l.c.), as הַבָּא "the coming; which came": "the letter of Nedabyahu ... which came to Shallum ... from the prophet!" A letter which came to Shallum from the prophet is the prophet's, not Nedabyahu's letter! There is no reason to take the prophet, from whom the letter comes, only as a distributor of official "circular" letters, and the summary of the letter's contents "saying beware", as only "the first word of the letter, used to identify it" (Albright). מֵאֵת "from" is used in the Bible as referring to the author of a message. There would also be no necessity in this case, where sender and addressee are named, to say in an impersonal way "a letter *which came* from A to B" instead of the simple: "which

59

A *sent* to B". And if "saying: beware" were only given for identification of Nedabyahu's (not the prophet's) letter, one certainly must have said: "And Nedabyahu's letter, saying: Beware, which came from A to B", not "and Nedabyahu's letter, which came from A to B, saying beware".

Thus it is the prophet's letter, the letter (which) Nedabyahu . . . had brought from the prophet to Shallum . . . saying (as its general contents): Beware. Such relative clauses without the relative pronoun אֲשֶׁר, as וְסֵפֶר גְּדַבְיָהוּ הֵבָא . . . are as frequent in Biblical Hebrew as in English. It is not without reason that Gesenius-Kautzsch, *Hebräische Grammatik*, 27th edition, 155 b, *page* 494, note 1, quotes for comparison the English example: "this is the *letter* [which] he wrote to me", in strict parallel to the passage in our letter.

Further, this explanation must be correct; for, as shown above, the main part of the letter deals with *the letters* which Hosha'yahu has forwarded to and from Ya'ush and the Piqqeaḥ, and which he denies having read and spoken about. And it is only in continuation of this general topic of the letters which came through his hands that he says: "And one of these letters, the letter which Nedabyahu brought from the prophet . . . thy slave has forwarded to my lord". It is the letter "saying beware", *i.e.* the warning letter of the prophet. Ya'ush had certainly ordered that all the letters coming from the Piqqeaḥ should be taken from their recipient and sent to him.

From the fact that the new subject Hosha'yahu wants to mention is not the arrival, but his dispatch of the letter which he took from Shallum, its recipient, to Ya'ush, we may perhaps conclude that the letter had come some time before.

LINE 19. נדביהו Nedabyahu is the same name as Nedabiah, mentioned as the name of a son of Jeconiah and grandson of the king Jehoiakim in I Chronicles III, 18. The reading of the following word (נכד (המלך) "the grandson (?) of the king" has been a matter of careful examination. At first one was inclined to read here the very frequent denomination עבד · המלך "the servant of the king", assuming that the two letters עב may not be completely visible. But after further examination, both Mr. Harding and I are satisfied that the reading עבד has to be definitely excluded. This result has been most carefully reconsidered, since some scholars (who did not, however, handle the original ostraca) expressed themselves in favour of the reading עבד, but finally I was led only to the same conclusion; neither ע nor ב seems possible, and thus our rare word נֶכֶד must be accepted here.

Our passage is therefore valuable for Hebrew lexicography, since נכד occurs in the Bible only in connexion with נִין: לְנִינִי וּלְנֶכְדִּי (Genesis XXI, 23); וְנִין וָנֶכֶד (Isaiah XIV, 22); לֹא־נִין לוֹ וְלֹא־נֶכֶד בְּעַמּוֹ (Job XVIII, 19). However, there certainly was such a word in Biblical Hebrew, otherwise phrases as נין ונכד, etc., now, unfortunately, the only relic of this word's use, could not have developed at all. And נכד is by no means the only ancient Hebrew word not occurring in the Bible or unrecognized by tradition (as עת כים; *cf.* the note on VI, 2), which we now have preserved in our letters. The *hapax legomenon* עֶקֶר which occurs, as נכד, only in Leviticus XXV, 47 וְנִמְכַּר לְגֵר תּוֹשָׁב עִמָּךְ אוֹ לְעֵקֶר מִשְׁפַּחַת גֵּר "and sell himself unto a stranger-sojourner[1] or to the stock of the stranger's family", and was therefore doubted by many scholars, has now reappeared in the Aramaic stele from Sudshin of the 8th century B.C., A, a, lines 2–3, as a regular word: "Treaties of Bar Ga'yah, king of KTK with Mati'-el the son of 'Attar-samakh, king of [Arpad] and treaties of the sons of Bar-Ga'yah with the sons of Mati'-el and treaties of the grand-children of Bar-Ga'[yah] with the עקר

---

[1] גר תושב is to be taken as *hendiadyoin*.

of Mati'-el . . .". *Cf.* H. Bauer, *Archiv für Orientforschung*, VIII (1932), *page* 3, who, however, while realising that עקר must mean "Enkel, Nachkommenschaft", did not recognize in it the Biblical עֵקֶר of Leviticus XXV, 47. It should also be kept in mind that when speaking of the *king's* family and court, unusual and even foreign words, like "prince" or "princess", or "infant" (of Spain), "dauphin" (of France) are considered rather better form than the simple "son of the king". Thus "Nedabyahu the נכד of the king" is quite probable; and, as both archaeological facts,[1] as well as the examination of the proper names of Letter I, undoubtedly point to the latter days of the kingdom of Judah, the question arises whether Nedabyahu, the נכד of the king, is to be identified with Nedabiah, the son of Jeconiah and grandson of Jehoiakim mentioned in I Chronicles III, 18; and, taken in a general way, this certainly seems possible and even probable.

However, in order to identify the king, to whom Nedabyahu is related, we have to know the proper meaning of נכד. Unfortunately this is not definitely established; inner Jewish tradition unanimously explains the Biblical word as "grandson, the son of the son"; thus, *e.g.* the Targumim, בר־ברי, Ibn Ezra and Samuel ben Meir, בן־בני; David Qimḥi, בן־הבן; however, LXX [2] gives the word as "offspring" in general, and most modern scholars have adopted this meaning. If the second explanation is true, and Nedabiah is only "seed" (LXX: σπέρμα) of the king, then the king may be either Jehoiakim, his grandfather (608–597 B.C.) (or less likely, Jeconiah, his father), or Zedekiah (597–587/6 B.C.), who, according to II Kings XXIV, 17, was the uncle (דדו) of Jeconiah, *i.e.* following I Chronicles III, 14–24, his (Nedabiah's) grandfather's brother. If, on the other hand, the translation "grandson" is correct, one would certainly, as I did at first, think of Jehoiakim, Nedabiah's actual grandfather. However, in such a message it would be quite possible for the sake of abbreviation to call somebody the "grandson" of his grandfather's *brother*. And therefore, even according to this explanation, the king could be Zedekiah, his grandfather's brother. Expressions for family relations in all languages are very often not used in one strictly circumscribed sense. Thus the German word "Enkel" for "grand*son*" as the Latin "avunculus" (and the English "uncle", derived from it) originally meant "the little grand*father*", and both are used for uncle and grandson: In German of the 16th–17th century the word "*Neffe*" (to-day only = nephew) still occurs for "grandson", which as the Latin "nepos" is the oldest Indo-German word for grandson,[3] but already in post-classic Latin means nephew. Thus, like the Latin "nepos", and German "Neffe", "grandson and nephew", the Hebrew נֶכֶד may certainly have been used at least for *grand-nephew* as well as for grandson.[4] *See* general remarks.

הבא. The apparent stroke between ה and ב is merely due to a fault on the surface of the pot and is not a trace of a letter.

LINE 20. שלם. This could be read שַׁלֻּם, a name very usual throughout all periods of Biblical history, and occurring especially in Jeremiah's time; *cf.* (*a*) Jeremiah XXII, 11; I Chronicles III, 15 (the same as Joahaz, king of Judah); (*b*) II Kings XXII, 14; II Chronicles XXXIV, 22 (husband of Huldah, the prophetess); (*c*) Jeremiah XXXII, 7 (father of Ḥanamel, uncle of Jeremiah the

---

[1] The main fact is the finding of the ostraca immediately beneath the burnt surface of the gate-room. The philological examination has been made independently, the archaeological facts having been withheld from me till my main conclusions were reached. However, *see later* and the notes to Letter VI.

[2] LXX to Genesis XXI, 23, μηᴅὲ τὸ σπέρμα μου μηᴅὲ τὸ ὄνομά μου.

[3] Kluge, *Etymologisches Wörterbuch der deutschen Sprache*, 9th edition, *page* 113: "Im 16. und 17. Jahrhundert begegnet für 'Enkel' noch *Neffe*, das mit lat. *nepos* das älteste idg. Wort für 'Enkel' ist."

[4] The same word in post-Biblical sources has been interpreted as "nephew". *Cf.* Ben-Yehouda, *Thesaurus totius Hebraitatis* VII, 3655 *b*.

prophet); (*d*) Jeremiah XXXV, 4 (father of Ma'aseiah(u) the doorkeeper). Another possible reading is שֶׁלֶם, which name, however, is not mentioned in Jeremiah's time, but before (Genesis XLVI, 24; Numbers XXVI, 49 [for this I Chronicles VII, 13, gives שַׁלּוּם], and this vocalization is established for a later period by the New Babylonian transcription Shilimmu (*cf.* Clay, *Babylonian Expedition of the University of Pennsylvania*, IX, 27, 21). The spelling שלם, pronounced by Cowley, No. 22, 39, as שֶׁלֶם, occurs also in Elephantine. On the whole, the reading שַׁלֻּם seems preferable. For the form of such names, *cf.* Lidzbarski, *Ephemeris*, II, 21. The most likely reading of his father's name ידע is, accordingly, יָדַע (*cf.* Nehemiah X, 21; XII, 11, 22); but the reading יָדָע (Orientals יָדָע) (*cf.* I Chronicles II, 28. 32) is also possible.

הנבא = הַנָּבִיא the prophet. The Hebrew word originally does not mean "the prophet, the man who tells the future or God's word in general", but as a passive adjective "the inspired one"; thus the verb הַנִּבָּא, הִתְנַבֵּא is used in the passive form, "to be inspired", only.

הִשָּׁמֵר "beware" gives in one word the contents of the "warning" letter. The meaning of this warning is clear from the context, while in itself it could be open for different interpretation (*see above*). Only for the sake of completeness it may be mentioned that the Hebrew word itself could be understood quite differently. Thus the prophet Isaiah's message (Isaiah VII, 4) הִשָּׁמֵר וְהַשְׁקֵט does not mean "take heed and keep quiet"—which would be a contradiction—but as David Qimḥi in his commentary has already seen, the same as שקט ... אל שמריו (Jeremiah XLVIII, 11) "to settle on his *lees*", to keep quiet; perhaps השמר in this sense has to be vocalized differently (הַשָּׁמֵר?). (*Cf.* notes on Letter VI, 6–7.)

In the last sentence (שלחה עבך אל אדני), עבך is undoubtedly a very interesting mistake for עבדך, showing that the letter had been written very quickly and was not revised by the writer. שלחה must certainly be pronounced שְׁלָחֹה "he has sent it".

GENERAL REMARKS

Letter III is not only the best preserved of the larger ostraca but certainly the most interesting and important document among the Lachish Letters, and may be considered almost as an authentic chapter of the Holy Scriptures.

However, the full import of this letter was not reached at once, and it may be of interest to give here a record of the way in which, bit by bit, its full significance emerged, and one fact after another became clear. The text on the reverse, being extremely well preserved, could be read immediately, but an understanding of it was handicapped because at first we considered it as a copy of a letter, independent of the text on the obverse, which created certain difficulties both in language and contents, and puzzled us for some time. The name "Nedabyahu (Nedabiah), the grandson of the king", seemed to point to Jehoiakim's time;[1] however, if so, only to his last year, when Nedabiah, the son of Jeconiah (then eighteen years old, *cf.* II Kings XXIV, 8) was at least a child of perhaps five years, possibly suited as an unsuspected messenger of secret letters. In line 20 "the prophet" was mentioned, about whose identity nothing as yet could be said.

On the obverse the "commander of the army", of whose name the letters "KBR . . ., the son of Elnatan", were legible and who "went down to come to Egypt", reminded one very strongly of the story about the prophet Urijah, as told in Jeremiah XXVI, 20–23:

---

[1] However, *see above*, notes on line 19.

וְגַם־אִישׁ הָיָה מִתְנַבֵּא בְּשֵׁם יְהֹוָה אוּרִיָּהוּ בֶּן־שְׁמַעְיָהוּ מִקִּרְיַת הַיְּעָרִים וַיִּנָּבֵא עַל־הָעִיר הַזֹּאת וְעַל־הָאָרֶץ הַזֹּאת כְּכֹל דִּבְרֵי

יִרְמְיָהוּ׃ וַיִּשְׁמַע הַמֶּלֶךְ יְהוֹיָקִים וְכָל־גִּבּוֹרָיו וְכָל־הַשָּׂרִים אֶת־דְּבָרָיו וַיְבַקֵּשׁ הַמֶּלֶךְ הֲמִיתוֹ וַיִּשְׁמַע אוּרִיָּהוּ וַיִּרָא וַיִּבְרַח וַיָּבֹא מִצְרָיִם׃

וַיִּשְׁלַח הַמֶּלֶךְ יְהוֹיָקִים אֲנָשִׁים מִצְרָיִם אֶת־אֶלְנָתָן בֶּן־עַכְבּוֹר וַאֲנָשִׁים אִתּוֹ אֶל־מִצְרָיִם׃ וַיּוֹצִיאוּ אֶת־אוּרִיָּהוּ מִמִּצְרַיִם וַיְבִאֻהוּ אֶל־הַמֶּלֶךְ

יְהוֹיָקִים וַיַּכֵּהוּ בֶּחָרֶב וַיַּשְׁלֵךְ אֶת־נִבְלָתוֹ אֶל־קִבְרֵי בְּנֵי הָעָם׃

"And there was also a man that prophesied in the name of the Lord, Urijah the son of Shemaiah of Kirjath-jearim, who prophesied against this city and against this land according to all the words of Jeremiah. And when Jehoiakim the king, with all his mighty men, and all the princes, heard his words, the king sought to put him to death: but when Urijah heard it, he was afraid, and fled, and went into Egypt; and Jehoiakim the king sent men into Egypt, namely *Elnathan the son of Achbor* (אלנתן בן עכבור), and certain men with him into Egypt. And they fetched forth Urijah out of Egypt, and brought him unto Jehoiakim the king; who slew him with the sword, and cast his dead body into the graves of the common people."

Here, too, a high officer is mentioned who went down to come to Egypt in the time of the king Jehoiakim, whose reign is dealt with in Jeremiah XXVI and XXVII,[1] and the officer's name is like the name mentioned in our letter. Could it be that the events underlying this message were parts of the actual story as told in the Bible? This seemed too good to be true, and at this time I was rather inclined to see in the "general" of line 15, KBR . . . the son of Elnatan, another officer, possibly a *son* of the Elnatan, son of Achbor, referred to in Jeremiah XXVI, 22, who also stood in a similar position in the service of Jehoiakim and who, too, went to Egypt on a similar errand. Why should this journey have any connexion at all with the prophet Urijah?

There was, it is true, also a prophet—whose name was not given—mentioned on the reverse, but at this time I had not yet recognized that Letter III, as we then called it, had any connexion with the obverse, then marked as III a. One blurred sign at the end of the obverse prevented me from connecting it with the reverse. But since then we learned both from archaeological evidence as pointed out first by Mr. Starkey, that Letters II, VI, VII, VIII and XVIII were written on sherds taken from the same pot, some being addressed to the same man,[2] and from the explanation of Letter IV, that the ostraca were not, as we thought first, copies of outgoing messages (which could be written two or more on one sherd) but original incoming letters, beginning, as is usual in this kind of inscription (*cf.* Lidzbarski, *Ephemeris* II, *page* 228; Wilcken, *Griechische Ostraka* I, *page* 18) on the outside and continued on the inside of the sherd. This fact naturally changed the situation. Not in a different letter, but in the continuation of one and the same message, and almost in the same sentence, the general who went down to Egypt and a prophet were mentioned. And how is this prophet introduced? No name is given, but he is simply called "the prophet". This certainly proves that it is the prophet with whom the whole letter really deals; and it is the prophet in connexion with whom the commander of the army went down to Egypt and wrote to Hodawyahu "and his men" to take them with him, exactly as it is told in the Bible, that the high officer, whose name corresponds so closely to the name of the general in our letter, "and men with him" went down to come to Egypt. Further, a letter of the prophet is quoted: "and a letter

---

[1] But *see pages* 68–72.

[2] It seemed improbable that copies of letters addressed to the same man and of the same origin should be found together at the writer's place. However, the actual fact that these sherds, originating from the same pot, reassembled at the addressee's place and remained here for 2,500 years is not less astonishing. For an explanation, *see* general remarks to this letter, *page* 73, and to Letter VI. *See* the reconstruction of the pot, *page* 220.

I

Nedabyahu, the grandson of the king, brought to Shallum, the son of Yaddua', from the prophet, saying: Beware!"[1] Why is this message of the prophet mentioned amongst political and military news? Is it his prophecy that played a part in this? However, his letter contains no prophecy, but a warning from the prophet to one of his friends, who is apparently in the same danger as he himself. It is, therefore, a prophet fleeing from his home and his friends, a prophet wanted by the military authorities, with whom we are dealing. And how is the prophet mentioned in this sentence? The order of words here is significant. "The prophet" is the last word in the sentence "and a letter Nedabyahu . . . brought to Shallum . . . from the prophet". The new fact upon which emphasis is here laid is only the letter, while the prophet is known as the man with whom the letter is concerned *from the very beginning*.

Can all this be mere coincidence?

But there is more evidence. Letter VI also mentions the same oath about somebody who did, or did not, read a letter, and this letter is written on a part of the same pot as II, and addressed, as II and III, to Ya'ush. This letter must, therefore, be dealing with the same matter. And here in VI, lines 5–6, we read: ". . . Behold, the words of the . . . are not good, (liable) to weaken the hands . . . the hands of the country and the city".[2]

הנה דברי ה]. . .[ ]. . .[לא טבם לרפת ידי־]. . . . .[

קט ידי האר]ץ[והעיר]. . .[

Who could have uttered such words, if not a prophet, and a prophet like Urijah, "Who prophesied against this city and against this land, according to all the words of Jeremiah", about whom the princes in Jeremiah XXXVIII, 4, say that "he weakeneth the hands of the men of war that remain in this city and the hands of all the people, in speaking such words unto them: for this man seeketh not the welfare of this people, but the hurt".[3]

The same Letter VI mentions "the king", who according to Jeremiah XXVI, sent the general, by whom Urijah was brought back and by whose order he was finally put to death, at the instigation of certain officers.

Furthermore, the birth-place of Urijah was Qiryat-Ye'arim (Kirjath-Jearim), which was certainly on the road from Jerusalem to Azeqah and Lachish. Already in a letter of the Amarna period, found as far south as Tell el-Hesi (Knudtzon, Amarna No. 333), a city Ya-ra-mi, usually identified with Qiryat-Ye'arim, is mentioned in connexion with Zim-ri-da of Lachish, thus showing a very old connexion between these two places. There is thus a possibility that Hosha'yahu's letters were written in the prophet's home town, Qiryat-Ye'arim, and that it is a friend living there whom he warns. His father's name, according to the Bible, was Shema'yahu, and it is interesting that in Letter IV a certain Shema'yahu is mentioned as going up to Jerusalem with Semakhyahu, a high military officer. (*See* the notes to Letter IV.)

From such a place between Jerusalem and Lachish Hosha'yahu might have written. If this were so, being nearer to Jerusalem he might have heard about the general's mission to Egypt before the rumour of it reached Lachish.

---

[1] This the previous translation, now corrected into: "and the letter (which) Nedabyahu . . . had brought, has thy slave sent to my Lord".

[2] For a full discussion of what then seemed still doubtful letters in these lines, omitted here, *see* notes to Letter VI.

[3] הוּא מְרַפֵּא אֶת־יְדֵי אַנְשֵׁי הַמִּלְחָמָה הַנִּשְׁאָרִים בָּעִיר הַזֹּאת,

וְאֵת יְדֵי כָל־הָעָם לְדַבֵּר אֲלֵיהֶם כַּדְּבָרִים הָאֵלֶּה כִּי הָאִישׁ הַזֶּה

אֵינֶנּוּ דֹרֵשׁ לְשָׁלוֹם לָעָם הַזֶּה כִּי אִם־לְרָעָה:

It must certainly be admitted that there was more than one prophet at this time. But the fact that the letters mention him as *the* prophet in this brief way affords certain proof of his activities having been the subject of frequent correspondence. And we may even say that where most of the Lachish Letters mention certain facts, those seem to concern this particular matter. In the fragmentary Letter XVI, line 5, even the name of the prophet is mentioned; unfortunately only the last letters, הנבא י[הו "... yahu the prophet", remain. There certainly have been many names compounded with יהו in this same way, and among them even names of prophets, *e.g.* Jeremiah (ירמיהו), and the false prophet חנניהו Hananiah (Jeremiah XXVIII); but there is only one prophet about whom the Bible relates that he prophesied in the same spirit as Jeremiah, that he fled to Egypt, and that an officer bearing a name very similar to that given in our letter went down with men after him. That prophet was Uriyahu (Urijah), son of Shemaʿyahu.

However, when I first ventured the assertion that not only in the last sentence, but also in the beginning of the letter, the real topic of the whole message was the prophet, this was founded on deduction only. But since then the difficulties of the first lines of the inscription have been fully elucidated, and the contents proved what before had been mere speculation. The prophet is in fact mentioned here, and this in a very interesting form; and it is the peculiar name given to him in this letter which at first prevented my recognizing in it the prophet. For, what could הפקח "the open-eyed", the שְׁתֻם־הָעַיִן or גְּלוּי עֵינַיִם "who has his eyes opened" (as Balaam the seer, Numbers XXIV, 3–4 and 15–16 says of himself) mean if not the prophet, the seer "the man whose eyes God had opened to see", in Hebrew הָרֹאֶה or הַחֹזֶה the seer? *Cf.* Genesis XXI, 19 וַיִּפְקַח אֱלֹהִים אֶת־עֵינֶיהָ וַתֵּרֶא בְּאֵר מָיִם "and God opened her eyes, and she saw a well of water"; II Kings VI, 17: וַיִּתְפַּלֵּל אֱלִישָׁע וַיֹּאמַר יְהוָה פְּקַח־נָא אֶת־עֵינָיו וְיִרְאֶה וַיִּפְקַח יְהוָה אֶת־עֵינֵי הַנַּעַר וַיַּרְא וְהִנֵּה הָהָר מָלֵא סוּסִים וְרֶכֶב אֵשׁ סְבִיבֹת אֱלִישָׁע "And Elisha prayed, and said, Lord, I pray thee, open his eyes, that he may see. And the Lord opened the eyes of the young man; and he saw: and, behold, the mountain was full of horses and chariots of fire round about Elisha" and l.c., v. 20: וַיְהִי כְּבֹאָם שֹׁמְרוֹן וַיֹּאמֶר אֱלִישָׁע יְהוָה פְּקַח אֶת־עֵינֵי־אֵלֶּה וְיִרְאוּ וַיִּפְקַח יְהוָה אֶת־עֵינֵיהֶם וַיִּרְאוּ וְהִנֵּה בְּתוֹךְ שֹׁמְרוֹן "And it came to pass, when they were come into Samaria, that Elisha said, Lord, open the eyes of these men, that they may see. And the Lord opened their eyes, and they saw; and, behold, they were in the midst of Samaria." It is to the prophet, the "seer", who has already left his home, that Hoshaʿyahu has sent a letter, referring to the letter received by him from Yaʾush; it is the prophet again, in pursuit of whom the commander of the army went down to Egypt, with men he has taken from the writer's town, perhaps Qiryat-Yeʿarim; and it is he who had sent the warning letter to his friend Shallum.

There certainly remained a few queries and difficulties connected with this letter which seemed to me not insuperable; but the main fact seemed certain, that in Letter III we have one of the actual documents connected with the Biblical story, as told in Jeremiah XXVI.

I had reached this point, in London, in July, 1935. But only in a final revision, particularly in April, 1936, in Jerusalem, while returning to the study of our ostraca with an open mind and ready to change my views entirely, if this should be suggested by the facts,[1] I reached a definite result about the reading and translation of lines 7–8 and 19–21,[2] concerning the real relations between Hoshaʿyahu, his lord Yaʾush and the Piqqeaḥ, the correct meaning of Hoshaʿyahu's oath,

---

[1] *Cf.* my statement in the *Bulletin of the Jewish Palestine Exploration Society*, 1935, *page* 92 (dated 18th December, 1935), showing that at this time I was quite ready to accept "a considerable part" (חלק חשוב) of the arguments against my hypothesis.

[2] This already in January 1936.

65

repeated in other letters, the contents of Letter II, and its connexion with Letter III. These results, far from destroying my working hypothesis, that most of Hosha'yahu's letters deal with the prophet as their main topic, and that this prophet shows all the "symptoms" characteristic of *Urijah*, and of him alone, all tend to strengthen it in such a way that this hypothesis must be taken as definitely proved by the ostraca of Lachish, and that if there are difficulties arising from other evidence, there must also be a way to meet them.

There can now be no further doubt that Letter III, from the beginning to the end, deals with the same matter, the prophet and his letters, the chief topic of his lord's letter, to which our message is the answer. In the beginning Hosha'yahu defends himself against the accusation of having read the letters of the Piqqeaḥ; and at the end he declares that he has sent the prophet's warning letter to his lord, according to his wish. Can it now still be doubted that the prophet, whose name is not mentioned, is the same as the Piqqeaḥ, the open-eyed, and that the warning letter mentioned in lines 19–21 is one of the Piqqeaḥ's confidential letters, that came to Hosha'yahu, but which he should not have read or mentioned? And can there be any doubt that Hosha'yahu, while speaking about the general of the army who went down to come into Egypt and on his way "sent to take from here" Hodawyahu and his men, still sticks to the topic of the prophet, the open-eyed and his unfortunate letters? Only this one matter is preying upon his mind and making his heart sick; this is the only topic he deals with in most of his letters, in Letter III as well as in Letters VI and XII, and as we now realize, in another form in Letter II. Hosha'yahu has been the trusted man, through whose hand the prophet's letter came, after the seer fled to Egypt. And his accusers say that through his indiscretion the prophet's flight to Egypt has been made known to the king and the mighty men in Jerusalem. Should his heart not ache and should he not repeat over and over again, writing to the prophet as well as to his lord Ya'ush and swearing, that he never said anything, that he himself does not know how to read, that nobody ever read any confidential letter to him? How could he have said "something which he did not even know!"? (Letter II.) This is the tragic part which Hosha'yahu seems to have played in Bible history.

Was there any other prophet who, arousing the anger of the king and his mighty men to such a degree that they wanted to kill him, fled into Egypt, was followed by a general of the army so much resembling in name and action Elnatan son of 'Akhbor, mentioned in the Bible, who, like this officer, took "men with him" in order to bring back the prophet and have him put to death? This is very hard to believe. Our prophet was surely Uriyahu of Qiryat-Ye'arim.

Thus it will be from Qiryat-Ye'arim, where Hosha'yahu lived, that his letters came. It is there that the prophet's friends lived, where letters from him are expected, and where Ya'ush writes, asking for news about him. From Letter III, as from the other ostraca, we may also conclude that Ya'ush and his men are the prophet's followers, and this also fits in well with the fact, shown by the proper names (*see* the remarks to Letter I), that all the men mentioned in the Lachish Letters are true and faithful worshippers of Yhwh.

This picture will receive still more colour from the examination of the following letters, particularly Letter VI. There, too, the same oath is given as in Letter III, addressed, as Letter III shows, to the Piqqeaḥ, the open-eyed. But in Letter VI the oath is given with the introductory expression חי יהוה אלהיך "Yhwh lives, *thy God*", an expression used in the Bible only while addressing a prophet, in Lachish the prophet Uriyahu.

66

Why Uriyahu fled into Egypt, as told in Jeremiah XXVI, 21, is puzzling, for according to the Bible he spoke "like all the words of Jeremiah", *i.e.* for peace with *Babylonia*, thus—as also our letter says—"loosening the hands of country and city". Why should he not have gone over to the Babylonian army instead of fleeing to Egypt, whence the enthusiasm to fight the Babylonians was fostered? This we do not know; but even this astonishing fact makes it all the more certain that there was no other prophet fitting all the conditions given in these letters.

Now for the remaining difficulties and problems connected with this unshakable understanding of our letters.

There is first the question of the *name* of the commander of the army, which in Jeremiah XXVI, 22, as well as in XXXVI, 12, is given as אֶלְנָתָן בֶּן־עַכְבּוֹר (XXXVI, 25 as אלנתן alone) while our letter gives, as is now clear, ‏[כבריהו בן אלנתן י].

However, we have (*a*) cases of similar changes in names compounded with the name יהוה in the Bible. Thus, the name of the king אחז is written in cuneiform inscriptions Yauḫazi, representing the Hebrew יהואחז. The name of the king כָּנְיָהוּ, יְכָנְיָה, כָּנְיָה, Jeconiah, is given also as יְהוֹיָכִין. Thus an abridged form יְכְּבָר for יכבריהו or כבריהו, "Yhwh is great" could easily have been misread into עכבר ("mouse"). The same error of a copyist explains the different spelling of the name "Yezanyah (יזניה), the son of Hoshaʿyah", Jeremiah XLII, 1, as "Azaryah (עזריה) the son of Hoshaʿyah" in XLIII, 2. (*b*) The inversion of the names of father and son also has parallels in the genealogies in the Hebrew Bible. *Cf.* II Samuel VIII, 17, where instead of Ebjathar, the son of Ahimelech, we read: Ahimelech son of Ebjathar; or the names, as given for the wives of Esau, (*a*) in Genesis XXVI, 34 and XXVIII, 9; (*b*) in Genesis XXXVI, 2–3.

(*a*) Genesis XXVI, 34; XXVIII, 9:

(1)	יהודית בת־בארי החתי	Judith, d. o. Beeri the Hittite.
(2)	בשמת בת־אילון החתי	Basemath, d. o. Elon the Hittite.
(3)	מחלת בת־ישמעאל . . . אחות נביות	Mahalath, d. o. Ishmael . . . sister of Nebajoth.

(*b*) Genesis XXXVI, 2–3.

(1)	עדה־בת־אילון החתי	Adah, d. o. Elon the Hittite.
(2)	אהליבמה־בת־ענה בת־צבעון החוי	Aholibamah, d. o. Anah, d. o. Zibeon the Hivite.
(3)	בשמת־בת־ישמעאל אחות נביות	Basemath, d. o. Ishmael, sister of Nebajoth.

We have here עדה instead of יהודית, אהליבמה for מחלת, החוי for החתי, etc., and Adah-Judith is here daughter of Beeri, there of Elon; Basemath's father is here Elon, there Ishmael, and so on.

Thus it is quite possible that the general's name, written in the Bible "Elnatan ben ʾAkhbor", was in fact "Yikhbar ben Elnatan" (*see later*).

However, there is another possibility, that some mistake was made by the scribe of our ostracon and not by the copyists of the Bible. Hoshaʿyahu is not copying from any official document; he has only "been told" about the officer going down; and why should it be impossible that he, or rather his scribe, mistook the name Elnatan ben Yikhbar (or even ʾAkhbor, Achbor) for Yikhbar(yahu) ben Elnatan, or wrote one for the other? Has not the same scribe made other mistakes as עבך, line 21 for עבדך?

If this were the case, the name Elnatan would be the name of a still living person composed with El instead of Yhwh;[1] but there can be no doubt that this commander of the army is one

---

[1] *See above* as to the proper names of Letter I.

67

of the mighty men, opposed to Uriyahu, the prophet of Yhwh. And it fits the picture as given in the book of Jeremiah that these men, who did not listen to Yhwh's word and persecuted the prophets, even then worshipped the queen of heaven and all the other deities as did their fathers, thereby arousing Yhwh's anger.

Another difficulty seems to lie in the *dating* of our letters. According to the report as related in Jeremiah XXVI, the events connected with the prophet Urijah occurred during the reign of Jehoiakim (608–597 B.C.). Now, while Chapter XXVI starts with events "in the *beginning of the reign of Jehoiakim*", which may mean in the first half of his reign (*cf.* Jeremiah XXVIII, 1, "in the beginning of the reign of Zedekiah king of Judah, in the fourth year"), the events told at the end of the chapter could from internal evidence belong to the end of Jehoiakim's reign,[1] the story of Urijah being put in as an independent parallel to Jeremiah's fate, and not bound to any particular date. But in the story itself the king Jehoiakim is mentioned: (v. 21) "and when Jehoiakim the king... heard his words"; (v. 22) "and Jehoiakim the king sent men into Egypt"; (v. 23) "... and they brought him unto Jehoiakim the king". So the king should be Jehoiakim,[2] although it could be his last year, particularly since the troubles caused by the prophet might well have extended for many years, just as Jeremiah kept repeating his "demoralizing" words from at least the thirteenth year of Josiah (628 B.C.) till after the destruction of Jerusalem and the death of Gedaliah (585). In July, 1935 there was no sufficient reason to disbelieve the Biblical statement that the events told in Jeremiah XXVI, forming the background to our ostraca, actually happened in the last year of Jehoiakim, immediately before the fortress fell into the hands of the Babylonians[3] in their first onslaught on Judah in 598–597 B.C. The Biblical reports about the fall of Lachish[4] are not sufficiently clear to exclude this possibility; the prophet's warning letter, sent some time *before* Letter III was written,[5] could have been sent while the prophet was still near his home town, through a little boy, most suited as an unsuspected messenger, just as such boys in II Samuel XV, 36; XVII, 17–21, deliver messages for David: such small boys are used also to-day in Palestine, often for quite responsible missions and it might be that the noun נכד used for Nedabyahu particularly meant a "little grandchild".

It was not until after November 1935 that the excavators of Lachish realized the importance of the evidence which lay under the floor beneath the burnt layer wherein the Lachish ostraca were found, and where another burnt level appeared, thus showing that the fortress during a short period of perhaps not more than 10 years had been *twice* destroyed by fire. This double destruction by fire (while other explanations may not be entirely excluded) seems to be accounted for by the assumption that Lachish had been attacked and burnt twice, about 597 B.C. and 588 B.C.; and thus the letters found between these burnings seemed to belong to the later date. No other destruction of Lachish is known to us from our very incomplete sources about this period, and this double burning and conquest is a new fact, not suggested before. While further knowledge may perhaps yet open up other views,[6] it seemed probable that our letters were written, not in the reign of

---

[1] *Cf. e.g.* Hans Schmidt, *Die Schriften des alten Testaments neu übersetzt und für die Gegenwart erklärt*, vol. II, 2, *page* 288: "Das Ereignis, von dem diese Notiz berichtet, wird *nicht in die ersten Jahre* der Regierung Jojakims fallen. Der König muss zu diesen Zeiten in guten Beziehungen zu Ägypten gestanden haben. Sonst hätten sie ihm den Flüchtling nicht übergeben. Er wird also nicht mehr Vasall der Babylonier gewesen sein."

[2] However, *see later*.

[3] This seemed required by the contents of Letter IV.

[4] *See the following*.

[5] *See above*, notes on lines 19–21.

[6] However, as will be seen later, the letters were not originally in this room. *See* the remarks to Letter VI.

Jehoiakim but of *Zedekiah*, not long[1] before the final destruction of Lachish in 588. And this would agree better with the somewhat cryptic notice in Jeremiah XXXIV, 6–7, "then Jeremiah the prophet spake all these words unto Zedekiah king of Judah in Jerusalem. When the king of Babylon's army fought against Jerusalem, and against all the cities of Judah that were left, against Lachish and against Azekah", showing that even after 597, Lachish was (at least once more) besieged by the Babylonians. Also for Nedabiah, called the נכד "nepos" of the king, which, as shown above, may equally well mean the grandson of Jehoiakim as the grandnephew of Zedekiah, as the messenger of the prophet's letter, one would prefer the age of 10–13 to that of 5 years.

If we should have to accept the date of 590–588 B.C. for our letter, and therefore the ninth or tenth year of *Zedekiah* for the flight of Urijah, instead of the end of Jehoiakim's reign, could it be reconciled with the facts as related in Jeremiah XXVI, 21, 22, 23, where all the events connected with this prophet are attributed to Jehoiakim? It most certainly could!

First, it is not mere hypothesis, but actual fact, recognized by every reasonable scholar, that in the same text of Jeremiah the name Jehoiakim has been erroneously put in, where originally Zedekiah had been written. Immediately after the report about Urijah (Jeremiah XXVI, 20–23); and divided from it only by one single sentence (v. 24) comparing Jeremiah's fate with Urijah's, there follows in XXVII, 1–3: "*In the beginning of the reign of Jehoiakim* the son of Josiah king of Judah came this word unto Jeremiah from Yhwh saying, Thus saith Yhwh to me: Make thee bonds and yokes, and put them upon thy neck, And send them to the king of Edom, and to the king of Moab, and to the king of the Ammonites, and to the king of Tyrus, and to the king of Zidon, by the hand of the messengers which come to Jerusalem unto *Zedekiah* King of Judah." The messengers which come *unto Zedekiah king of Judah*—in the reign of Jehoiakim? Certainly not! And thus all the contents of Jeremiah XXVII and XXVIII deal with matters fitting only for the reign of Zedekiah; his name, as king, is mentioned in XXVII, 12, and at the beginning of Chapter XXVIII: "and it came to pass *the same year*, in the beginning of the reign *of Zedekiah*, king of Judah". There is, I think, no doubt that in verse 1 one of the copyists rewriting the book of Jeremiah or this part of it, *erroneously* put in Jehoiakim's name instead of Zedekiah's.

And what about the story of Urijah, told immediately before this passage? Is it given with any definite date? No, it is only told as a *parallel* to Jeremiah's not less dangerous position, *beginning* in the time of Jehoiakim, but continuing through the reigns of Jeconiah and Zedekiah. Could not the copyist who, following the beginning of Chapter XXVI, also in XXVII, put in king Jehoiakim's name, have done the same in the report about Urijah, while his original text only anonymously said: "And when the king . . . heard his words . . . And the king sent men into Egypt . . . and they brought him unto the king"? If what follows in XXVII was, as he thought, still in Jehoiakim's time, might he not have included the passage which precedes it? It need not be emphasized that the division into chapters is very late, adopted only for reference in the XIIIth century A.D., and is of no historical importance.

And it is even simpler than this. As Jeremiah, who prophesied during at least 43 years (628–585), so Urijah could have uttered rebellious words for a long time. The troubles he caused made the king and his mighty men realize the danger; they decided to put him to death, and —as he had fled into Egypt—to send later on, after friendly relations had been established with this

---

[1] *See* Letter IV, and *page 86*.

69

country, an officer with men to have him brought back and killed. They considered him dangerous even after he had left the country; thus Urijah's religious influence must have been of great extent and long standing! There is no objection to this from the fact that his activity is mentioned in only a few passages in Jeremiah's book, which records none of his prophecies or the facts concerning him; it is only to make the reader realize Jeremiah's great danger that Urijah's tragic fate is mentioned, which, but for Ahikam's intervention (Jeremiah XXVI, 24), might also have been Jeremiah's.

However, what would we know of the great Jeremiah himself, if we only had the Books of Kings, and what would be our opinion about his influence and position, if his name should then chance to appear in an ancient document? We should know nothing at all about him, because his name is not even once mentioned in these books; if we found his name on any inscription, we should take him for an entirely unimportant person. When the Book of the Covenant of Yhwh was found, at a time when Jeremiah, according to his book, is already well known to the king as God's prophet (622 B.C.), Josiah, the good and true king and his officers did not appeal to him, but to "the prophetess Huldah, the wife of Shallum the son of Tikvah, the son of Harhas, keeper of the wardrobe" (II Kings XXII, 14), an otherwise quite unknown figure.

Urijah was a very influential prophet, whose undermining activity continued for a long time; therefore his policy became increasingly dangerous to the king. Thus we may assume that "Jehoiakim the king heard . . . . . . his words" (Jeremiah XXVI, 21) and even that this king and his mighty men *wanted* to put him to death, just as "all the mighty men" in Jehoiakim's time would have put Jeremiah to death (XXVI, 11 *sqq*.) but for his clever answer and the help of Ahikam who saved him.

Thus also Urijah may have found protectors, or may have hidden in the hills of Western Judah, where he had friends and followers, for a long time. But the king, who heard of his flight to Egypt and had him brought back and slain, may well have been Zedekiah.

Is it too much to assume, in the face of the overwhelming evidence of the Lachish Letters (if this later dating is correct), that the same copyist who wrote about king Jehoiakim throughout the whole story, till he erroneously put the same name instead of Zedekiah in XXVII, 1, also between both quotations of Jehoiakim put in this king's name, where originally the story only said: "the king"? The text of our book of Jeremiah has been compiled from many sources, written in the Hebrew characters, now well known from our ostraca; it has been rewritten in a different alphabet, the square characters of the Aramaic (Assyrian) types, transcribed into different spelling, *i.e.* changing the defective orthography of these times into fuller and different spelling, עבדה into עבדו, writing גמריה, ירמיה, etc., according to the later *Aramaic* forms, instead of the original גמריהו, ירמיהו,[1] introducing a differentiation in some signs when used at the beginning, middle or end of the word, and even putting other, more "modern" words instead of obsolete expressions often not fully understood?[2]

More than this: we have complete paragraphs in our book of Jeremiah where the copyists, trying to clarify and render more precise the prophet's words, which they themselves did not correctly understand, completely destroyed their whole sense. Thus in Jeremiah XXIII, 33–40 Jeremiah seems to speak in a very peculiar way against prophet, priest and people (v. 33),

---

[1] *See above*, Letter I.   [2] *See* the note on VI, 2, about עת כים.

that " shall ask thee, saying, What is the burden (the word, the speech) of Yhwh (Hebrew: *massā'
Yhwh* מַשָּׂא יהוה)? thou shalt then say unto them, What burden? I will even forsake you, saith
Yhwh. (v. 34) And as for the prophet, and the priest, and the people, that shall say, The burden
of Yhwh, I will even punish that man and his house. (v. 35) Thus shall ye say every one to his
neighbour, and every one to his brother, What hath Yhwh answered? and, What hath Yhwh
spoken? (v. 36) And the burden of Yhwh shall ye mention no more: for every man's word shall
be his burden; for ye have perverted the words of the living God, of Yhwh of hosts our God.
(v. 37) Thus shalt thou say to the prophet, What hath Yhwh answered thee? and, What
hath Yhwh spoken? (v. 38) But since ye say, The burden of Yhwh; therefore thus saith
Yhwh: Because ye say this word, The burden of Yhwh, and I have sent unto you, saying, Ye
shall not say, The burden of Yhwh; (v. 39) Therefore, behold, I, even I, will treat you as a
loan,[1] and I will forsake you, and the city that I gave you and your fathers, out of my presence:
(v. 40) And I will bring an everlasting reproach upon you, and a perpetual shame which shall
not be forgotten."

How is it that the prophet here in such angry words condemns—till he makes the whole city
perish for ever for this sin—the use of a harmless word, the word *massā Yhwh*, which in so many
passages of our Biblical and even prophetic writings is used without any scruple, as in Zechariah
IX, 1; XII, 1; Malachi I, 1, "the burden, the word of Yhwh (מַשָּׂא דְּבַר יְהֹוָה)", or even with the verb
II Kings IX, 25–26: "and Yhwh said (not: laid) this burden (= word) about him (וַיהֹוָה נָשָׂא
עָלָיו אֶת־הַמַּשָּׂא הַזֶּה): Surely I have seen yesterday the blood of Naboth, and the blood of his sons,
saith Yhwh ".

As I have shown in an article about *Massā Yhwh* in *Monatsschrift für Geschichte und Wissenschaft
des Judentums* 1932, *pages 273–284*, the original meaning of Jeremiah's words was undoubtedly quite
different. What he condemns is the use of the word *massā' Yhwh* or *mashshā' Yhwh* (מַשָּׂא יהוה), not in
the sense of " Yhwh's burden (or: word)", but of " *Yhwh's loan*", and not as just a harmless
expression in the people's vocabulary, but as a *religious political slogan*. Priests, prophets and people
said: "even after God has given us, the king Jeconiah and the nobility, into the hands of the
Babylonians, we still are Yhwh's own property, his house and his heritage; we are only *Yhwh's
loan* in the hands of our enemies, and *he must redeem us*". However, just as Jeremiah says in God's
name in XII, 7: "I have *forsaken* mine house, I have *left* (נָטַשְׁתִּי) my heritage, I have given the dearly
beloved of my soul into the hand of her enemies", thus he in XXIII, 33–40, says, using the same
expression: "Why, you say, you are God's loan? Yea, I will take you as such. But I shall treat
you as a loan shall be treated (וְנָשִׁיתִי אֶתְכֶם נָשֹׁא v. 39) (according to Deuteronomy XV, after some
time passes), and I will forsake you (וְנָטַשְׁתִּי אֶתְכֶם) and the city that I gave you and your fathers out
of my face!"[2] But this expression, to say *massā' Yhwh*, "Yhwh's loan", has been misunderstood by
the men who copied our text for: "do not say *massā' Yhwh*, Yhwh's burden or speech, instead
of Yhwh's word", and to make this clear, they added quite in good faith: "thus shalt thou say
to the prophet, What hath Yhwh answered thee? and, What hath Yhwh spoken?" (v. 37).

And could not such men, who, in order better to express the prophet's intention, put in whole
sentences, have inserted in the same good faith, in order to make things clearer, the name of
the king missing in their sources?

---

[1] Not: "utterly forget you" (Hebrew: *venashiti ethkhem nasho'* וְנָשִׁיתִי אֶתְכֶם נָשֹׁא).

[2] For full argument *cf.* my article quoted above.

And are there not many reports given twice in the Bible, *e.g.*, in the book of Kings and in Chronicles, where the second report adds words, not to be found in the first book, which undoubtedly served as the main source of the latter?

There is no real chronological difficulty connected with the certain evidence, that our letters deal with the tragic fate of Uriyahu, the son of Shema'yahu, the prophet from Qiryat-Ye'arim. And if our letters show that later hands may have put the name of a king into our Biblical text, where originally no name stood, they fully repay us for this loss by proving in a unique way the inner truth of one of the most interesting religious and political episodes told in the Bible.

Letter III is an actual document dealing with the prophet Uriyahu's flight to Egypt and the part Hosha'yahu, the sender of the letter, may have played in his tragic death. But more than this seems now proved. Not only Letter III, but also Letter II, repeating the main statement of III in one sentence, VI and XII giving the same oath as III, the Letters VIII and XVI, also mentioning "the prophet", deal with the same topic, and are certainly written by the same man, Hosha'yahu. Further, as the potsherds II, VI, VII and XVIII are adjoining pieces of one and the same pot as II, VI and VIII, they must also be letters of Hosha'yahu, dealing in the main with the same theme.

Now, if II, III, VI, VII, VIII, XII, XVI and XVIII, that is the majority of our legible ostraca, are proved to be written on behalf of the same man about the same matters, would it not be a fair *working hypothesis that all our ostraca are essentially a one-man correspondence written by Hosha'yahu to Ya'ush*? Let us see where this hypothesis will lead us, whether it will help to clear the difficulties remaining in our letters and thus prove its truth.

For Letter II the connexion with Letter III has already been shown as very probable. Letter II actually gives in one sentence the gist of Letter III. Why this has been done will become clearer from the study of Letter V and its connexion with Letter IX.

The writing of Letter I, the list of names, strongly resembles that of Letter VIII, which in line 3 mentions the prophet, and therefore may even have been the letter accompanying the list of names. On the reverse line 1, one perhaps reads[1] אכתב "I am writing", and this may refer to Hosha'yahu's "writing" on a separate potsherd the names of men connected in some way with the incident about the prophet. (*See* the notes to Letter VI.)

And now we can better understand why the names mentioned in this list, in connexion with Ya'ush and Hosha'yahu in general, bear exclusively "Yahwistic" names, formed according to a certain rule, while among the non-believers in Jerusalem, in spite of Josiah's reformation, "heathen names" may also have been retained. The people mentioned at Lachish and from Hosha'yahu's post may belong to the prophet's party of zealous worshippers of Yhwh alone.

For the other letters, *see* the commentary following them. Their contents will add still further details to this picture and fully support the conclusions founded upon the examination of Letter III.

One other point: the letters are part of one particular correspondence, which—if taken together with those quite large sherds, upon which the writing is no longer visible—is to a great part preserved, and since no other document has been found in this room, it seems probable that these letters were originally kept together in some kind of receptacle,[2] like the documents which Jeremiah (Jeremiah XXXII, 14) puts "in an earthen vessel, that they may continue many days". Therefore there certainly is a possibility that the vessel containing this correspondence belonged to other

---

[1] *See* the notes on this letter.

[2] That Ya'ush must have kept letters in some kind of archives is shown expressly by Letter V. (*See* notes on this letter.)

similarly portable files, containing other documents, but that these special documents had been brought from another place. If this were the case, the archaeological evidence for dating the letters immediately before the second and last destruction of Lachish in 588 B.C. would not be conclusive. (*See* notes on Letter VI.)

The writing of Letter III presents only small differences from that of Letter II, and both could easily have been written by the same hand. Of particular interest is the difference in the writing of the נ as seen on the obverse, from the reverse. While on the obverse it is usually triangular, on the reverse it is one curved stroke. Is this a sign of greater hurry at the end of the letter, as was the mistake עבך for עבדך in line 21? Or did another scribe write the last lines?

LETTER IV

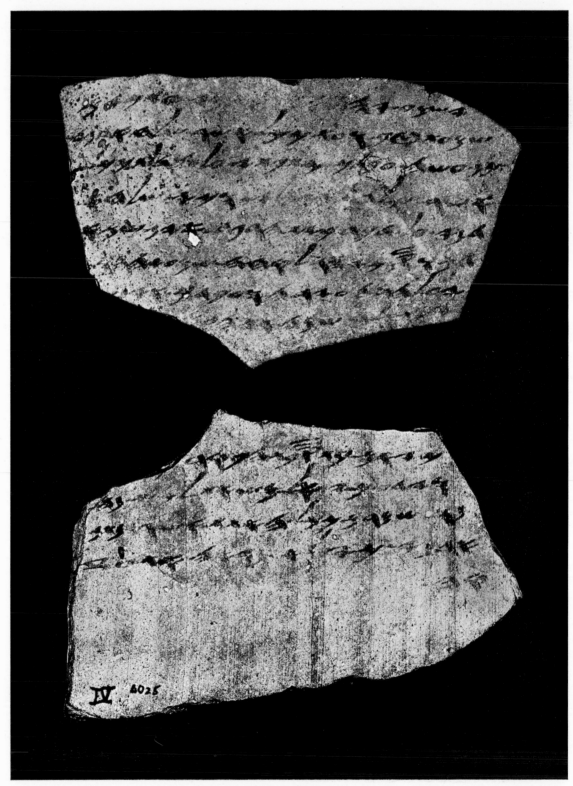

Photo: S. W. Michieli

76

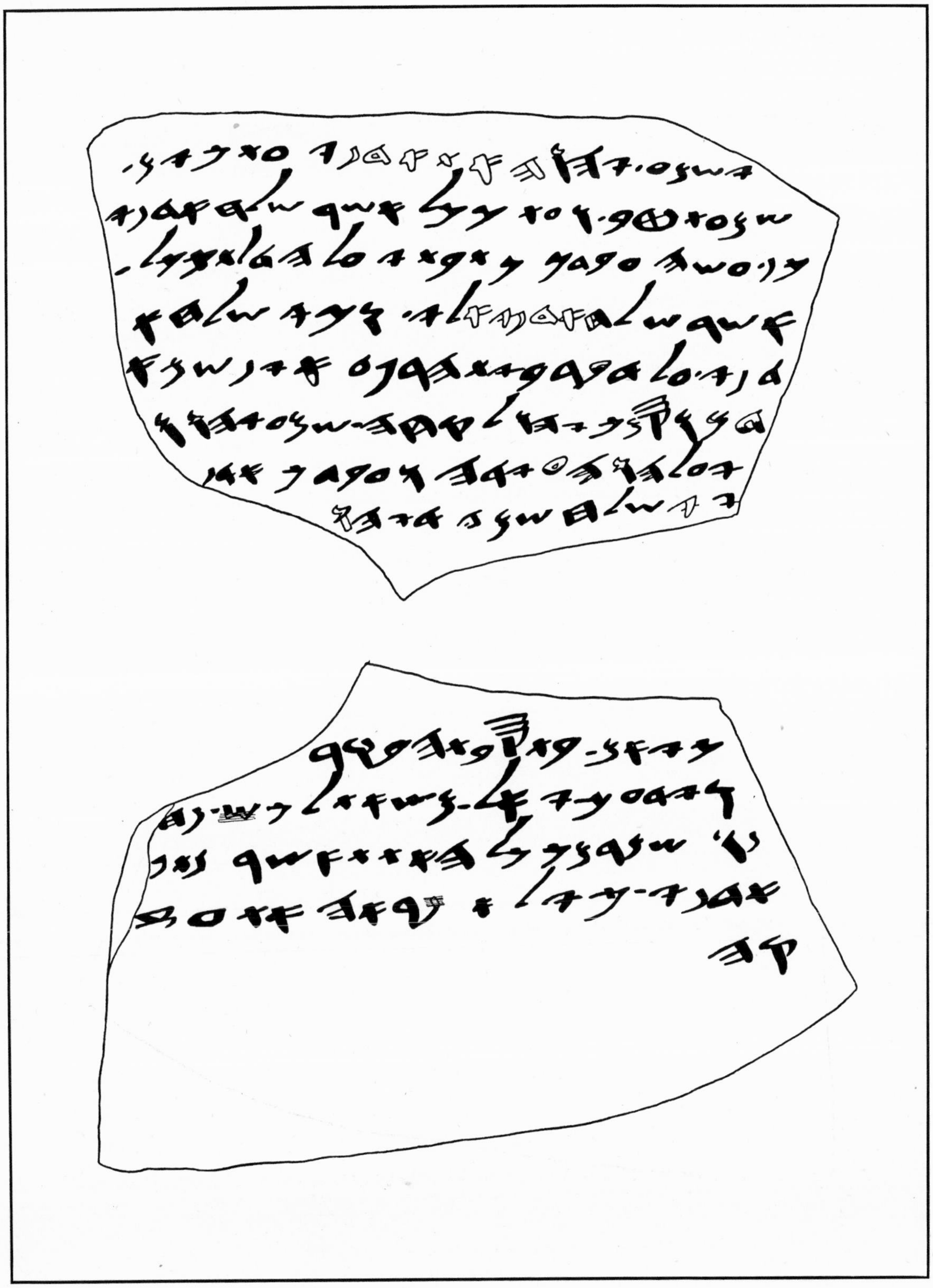

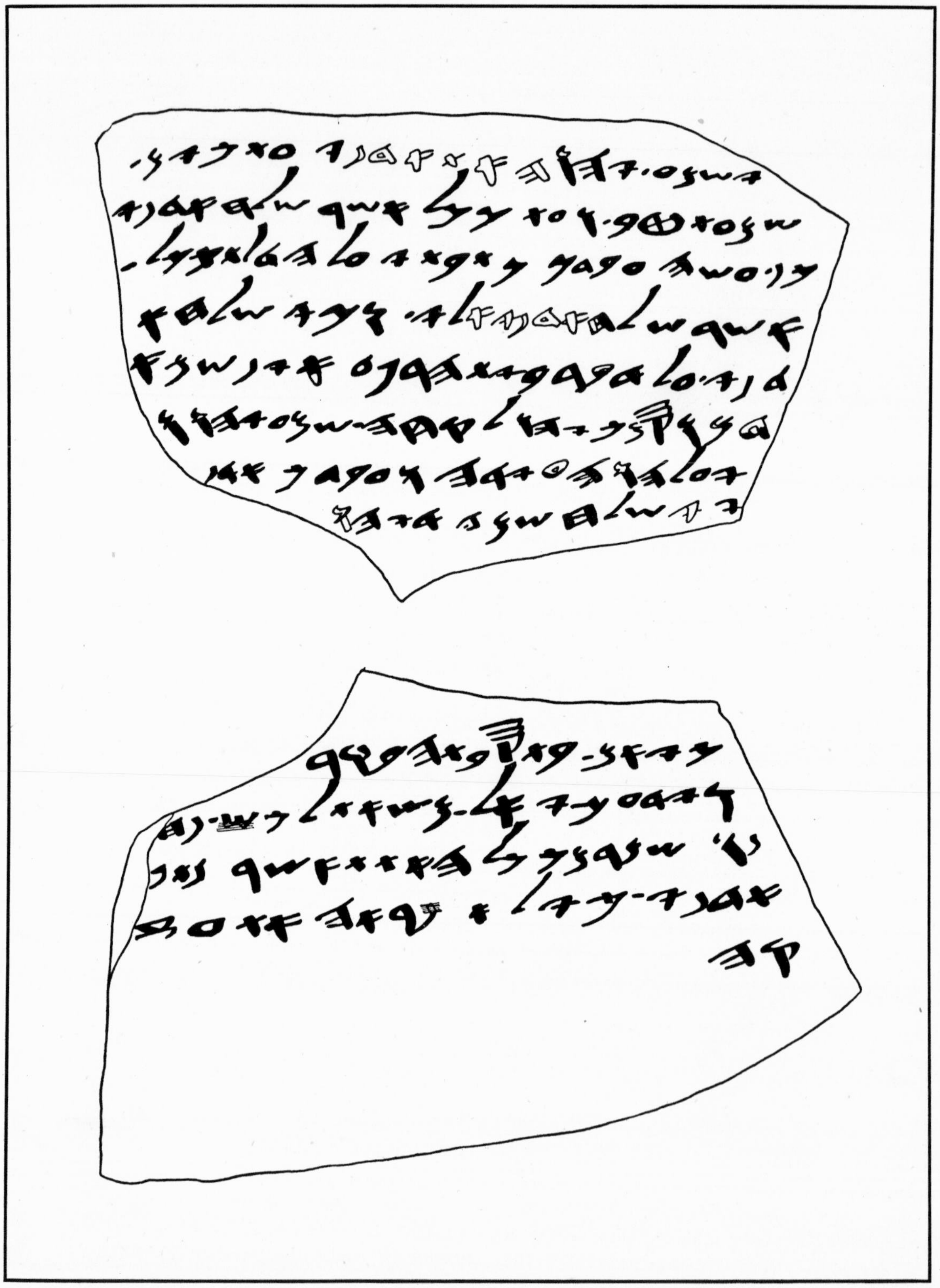

LETTER IV

TRANSLITERATION

OBVERSE

1. ישמע · יהוה [את] אדני עת כים ·
2. שמעת טב · ועת ככל אשר שלח אדני·
3. כן · עשה עבדך כתבתי על הדלת ככל ·
4. אשר שלח אדני אלי · וכי · שלח א
5. דני · על דבר בית הרפד אין שם א
6. דם וסמכיהו לקחה · שמעיהו ו
7. יעלהו העירה ועבדך אדן
8. י ישלח שמה איהו ·

REVERSE

9. כי אם · בתסבתה בקר
10. וידע כי אל · משאת לכש · נח
11. נו שמרם ככל האתת אשר נתן
12. אדני · כי לא נראה את עז
13. קה

TRANSLATION

1. May Yhwh let hear my lord even now
2. tidings of good. According to whatever my lord has sent (= written)
3. thus has thy slave done. I have written on the page according to what-
4. ever my lord has sent to me. And when my lord has sent
5. about the sleeping house, there is nobo-
6. dy. And Semakhyahu, him has taken Shemaʿyahu and
7. brought him up to the city, and thy slave, my lord,
8. shall write thither, (asking), where he is;

9. because if in his turning he had inspected,
10. he would know, that for the signal-stations of Lachish we
11. are watching, according to all the signs which my
12. lord gives, because we do not see (the signals of) Aze-
13. qah.

L

NOTES

LINE 1. For the greeting-formula, *cf.* the notes to Letters II and VI.

LINE 2. טב; according to the Massoretic vocalization the pronunciation טוֹב is alone possible, not טוּב as used in the Bible only in st. cstr., or with pronominal suffix and in combination with כָּל־טוּב: כל. וְעַתָּ leads to the following, as is usual in letters in Biblical Hebrew (Isaiah XXXVI, 8, 10) and Aramaic (כען, כענת, כעת) (Ezra IV, 13 *sqq.*), and similar expressions in Babylonian letters, *e.g.* Amarna (*cf.* Letter III, 4). The defective spelling עת for the usual עַתָּה occurs also in the Bible (Ezekiel XXIII, 43; Psalms LXXIV, 6 *Kethībh*). (*Cf.* also the notes to VI, 2.) The following sentence כְּכָל־אֲשֶׁר שָׁלַח אֲדֹנִי כֵּן עָשָׂה עַבְדֶּךָ has many parallels in Biblical style, *cf.* כְּכָל־הַדָּבָר אֲשֶׁר יִשְׁלָחַךָ יְהֹוָה אֱלֹהֶיךָ אֵלֵינוּ כֵּן נַעֲשֶׂה "according to all things for which Yhwh thy God shall send thee to us thus we shall do" (Jeremiah XLII, 5), *cf.* Esther III, 12; VIII, 9.

LINE 3. The wording כָּתַבְתִּי עַל הַדֶּלֶת is most interesting. דלת, originally door-board, then board in general, occurs in the sense of a sheet or page of papyrus only once in the Bible: Jeremiah XXXVI, 23: וַיְהִי כִּקְרֹא יְהוּדִי שָׁלֹשׁ דְּלָתוֹת וְאַרְבָּעָה יִקְרָעֶהָ בְּתַעַר הַסֹּפֵר וְהַשְׁלֵךְ אֶל הָאֵשׁ אֲשֶׁר אֶל הָאָח עַד תֹּם כָּל־הַמְּגִלָּה "And it came to pass, that when Jehudi had read three or four leaves, he cut it with the penknife, and cast it into the fire that was on the hearth, until the roll was consumed in the fire that was on the hearth". This meaning of דֶּלֶת is certainly the most probable where political or military secrets form the topic of the correspondence, not writing on a "door-board". In this unlikely case one would also expect: "I have written upon the *gate*" (שער), or at least "upon the door-boards of the gate" (דלתת השער); but it is the sign of a madman that he "scrabbled on the (wooden) doors of the gate" (I Samuel XXI, 14: וַיְתָו עַל־דַּלְתוֹת הַשָּׁעַר). Why should the sender of the letter write upon the door-board of his home town what he could easily proclaim personally?

The original meaning of דלת (Accadic *dalāte*, pl. of *daltu*, door-board) may be "locking" from *wdl* or *ydl*, the Accadic *edelu* "to lock, to shut".[1] The origin of the noun is in the plural or dual, the singular is the *nomen unitatis* to the plural (*cf.* my *Der Numerus im Problem der Sprachentstehung*, Berlin, 1928, *page* 20).

Nothing can be said definitely about the kind of writing to which the sender of this letter refers; it may even have been official letter-writing. The use of the word כתבתי instead of שלחתי necessarily results from the original meaning of שלח "to send" which was still being understood; thus שלח could not be used without the complement אל "to send *unto*", whilst here no addresses are mentioned. But *cf.* VI, lines 8–9, where כתב is used even for "writing to somebody" like שלח. Certainly שלח in many instances implies also the meaning: "to order, to send an order". However, the phrasing: "I have written on the page according to *whatever* my lord has sent to me", or, literally, according to *all* that my lord had sent (written)" one would expect a longer text probably recorded on papyrus. It is not likely that "all that" should be written on the door-board or upon an ostracon. As the passage suggests, papyrus may still have been available to the writer; however, he does not use it for a short message to Ya'ush, but keeps this material, valuable and scarce in wartime, for special purposes. It is even possible, as the determined "*the* page" suggests, that Ya'ush had sent the papyrus for this special writing, which perhaps had to be sent to Jerusalem. We may also take it that potsherds were used particularly in cases where sealing was not necessary, which could conveniently have been done on papyrus, but not on potsherds.

---

[1] As suggested before in the notes on Letter III, 4, the word may be an ancient loan-word in Hebrew.

"I have written" must certainly not be meant as "written by my hand", but may well be "I made (my scribe) write" as in many similar examples in the Bible, and in all ancient literature. Thus God says to Jeremiah—who did not write himself: "Write thee (כְּתָב־לְךָ) all the words that I have spoken unto thee in a book (אֶל־סֵפֶר)" (Jeremiah XXX, 2), and the king, knowing that Jeremiah has not himself written the roll, is quoted as saying to the prophet: "Why hast thou written therein? (מַדּוּעַ כָּתַבְתָּ עָלֶיהָ)" (Jeremiah XXXVI, 29), and in Jeremiah LI, 59–62, it is even told that Jeremiah wrote (וַיִּכְתֹּב יִרְמְיָהוּ) a "book" and gave it to Seraiah, the son of Neriah, the brother of his regular scribe Baruch, where the implied meaning certainly is that Jeremiah "gives" his words to Seraiah, and it is he who writes them on a "book".

LINE 4 *sqq*. The next sentence deals with the question asked by Ya'ush about certain men who were supposed to be in (the) בית הרפד. At first I was inclined to read here בֵּית הָרְפָא and to connect this, as the name of a place (*cf*. the following: *there* is nobody), with בֵּית רָפָא mentioned among names of families and places in Judah in I Chronicles IV, 12.[1] But further examination showed, as the excellent photograph reproduced here makes clear, that the last letter certainly is ד, not א or ע: בית הרפד. Now רפד is a usual Hebrew word for "bedding" (*cf*. Job XVII, 13, בַּחֹשֶׁךְ רִפַּדְתִּי; Song of Solomon II, 5, סַמְּכוּנִי בָּאֲשִׁישׁוֹת רַפְּדוּנִי בַּתַּפּוּחִים יְצוּעַי "Lean me to the vines, bed me at the trees" [this is the correct translation]). רְפִידָתוֹ in Song of Solomon III, 10, "he made the pillars thereof (of his אַפִּרְיוֹן, a sedan-chair) of silver, the *bottom* thereof (רְפִידָתוֹ) of gold" is originally the bedding, whereupon he reclines. Thus בֵּית הָרֶפֶד "the beddinghouse, sleepinghouse" would certainly be a fitting name for a place or room where incoming guests or soldiers would be lodged. And it is most natural that Ya'ush, inquiring for men coming from elsewhere (Jerusalem?) referred to such a place, where he thought they would most probably stay. However, nobody is there.

Mr. M. Kutscher, Jerusalem, calls my attention to *Festschrift A. Schwarz* (Vienna), 1916, *page* 301, where F. Perles discusses a passage in MS. Munich of the Babylonian Talmud Megilla 10 b, which instead of שרף רפידת בית ה׳ of our usual editions gives שרף בית מרפדו של הקב״הו (הקדוש ברוך הוא =)—"(Nebuchadnezzar) who burned the *Bet Marped* (or *Mirpad*) of the Holy one, blessed His name". Perles, following Montgomery, *Aramaic Incantation Texts from Nippur* (Philadelphia, 1913), *page* 126, explains *Bet Marped* as "Dwelling Place". Taken together with the passage in our letter it shows that בית רפד or בית מרפד was a regular Hebrew expression for "sleepinghouse, dwellinghouse". *Cf*. also the Biblical use of מָלוֹן which, if not a Khan proper, at least means a special place, where travellers usually passed the night. The fact that such a "sleepinghouse", at least for soldiers, existed where the writer lived is in itself of great interest.[2]

Among the men supposed to be in the sleepinghouse was one Semakhyahu (*i.e.* Semachiah), who is mentioned also in the small fragment XI, and probably also in Letters V and IX. He was, according to the following lines on the reverse, a man of high position entrusted with the inspection of the place from which the sender of the letter writes. But he is no longer there; Shema'yahu has taken him and brought him up to the city, certainly to Jerusalem (*cf*. VI, 5). Shema'yahu is also the name of the father of the prophet Uriyahu (Jeremiah XXVI, 20) (*see later*). Note also Shema'yah, the son of Obed-Edom (time of David) (I Chronicles XXVI, 4, 6, 7), among whose sons in v. 7 even a Semakhyahu is mentioned. ויעלהו, in line 7, also איהו, in line 8, show the difference between the spelling of the pronoun after the vowel *ē* and in contracted forms as עבדה

---

[1] This reading and explanation was first given by me in my lecture to the Palestine Oriental Society, Jerusalem, May 6th, 1935.

[2] *Cf*. also the Summary *page* 206.

"his slave", so far consistent with Biblical Hebrew, where also the *hē* and *waw* are preserved in אַיֵּהוּ and וַיַּעֲלֵהוּ, though not in the other cases, where the *waw* may have been contracted with the preceding original *a* to one vowel. Note also the *waw consec.* in ויעלהו and also the full spelling of העירה. Was there a form עָיִר for עִיר, or was it the influence of the guttural ע which made them pronounce a diphthong "'ayr"?

The last sentence, lines 7–8: "And thy slave, my lord, will write thither where he is", is certainly a kind of elision instead of " . . . [asking] where he is" (*cf.* the notes to VI, 6). It is the same kind of abbreviated expression as in Job XV, 23: נֹדֵד הוּא לַלֶּחֶם אַיֵּה "He wandereth abroad for bread [asking] where [is it]", here even simpler, as ישלח "he will send", *i.e.* "write" in itself implies the expressing of words and does not necessarily need the addition "saying" or "asking". For another, even more striking parallel, *see* notes on Letter IX, line 9.

The first line of the reverse presented considerable difficulties, which here, as in Letter III, for some time prevented my seeing the connexion between obverse and reverse. At the beginning of the reverse, then insufficiently cleaned, one could recognize the letters כי אם (perhaps כי ים). However, the more probable reading כי אם usually means in Hebrew "but". How could this be connected with the facts told on the obverse? At the end of line 9, where no word-dividing dots could be seen, בקר or rather הבקר seemed to suggest itself. This could be either הַבָּקָר "the cattle" or הַבֹּקֶר "the morning". But what could be the meaning of בתסכת or בתסבת (הבקר) which also seemed possible?[1] In line 10 a flaw in the pot made the reading of משאת at first impossible. In 11–12 one could recognize ככל ה . . ת . . אשר נתן אדני, "according to all the . . . which my Lord has given (or giveth)". The object which suggested itself was something like מתת "gift", the gift which he has given. Only after a final cleaning of this side of the letter did I recognize the names of Azeqah and Lachish, and how astonished was I to find the signal-stations משאת as mentioned in the Mishnah. And then at last I realized that בקר without the ה was neither בָּקָר nor בֹּקֶר but the verb בִּקֵּר, "he had inspected". For details, *see* the following remarks. כי אם is here not "but",[2] it stands here for "because if". It is rather unusual that אם should stand in the sense of לוּ(א) introducing an unreal condition: אם . . . בקר וידע "if he had inspected he would know", although in the Bible אם is sometimes used almost in the same sense as "though"; but there is again in Jeremiah one passage beginning like our sentence with כי אם where אם is used exactly in the same sense: Jeremiah XXXVII, 10: כִּי אִם הִכִּיתֶם כָּל־חֵיל כַּשְׂדִּים הַנִּלְחָמִים אִתְּכֶם וְנִשְׁאֲרוּ־בָם אֲנָשִׁים מְדֻקָּרִים אִישׁ בְּאָהֳלוֹ יָקוּמוּ וְשָׂרְפוּ אֶת־הָעִיר הַזֹּאת בָּאֵשׁ "For though ye had smitten the whole army of the Chaldeans that fight against you, and there remained but stabbed men among them, they will rise every man in his tent and will burn this city with fire". A similar case is Hosea IX, 12: כִּי אִם יְגַדְּלוּ אֶת־בְּנֵיהֶם וְשִׁכַּלְתִּים מֵאָדָם "For though they bring up their children, yet will I bereave them (that there shall) not (be) a man (left)". בְּתִסְבָּתֹה "in his turning", from תְּסִבָּה to סבב "to turn", a new word, not found in the Bible. The meaning can be "survey-tour"[3] or like the Babylonian *tayartu* (from *tāru*, Hebrew תור, to turn round) the "turning off" or "turning back" in another direction. בִּקֵּר "he inspected"; the word was originally used for the shepherd who inspects and searches his sheep as in Ezekiel XXXIV, 11, 12, "For thus saith the Lord God: Behold I, even I, will both search my sheep and seek them out (וּבִקַּרְתִּים). As

[1] It is now much easier to control these readings from the excellent photographs reproduced here, than to find them from the then insufficiently cleaned originals.

[2] Considered only from a linguistic point of view, one could translate "But in the turning of the morning בְּתִסְבַּת הַבֹּקֶר *then*

he will know", although the ו of וידע requires a preceding verb; but how is this to make sense?

[3] The same as Arabic دَوْرَة or Pal. Arabic *duarieh*, used to-day for "patrol"?

a shepherd seeketh out his flock (כְּבַקָּרַת רֹעֶה עֶדְרוֹ) in the day that he is among his sheep that are scattered; so will I seek out (אֲבַקֵּר) my sheep"; it is used also of the priest looking for symptoms of the leper (Leviticus XIII, 36) and for the search for a better or a worse sheep to be used as offering (Leviticus XXVII, 33). *Cf.* also the notes on Letter II, 5–6.

LINE 10. וידע. *Waw consec.* in the sense of Arabic ف *fa*, occurs frequently in the Hebrew Bible, particularly after conditional clauses beginning with אם or כי (*cf.* Genesis XXXI, 8; XXXVIII, 9; XLIII, 9). משאת. The word in this sense is known particularly from the Mishnah Rosh Hashanah II, 2–3, where we have a full description of the *massu'oth*, used to inform the Jews in Exile of the appearance of the new moon in Jerusalem: בראשונה היו משיאין משואות · משקלקלו הכותם התקינו שיהו שלוחין יוצאין : כיצד היו משיאין משואות? מביאין כלונסאות של ארז ארוכין וקנים ועצי שמן ונעורת של פשתן וכורך במשיחה ועולה לראש ההר ומצית בהן את האור ומוליך ומביא ומעלה ומוריד עד שהוא רואה את חבירו שהוא עושה כן בראש ההר השני · וכן בראש ההר השלישי: or in Professor H. Danby's translation: "Beforetime they used to kindle fires, but after the evil doings of the Samaritans they enacted, that messages should go forth. After what fashion did they kindle the flares (מַשְׂאוֹת)?[1] They used to take long cedarwood sticks and rushes and oleander wood and flax tow; and a man bound these up with a rope and went up to the top of the hill and set light to them; and he waved them to and fro and up and down until he could see his fellow doing the like on the top of the next hill. And so, too, on the top of the third hill."

This testimony of the Mishnah, in itself of later origin (2nd century A.D.) refers to an earlier time, "at first, before the Kuthaens (*i.e.* the Samaritans), did their wrong". And it is certainly the same thing which is mentioned in Jeremiah VI, 1: "O ye children of Benjamin, gather yourselves to flee out of the midst of Jerusalem, and blow the trumpet in Tekoa, and set up *a sign of fire* in Beth-haccerem" (וְעַל־בֵּית הַכֶּרֶם שְׂאוּ מַשְׂאֵת). *Cf.* also Judges XX, 38: "Now there was an appointed sign between the men of Israel and the liers in wait, that they should make a great flame with smoke rise up (לְהַעֲלוֹתָם מַשְׂאַת הֶעָשָׁן) out of the city", and v. 40, "But the flame began to arise up out of the city (with) a pillar of smoke" (וְהַמַּשְׂאֵת הֵחֵלָּה לַעֲלוֹת מִן־הָעִיר עַמּוּד עָשָׁן). It may be doubtful whether the Biblical or the Mishnaic vocalization be accepted for our letters. It is also possible to read the singular instead of the plural; but the description of the Mishnah and the fact that the writer should ordinarily be able to see the משאת transmitted from both Lachish and Azeqah, support the assumption that not only a main station but all the intermediate fire beacons on the hills are intended. לכש. ל and כ are quite clear and ש also is certain. נַחְנוּ (lines 10–11) is very interesting, as this form occurs only five times in the Bible (Genesis XLII, 11; Exodus XVI, 7, 8; Numbers XXXII, 32; Lamentations III, 42). שמרם read שֹׁמְרֵם. The construction שמר אֶל "*to watch for, to look out* for"[2] occurs rarely in the Bible (there is no need to look for later parallels) in passages which now have a special significance. *Cf.* II Samuel XI, 16 וַיְהִי בִּשְׁמוֹר יוֹאָב אֶל־הָעִיר "And it came to pass when Joab was watching for the (besieged) city", and Psalms LIX, 10, עֻזּוֹ אֵלֶיךָ אֶשְׁמֹרָה כִּי אֱלֹהִים מִשְׂגַּבִּי "His strength, for thee I am watching because God is my stronghold", words which now get a

---

[1] But probably מַשּׂוֹאֹת is intended, *cf.* Mishnaic מַשּׂוֹא for Biblical מַשְׂא.

[2] This explanation was given by me from the first both in my lectures in Jerusalem (May 6th, 1935), London (July 9th, 1935), and in my preliminary articles in English (*Jewish Daily Post*, London, July 3rd, 1935, *page* 6) and in Hebrew (*Kenesset*, pages 387–388) thus explaining Psalms LIX, 10: "The praying psalmist is watching for signs which God, his fortress and stronghold, will give him, just as the watching men are looking out for the fire-beacons and the *signals given from the mountains*." Unfortunately, some scholars misunderstood my Hebrew notes, thinking I had explained שמר אֶל as "*to keep guard over*" and offered their corrections.

fuller meaning from our Lachish Letter, such as "Thou, O God, art my fortress and for the signals Thou givest me I am watching". The same meaning has also ל שמר in Psalms CXXX, 6 נַפְשִׁי לַאדֹנָי מִשֹּׁמְרִים לַבֹּקֶר שֹׁמְרִים לַבֹּקֶר "My soul is (waiting) for Yhwh more then they that watch for the morning, (they that) watch for the morning". האתת are the particular signs or signals given by the אשר נתן. משאת: according to the present tense in נחנו שמרם "we are watching", we may have to pronounce אֲשֶׁר נֹתֵן "which my lord giveth", although this construction is less usual than אֲשֶׁר נָתַן "which he has given", which is also possible.

LINES 12–13. כי לא נראֶה אֶת עזקה "Because we do not see Azeqah"; G. R. Driver, already in July, 1935, kindly pointed out to me the possibility (considered, but rejected by me) of translating "because there is not visible (נראה as Nifʿal) a sign (אֹת) of Azeqah", as "for we cannot see Azeqah" would be a truism. However, after "for the signals of Lachish we are watching" the following "for we do not see Azeqah" in the short language of these messages (there is a world of tragedy in these few lines!) certainly means "we do not see Azeqah *in its signals*", which obviously is no truism; thus Lachish itself also is not visible, but only its signals. Further, in such a case the sentence should speak not of one sign (את) but of the signs (אתת) or the beacon(s) (משאת) of Azeqah, and in the better Hebrew wording: (or תֵּרָאֶנָה) כי אתת עזקה לא יֵרָאוּ "for the signs of Azeqah are not visible", putting the subject at the beginning; also, nowhere in the Bible amongst the many references to "signs" is a possessive genitive added. There is "a sign or token of truth" (אות אמת) Joshua II, 12, "a token of (=for) the covenant (אות ברית)" Genesis IX, 12, and often, but only "a token (demanded) *from* Yhwh (מֵעִם יהוה)" (*see* the notes to Letter VI, line 2). Finally, the sentence, starting in the first person plural, "we are watching", should normally continue in the same way: "because we do not see", the active form "we see" as a general rule being more likely than the passive and incomplete "it is not visible (to us)".

Note that whilst the description in the Mishnah only proves that some signals had been given which were understood as announcing the appearance of the new moon, our letter shows without doubt that fire was used to transmit signals in a type of semaphore, thus proving the existence of a system of communication by beacons and signs, of which we previously had no knowledge.

GENERAL REMARKS

Just as Letter III is of singular importance for the study of Biblical history, so is Letter IV for the topography and military history of Lachish as well as of ancient Judah. Here, too, particularly in the five lines on the reverse, we see Judah as she was in Jeremiah's time, in the midst of her struggle and suffering, depicted with all the vividness of real life.

After the customary greeting, the writer observes that he has carried out all his lord's instructions and duly recorded on a sheet of papyrus whatever his lord ordered.

With regard to one question, however, concerning persons of high standing, visiting the writer's place and certainly staying at the "sleepinghouse", he replies to his questioner, Ya'ush, that none of them is there. One particular officer, Semakhyahu, who should have inspected the place whence this letter had been sent, had been there, but a certain Shema'yahu had taken him to Jerusalem.

The following lines give positive proof that Tell ed Duweir, where the letters were found, really is the site of ancient Lachish. The sender says that if the officer had only carried out his inspection of the station whence he writes, "he would have known that we are watching for the signal-stations of Lachish for all the signs that my lord gives". It is clear from this that the place where Ya'ush lives is none other than Lachish.

The writer adds: "(we are watching for the signal stations of Lachish . . .) because we do not see Azeqah". Here Lachish and Azeqah, the last fortresses left in Judah besides Jerusalem, are mentioned together as in the striking words of Jeremiah XXXIV, 7: "And the king of Babylon's army fought against Jerusalem, and against all the cities of Judah that were left, against Lachish and against Azeqah; for these alone remained of the cities of Judah as fenced cities".

וְחֵיל מֶלֶךְ־בָּבֶל נִלְחָמִים עַל־יְרוּשָׁלַם וְעַל כָּל־עָרֵי יְהוּדָה הַנּוֹתָרוֹת אֶל לָכִישׁ וְאֶל־עֲזֵקָה כִּי הֵנָּה נִשְׁאֲרוּ בְּעָרֵי יְהוּדָה עָרֵי מִבְצָר:

It seems certain that the writer does not intend to inform Ya'ush whether the fortress of Azeqah is visible or not, as this must have been known to the officer. If Azeqah is invisible, then also, Lachish cannot be seen, except for its signals, sent through intermediate stations. It is the signals of Azeqah that are no longer to be seen, and therefore he has to watch for those of Lachish; this fact may suggest that Azeqah was already in enemy hands, or at least so closely beset that it was no longer possible to send out signals.

The sentence ". . . for the signal-stations of Lachish we are watching . . . because we do not see (the signs) of Azeqah", implies, further, that the natural thing for the writer to do, would be to watch for the signals of Azeqah. Azeqah is therefore presumably nearer to him than Lachish. But how could "watching for the signs of Lachish" transmitted over the hills be only a substitute for the signs of Azeqah, if Azeqah originally did not normally pass on the messages sent there from Lachish? Azeqah therefore is the intermediate station between Lachish and the writer's place; thus the sentence seems to say fully: we are watching Lachish, because we do not see the middle station Azeqah. The writer's place itself seems to be a middle station between Lachish and Azeqah on one side and Jerusalem on the other. It is from here that he will send to Jerusalem to inquire about Semakhyahu "where he is".

The message of Letter IV, saying, "We have no direct signals from Azeqah, we can watch only for the signals which my lord in Lachish gives" implies also an *appeal* to the men at Lachish, *to send signals*: "We have no other signals than those, which my lord sends".

After having examined the contents of Letter IV independently, we now have to consider whether the working hypothesis based so far upon the evidence of Letters II, III, VI, VII, VIII, XII, XVI and XVIII and made plausible also for Ostracon I, applies equally to Letter IV, and if so, what can be learned from it for a better understanding of the message.

There is certainly nothing in our letter inconsistent with the hypothesis that Letter IV was also written by Hosha'yahu to Ya'ush, and, though not making the same statements as II, III, VI and XII, belongs essentially to the same correspondence which also dealt with the prophet, his flight and the troubles connected with it; and this hypothesis would be probable even if we could not as yet see any connexion in the rather vague allusions in our letter. But there are even some points which remind us of Hosha'yahu and his connexion with the prophet.

First, the situation of the writer's place as an observation post and middle station between Azeqah and Jerusalem fits in well with the site of Qiryat-Ye'arim, the prophet Uriyahu's home-town. Without laying particular stress upon any actual identification of Qiryat-Ye'arim, it is generally accepted that, according to the boundary of Judah denoted in Joshua XV, 8–10, this town was situated to the west of Jerusalem, in the hills, while the frontier was still farther west towards Beth-Shemesh in the foothills. Thus Qiryat-Ye'arim would lie north-east of Azeqah (Tell Zakariya) which itself lies about 11 miles north-north-east of Lachish (Tell ed Duweir).

However, could the signals given from Lachish and Azeqah be observed by men watching for them in Qiryat-Ye'arim? If this place is to be identified with Abu-Ghosh, Lachish and even Azeqah could not be seen from Qiryat-Ye'arim itself. Now, as for receiving the signals sent from Azeqah, this is in no way necessary. As seen from the Mishnah, the signals were not transmitted directly from the main station, but were relayed from hill to hill, till they reached their destination, and by signs given it could be recognized, whether they came from Lachish or Azeqah. Still the words in lines 12–13, "because we do not see Azeqah", while meant as "we do not see the signals of Azeqah" might apply to the main fire beacon erected in Azeqah itself or very near to it. But the men in Qiryat-Ye'arim, behind the lines, were still free to observe the signals sent, directly or indirectly, from Azeqah and Lachish, since their messengers were still coming and going from Lachish and Jerusalem. The site of Beit-Mahsir, south of Bab-el-Wad, where now the way to Tell Zakariya, Beit Jibrin, and Tell ed Duweir branches off from the main Jaffa–Jerusalem road, is an exceptional vantage point, and may well have been used as an observation post for Qiryat-Ye'arim; from it all the main forts of the western frontier were visible.

It is no coincidence, either, that the prophet appeared in Qiryat-Ye'arim, and that there his words "weakened the hands of the men of war", for Qiryat-Ye'arim was both a small fortress and an ancient holy place, where Obed-Edom and his sons—among them one Shema'yahu and his son Semakhyahu (I Chronicles XXVI, 7)—guarded the ark of God.

Shema'yahu is also the name of the prophet's father, and thus it is just possible that what Hosha'yahu refers to in lines 6–7 is that the prophet's father has taken this important person and brought him up to the city in order to use his influence with the king and his officers in matters connected with his son's fate. To Semakhyahu Hosha'yahu should also have reported about other matters; therefore he should have applied to him. But he is no longer here. Had he on his rounds, his "[re]turning" inspected he would have known that Hosha'yahu and his friends were trying to observe all the orders of Ya'ush. While the connexion of Letter IV with the writer of the other ostraca mentioned above could not be based upon such possibilities alone, the testimony of so many other letters is so strongly in favour of it that it must be considered as highly probable. Also in XI (*see above*) as in V (and IX, *see* notes to Letter V) and XIII, Semakhyahu is mentioned; all this shows that these ostraca belong to one and the same correspondence between Hosha'yahu and Ya'ush.

However, this letter was probably not written during the same few days as Letters II, III, VI and XII (making the same statement on oath), but rather later (hardly before). There is no further need for Hosha'yahu to protest so fervently against the accusation referred to in Letter III, the message written the day after Ya'ush wrote to him about it. While Letter III and Letters II, VI and XII give the same oath, and the other Letters VII, VIII and XVIII (on fragments of the same pot as II and VI) must have followed immediately and dealt with the same unchanged situation, others could have arrived later and be based upon an altered position. (*See also* Letters V and XVI.)

If the explanation given on *page* 73 is true, the ostraca found in the gate-room are not just the last letters left there before the destruction of the fortress, but a part of one correspondence collected and preserved in one vessel. Otherwise, we should have expected that the letters would deal with more varied topics, and it is hardly likely that nine out of twelve documents[1] should belong to the same correspondence, while the remaining few letters show similar characteristics and the same relation of writer to receiver. Though found together, there may be a certain lapse of time between the arrival of some of them. Thus there is no necessity, on archaeological grounds, to date the letters dealing with the prophet to the year before the final destruction of Lachish (*see* notes to Letter VI) as is the case with Letter IV.

The last lines of Letter IV would most naturally be understood in a military sense: it is already difficult to send letters between Lachish and the writer's place. The writer and his men are watching for fire-signals given, perhaps, in a secret code. Azeqah, which formerly transmitted the orders from Lachish, no longer gives signals. So it seems that in this letter we are dealing with a very critical phase of the siege of Lachish, if not actually its last days. Letter IV also shows us clearly the position of Ya'ush and his relation to the writer of the letter, Hosha'yahu. Ya'ush's letter referred to in Letter III, and dealing with the offence committed by Hosha'yahu against the prophet, could still be understood as a token of Ya'ush's unofficial leadership among a religious party of followers of the prophet only; Letter IV, however, shows his real position as the writer's official and military superior. Ya'ush sends signals from Lachish, which have to be transmitted by Azeqah and watched for and obeyed by a small outpost to the north of Azeqah, in all probability Qiryat-Ye'arim. A high officer, Semakhyahu, is ordered by Ya'ush to inspect and see whether Hosha'yahu, in whom we shall have to recognize the commander of Qiryat-Ye'arim, actually observed and obeyed the orders given by Ya'ush through the beacons of Lachish. Thus Ya'ush must be the military governor of Lachish, commanding from this greatest fortress of Judah also the other fenced cities and watch-posts of the western frontier along the border of the Philistine plain.

The writing of Letter IV again shows a few peculiarities, *e.g.* the כ and the double-sided ק, differing from the alphabet of Letters II–III, but not sufficiently to permit a definite decision as to whether these letters were written by the same hand.

---

[1] The others are IV, V and XIII, Letter IX being only a duplicate of V. (*See* the notes on these documents.)

LETTER V

Photo: S. W. Michieli

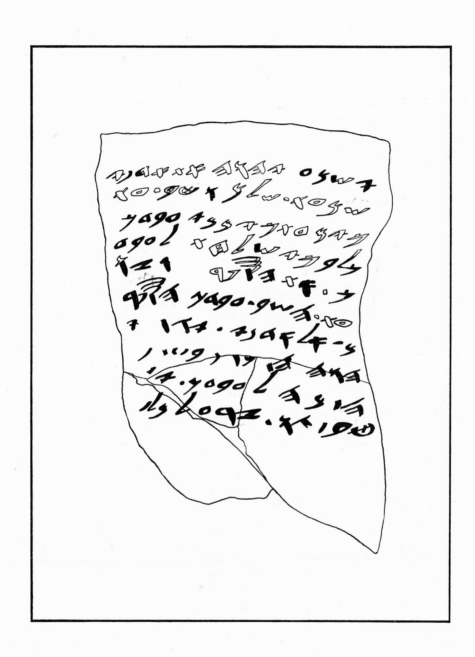

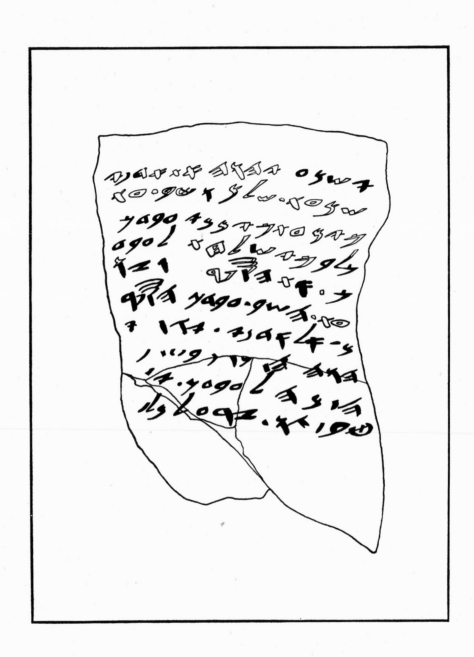

LETTER V

PRELIMINARY TRANSLITERATION[1]

1. ישמע יהוה [א]ת [אד]ני
2. שמ[ע]ת· [שלם] וטב [עת]
3. [כים עת כים] מי עבדך
4. כלב כי [של]חת אל עבד
5. [ך ·] את ס[נ]פרי – – –]יהו
6. [עת] השב · עבדך הספר
7. ם · אל אדני · יד – (-)[ך י
8. הוה [– – ֥ (-)] [(-)] – ע – (-)
9. ה · מה לעבדך · יא
10. – · ביהו · זרע למלך

---

[1] For fuller reconstruction and translation of this letter, *see* the following. Mr. Harding's hand copy here and for the following letters gives what he believes he sees on the sherd, differing in details from my readings. *See page* 102.

NOTES

The most interesting contents of this very difficult letter only became clear after it was observed that, just as the contents of Letter III are repeated in another version in Letters VI and XII, so also the contents of Letter V apparently are given in Letter IX. By comparing both versions we are able to reach almost their full meaning.

The fact that not only this message, but also the other letters, are repeated in more than one ostracon is in itself very significant. These repetitions are not literal copies of one definite version, giving the same text and even the same details, but renewed renderings of the same facts in different form. Therefore, they cannot be regarded as mere duplicates, sent by different messengers, because their sender feared that some of them might not reach their destination—although this may also have caused the double message—but rather as repetitions urged by the great importance of the letters, and by the writer's need to make his lord take notice of his plea. From the circumstance that more than one example of such repetitions occur, we may perhaps infer that the greater part of at least one side of this particular correspondence has been preserved in the gate-room of Lachish, though some of the letters are no longer legible. (*See* the notes on Letter VI.)

Only faint traces of the first sentence (lines 1–3) are visible, but the beginning of the next sentence in line 3 shows that not less than two and a half lines were filled with the customary greetings, which can be restored from the traces and other examples. "May Yhwh let hear my [lord tidings of peace and good, even now, even now]." This is also the case with the following question, lines 3–5, which as a whole may be correctly reconstructed: "Who is thy slave, a dog, that thou hast sent the letters of . . . to thy slave. Thy slave has now returned the letters to my lord." The latter sentence (lines 6–7) "Thy slave has returned the letters" is quite clear and shows that also the former passage must be approximately reconstructed as given above. It is somebody's "letters" (*cf.* Letter VI, 4) that are spoken of, not "one" or "the" letter. The letters cannot be the king's or the officers' as the traces at the end of line 5 can be neither those of המלך nor of השרם. Thus only a personal name can be mentioned, and in this case the traces should probably be interpreted as those of יהו, ending a proper name. The traces at the probable beginning of the name look to me as parts of the letter ס followed by two other, now effaced signs. (*See* General Remarks.)

It is also interesting that in this short message the writer apparently says שׁל[חת] "thou hast sent" instead of the usual שׁלח אדני "my lord has sent"; thus also in line 7 we have "may he let thee know" instead of "may he let my lord know". This explains itself naturally by the assumption, made probable by the comparison of other doubles, that both Letters V and IX are *shortened* recapitulations of another longer letter, perhaps even of one of the larger ostraca, which now show only traces of effaced writing. At the beginning of line 6 עת "now" is most likely.

The following sentence, lines 7–9 (first sign), starts with the verb יד־(־)ך[1] followed by יהוה, thus certainly stating a wish: "may Yhwh". But the reading of the verb and of its object was for a long time very doubtful. I could only see that this sentence, as in Letter II, 5–6, may intend to confirm something in a positive form through Yhwh's intervention, which the following sentence denies about the writer himself.

It was now that the great similarity of Letter V and Letter IX became apparent to me. After the greeting and an introduction, which —while in particulars it could be different—also mentions letters sent to the writer, Letter IX gives as its main sentence the following letters, compared here

---

[1] About the number of letters in this verb, *see* following.

94

to what is visible in Letter V, middle of line 7 to the beginning of line 9.[1] Letter V, 7–9 יד־(־)ך
יהוה; .... ה מה; Letter IX מה נעשה אשר יהו ך(־)ידע. This seemed no coincidence; both letters gave
apparently the same meaning. And for both letters we certainly reached the perfectly fitting
sentence "May Yhwh let thee know (ידעך יהוה) what had been done (what happened)". יֹדְעֶךָ[2] "May
he let thee know" Hif'il imperf. 3. p. sg. masc. with suff. 2. p. sg. masc. seemed clear. נַעֲשָׂה perf.
3. p. sg. masc. Nif'al seemed here more likely than נַעֲשֶׂה "we do". Of the שה at the end of line 8 no
definite trace is visible; what looks like a rather vertical stroke is no letter but only a scratch on
the surface of the potsherd. מה, line 9, belongs to the following sentence.

The reading of the verb ידע (see above) so far agreed with the traces, and no other plausible
verb could be found, which would fit into the frame given by the clear letters יד־(־)ך[3]; but while
there is no room at all between the letters י, ד, and ע, and while also the following י, beginning *a new
word*, is written very close to the preceding ך, there is plenty of room between the ע and the ד of
ידע. And this suggests that probably another narrow sign, of which traces could be recognized,
stood between these two letters.

Now, in Letter IX, reverse, line 1, the space between ידע כ shows that another sign stood between
ע and כ.[4] Must the suggested reading, therefore, be abandoned (see notes to Letter IX) at least for
Letter IX, and must ידע there be understood as a verb in itself, not connected with the following
כיהו, thus destroying the striking similarity between Letters V and IX?

However, even in Letter V there seemed to be another letter before the כ; but here ידע־ך must
be one single verb as the predicate to the following יהוה. Thus we shall have to recognize here and
in Letter IX the very interesting energetic form: יֹדְעֶנְךָ "may he let thee know". This *nun energicum*,
often preserved before the suff. 3. p. sg. (masc. and fem.) as in יִסֹּבְבֶנְהוּ and יִצְּרֶנְהוּ Deuteronomy
XXXII, 10; יַעַבְרֶנְהוּ Jeremiah V, 22; יְבָרְכֶנְהוּ Psalms LXXII, 15, and even in the regular contracted
forms as אֶצֳּרֶנָּה Isaiah XXVII, 3; אֶתְּנֶנּוּ Judges XX, 28; תְּתְנֶנּוּ Psalms LXXIV, 14; אֶזְכְּרֶנּוּ Jeremiah
XX, 9; XXXI, 20 (19), etc., is usually contracted with the following כ of the suff. 2. p. sg. and *nk*
assimilated into *kk*, as in וִיחֻנֶּךָּ Numbers VI, 24; אֶעֶזְבֶךָּ Joshua I, 5; II Kings II, 2, 4, 6; IV, 30;
יְצַוֶּךָּ Deuteronomy XXXI, 6, 8; I Chronicles XXVIII, 20, and often for original יעזבנך, אעזבנך, ויחננך.
Jeremiah XXII, 24 still shows also the original form אֶתְּקֶנְךָ and thus here also we shall have to accept
the reading יֹדְעֶנְךָ, which we should have expected with other characteristics of ancient Hebrew
spelling appearing in our letters. (For other particulars, see the notes to line 10 and Letter IX.)

Instead of אשר נעשה (or את אשר) also other words of the same meaning as *e.g.* הדבר הנעשה "the
thing (which has been) done" might have stood in Letter V, line 8. The traces left in this
line are very deceiving and what looks like letter strokes may in part be mere scratches on the
surface of the sherd. The last two signs, lines 8–9, may even be פה "(what) here (occurred)",
but I am not quite satisfied that the last "sign" on line 8 really is a letter. Also מה "what" or מהו
"what it is" (cf. Letter IX, 9) does not seem impossible and may even be the correct solution.

Now the final, and as it seems essential, sentence (lines 9–10) starts with the question: מה לעבדך
"What has thy slave?" *Cf.* Biblical passages as Judges XVIII, 23, מַה־לְּךָ כִּי נִזְעָקְתָּ. "What aileth thee
that thou hast assembled?"; I Samuel XI, 5, מַה־לָּעָם כִּי יִבְכּוּ "What aileth the people that they weep?";
II Samuel XIX, 29, וּמַה־יֶּשׁ־לִי עוֹד צְדָקָה וְלִזְעֹק עוֹד אֶל־הַמֶּלֶךְ "What right therefore have I yet to cry unto the

---

[1] Notice that lines 8–10 of Letter V are written in particularly
broad letters with large spaces between the words.

[2] *See page* 136.

[3] The second letter can hardly be ר, the only possible reading

besides ד. The third letter could be also ק, but no verb fitting this
possibility could be found.

[4] For this objection to the offered reading, as for other helpful
criticism, I am indebted to Mr. L. Harding.

king?"; Isaiah III, 15, מַלְכֶם תְּדַכְּאוּ עַמִּי "What mean ye that ye beat my people to pieces?"; Isaiah XXII, 1, מַה־לָּךְ אֵפוֹא כִּי־עָלִית כֻּלָּךְ לַגַּגּוֹת "What aileth thee now, that thou art wholly gone up to the housetops?"; Jeremiah II, 18, מַה־לָּךְ לְדֶרֶךְ מִצְרַיִם . . . וּמַה־לָּךְ לְדֶרֶךְ אַשּׁוּר "What hast thou to do in the way of Egypt . . . or what hast thou to do in the way of Assyria . . .?"; Ezekiel XVIII, 2, מַה־לָּכֶם אַתֶּם "What מְשְׁלִים אֶת־הַמָּשָׁל הַזֶּה mean ye, that ye use this proverb?"; Jonah I, 6, מַה־לְּךָ נִרְדָּם "What meanest thou, sleeping?"; Psalms L, 16, מַה־לְּךָ לְסַפֵּר חֻקָּי "What hast thou to declare my statutes?"; Psalms CXIV, 5, מַה־לְּךָ הַיָּם כִּי תָנוּס "What ailed thee, O thou sea, that thou fleddest?"; Ecclesiastes VI, 8, מַה־לֶּעָנִי יוֹדֵעַ "What hath the poor, knowing . . .?"

According to these examples, one expects here such a sentence as, "What has thy slave, that he should . . ."; the "that" follows the question in most of the quoted passages, but is, for instance, missing before an imperfect verb in Isaiah III, 15; it would be implied here between ך of עבדך and י of the following verb. The writer, pronouncing the intended 'abdak ky ye . . . as 'abdakye, may easily have left out the letters כי (cf. to II, 4, etc.). יא at the end of line 9, however, could only be the beginning of a verb; the rest must then be sought in line 10. But what follows in line 10 seemed at first to be the well-known proper name טֹבִיָּהוּ [1] Ṭobiyahu, which here was impossible. No proper name could follow here; the subject of the sentence must be the "slave" himself, and the object was given by זרע "seed". It could hardly be expected that one man (Ṭobiyahu) should be called "seed to the king", not only because "seed of the king" instead of "seed to the king" would be expected, but particularly because of the regular collective meaning of "seed" זרע, which only stands for all the seed, all the offspring, of somebody. After the general meaning of the preceding sentence became clear, one had to accept at least the first letter of line 10 as belonging to the verb.[2] And as the following ביהו (or פיהו?) could apparently not be understood as a part of the same verb, no other interpretation of lines 9–10 at first seemed possible than: "What aileth thy slave that his mouth(?) should curse (יָאֹר פִּיהוּ) seed to the king?"[3] Cf. for פִּיהוּ "his mouth", Exodus IV, 15; I Kings VII, 31, and often; for ארר "to curse" particularly Exodus XXII, 27 וְנָשִׂיא בְעַמְּךָ לֹא תָאֹר "and a ruler in thy people thou shalt not curse"; cf. Job III, 1, "And Job opened his mouth (פִּיהוּ) and cursed (וַיְקַלֵּל) his day"; or II Samuel XVI, 9 לָמָּה יְקַלֵּל הַכֶּלֶב הַמֵּת הַזֶּה אֶת־אֲדֹנִי הַמֶּלֶךְ "why should this dead dog curse my lord the king?"

The first letter of line 10 can be ר followed by a rather large (as in line 9) word-dividing dot. However, the traces of the following sign point rather definitely to ב and not to פ. Is there no way to accept ביהו as a word in itself, since יא–ביהו cannot be understood as one word? And here we have to concede that such a possibility exists, if we recognize that the God-name Yhwh, usually written יהוה, but in proper names spelt יהו, and later in the Elephantine papyri found only in this abbreviated spelling, could also here sometimes have been written by some scribes יהו. And this would solve another difficulty: in Letter IX which, as shown above, may be a recapitulation of our letter, and is apparently written by the same scribe, we have instead of lines 7–8 of our Letter V ידע[נ]ך . יהו . . . . . in IX, rev. 1–2 נעשה אשר יהו ידע[נ]ך, i.e. יהו instead of יהוה. And thus we could read and translate: מה . לעבדך . יאר ביהו . זרע למלך "What aileth thy slave that he should curse in (the name of) Yhwh seed to the king". And this is the correct explanation. Cf. II Kings II, 24 "And he turned back and looked on them, and *cursed them in the name of Yhwh* (וַיְקַלְלֵם בְּשֵׁם יהוה)"; Isaiah VIII, 21,

---

[1] The first sign is not clear. For the second letter, *see* the following discussion.

[2] For some time I considered also the reading יַךְ "that he should slay". But the sign is א, not כ.

[3] For the meaning of "to curse seed to the king", *see* later.

"he shall fret himself, and curse in (the name of) his king and God" (‏וְקִלֵּל בְּמַלְכּוֹ וּבֵאלֹהָיו‎);
Leviticus XXIV, 11 "And the Israelitish woman's son spoke the name and cursed " (‏וַיִּקֹּב בֶּן־הָאִשָּׁה‎ ‏הַיִּשְׂרְאֵלִית אֶת־הַשֵּׁם וַיְקַלֵּל‎).

Now, how can we understand the expression "to curse seed to the king?" Hardly as "to curse somebody who is seed (offspring) to the king". As mentioned above, one would in this case expect "an offspring of the king" and not the word ‏זרע‎ "seed", which is only used in a collective sense. However, we have an interesting Biblical parallel in Malachi II, 2–3: "If ye will not hear . . . I will even send a curse upon you, and I will curse (‏וְאָרוֹתִי‎) your blessings: yea, I have cursed them already (‏וְגַם אָרוֹתִיהָ‎), because ye do not lay it to heart. Behold, *I will scold*[1] *to* (= *for*) *you the seed* (‏הִנְנִי גֹעֵר לָכֶם אֶת־הַזֶּרַע‎) . . ." Thus ‏ארר ביהו זרע ל‎ "to curse the seed to somebody in (the name of) Yhwh" apparently means to curse saying: "may Yhwh curse (or destroy) thee thy seed" (‏יָאֹר יהו(ה) לְךָ זֶרַע‎), and this seems to have been a special kind of curse used in ancient Israel, similar to the frequently heard vulgar Arabic curse: *Yikhrib bētak* "May [Allah] destroy thy house ". And thus the crime of which the writer is accused is — as in Exodus XXII, 27; II Samuel XVI, 9, or, in the case of Naboth, I Kings XXI, 10 — cursing of the king.[2]

Thus we reach the following reconstruction of Letter V:

RECONSTRUCTION

1. ‏ישמע יהוה [א]ת [אד]ני‎
2. ‏[שמ]עת · [שלם וטב · עת]‎
3. ‏[כים · עת כים ·] מי עבדך‎
4. ‏כלב כי [של]חת אל עבד‎
5. ‏[ך] את ס[פרי] סֹ ־ ־ יהֹו‎
6. ‏[עת] השב · עבדך הספר‎
7. ‏ם אל אדני · ידע[נ]ך‎
8. ‏הוה ־ ־ ־ ־ ־ מ‎
9. ‏ה · מה לעבדך · יא‎
10. ‏ר · ביהו · זרע למלך.‎

TRANSLATION

1. May Yhwh let hear my [lord]
2. [tid]ings of [peace] and good, [even
3. now, even now.] Who is thy slave
4. a dog, that thou [hast s]ent to thy sla-
5. ve the le[tters of . . . yahu]?
6. [Now] has thy slave returned the let-
7. ters to my lord. May Yh
8. wh let thee know [what] [happen-
9. ed] what it is. What has thy slave that he should
10. curse in (the name of) Yhw seed to the king?

---

[1] ‏גער‎ "to scold (and by it destroy)", synonymous to the preceding ‏ארר‎ "to curse", not "to corrupt".

[2] It may not be necessary to mention that ‏זרע למלך‎ could be understood also as "seed for the Molech" (whether this be interpreted as the name of a god or a kind of sacrifice), *cf.* Leviticus XVIII, 21, "And thou shalt not let any of thy seed pass through to Molech!": (‏מִזַּרְעֲךָ · · · לַמֹּלֶךְ‎). However, I do not see how this could make sense here. ‏זרע‎ itself also could be ‏זְרֹעַ‎ "arm".

GENERAL REMARKS

The meaning of Letter V (and IX) is now approximately clear. Ya'ush had received from . . . yahu, apparently a high officer, letters accusing the writer of Letter V of uttering curses against the king. Ya'ush sent the incriminating letters to the writer, who denies the accusation. Similarly, as in Letter II, he first invokes Yhwh to clear the matter for him: "May Yhwh tell thee, what really happened!" and to it he adds the logical argument: "Why should thy slave in Yhwh's name curse seed to the king?"

Who is the sender of the letter mentioned here? If I am not mistaken the sign at the beginning of the name in line 5 ending with -yahu is ס, and in this case no other name than סמכיהו *Semakhyahu* would be possible. Now, Semakhyahu is, according to Letter IV, a man of high position, who with Ya'ush's knowledge came to the place from which Letter IV is written, in order to inspect the troops, and then went up to Jerusalem. It is probable that our Semakhyahu may be the same man as the officer mentioned in Letters IV and XI (*see also* XIII), thus again showing that the Letters IV, V (and IX) and XI were in all probability written from the same place and by the same man. And as all the other nine letters of Lachish which can be read with certainty are written by Hosha'yahu, it becomes even more likely that the ostraca which at the most might be considered as coming from two persons, actually are parts of a one-man correspondence: From Hosha'yahu to Ya'ush. (For Letter XIII, *see later*.)

However, the situation and therefore also the dating of Letters V and IX differ from that of both Letter IV and the letters dealing with the prophet. The alleged cursing of the king that Semakhyahu (?) had heard may have happened at a time when this man actually met the writer, perhaps at another visit to the writer's place or before he left it. There is no possibility of "written" cursing, as for this there would be documentary proof and as the writer refers to "what (really) happened". Semakhyahu may have written his incriminating report directly after his tour of inspection, or later on from Jerusalem. That recriminations about the writer are sent to Ya'ush again shows that actually he is "his slave's lord" and commander, and that such phrases are not to be taken as mere courtesy. There also is no possibility of connecting this letter's contents directly with the messages about the prophet, although in these letters accusations sent by other persons (*see* Letters III and VI) had caused Ya'ush to request explanations from Hosha'yahu. But there the accusations are of a different nature: (*a*) that Hosha'yahu had read confidential letters, (*b*) that apparently the words of a third person—in all probability the prophet—are demoralizing land and city. While the position, as far as the writer is concerned, is similar, the situation behind it is different. The letters are most probably sent by the same person, but Letter V (and IX) may be connected more with the contents of Letter IV than of II, VI, XII, and may therefore belong to a later date. Considering all points, it seems possible that Letter V may have been written some time before Letter IV.

There is also no way to connect the words of Letter V, 7–9 "May Yhwh tell thee what (really) happened" more closely with the similar sentence of Letter II, lines 5–6, יבכר . יהוה את אנ[~ ~]י, דבר . אשר לא . ידעתה.

There, as here, the writer appeals to Yhwh to clear for him the incriminating affair. But it is impossible to find in Letter II, 5–6, exactly the same meaning as in Letter V, 7–9. Neither יבכר nor the impossible יזכר[1] could have the meaning of יְדִעֲךָ in our letter: "may Yhwh tell my lord

---

[1] *See* the discussion of this passage above, *page* 41–43.

98

(what really happened)"; nor, if "what really happened" were meant, would the writer refer to it by the words "something which thou dost not (canst not) know"[1]—this would be mere impudence—or "something which I do not know"; he knows what happened. Thus Letter II, written upon a piece of the same pot as Letter VI, must be connected with the matters dealt with in *this* Letter (VI), not with the different contents of Letter V.

The writing of Letters V and IX is characterized by the breadth of the letters, the space between them, the almost horizontal down-strokes of the מ and the horizontal, angular ע. In view of these points I am rather inclined to see in Letters V and IX the work of a different hand than that of the scribes who wrote the Letters I–IV.

---

[1] Here certainly is no possibility to *read* לא ידעתה in lines 8–9.

LETTER VI

O

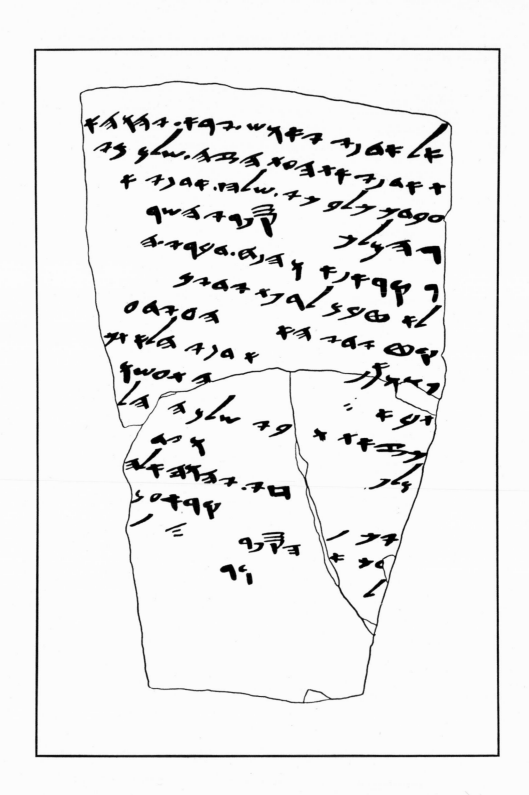

LETTER VI

PRELIMINARY TRANSLITERATION[1]

1. אל אדני יאוש · ירא · יהוה א
2. ת אדני אתהעתהזה · שלם מי
3. עבדך כלב כי · שלח · אדני א]‏- -[
4. ר המלך ואת ספרי השר]‏- - -[
5. ר קרא נא והנה · דברי · ה]‏- - -[
6. לא טבם לרפת ידי -]‏- - -[
7. קט ידי הא]‏- - -[העיר ע]‏- - -[
8. וננ אַ]‏- - - -[אדני הלא תכ - -
9. תב א -]‏- - - - - - התעשו
10. כזאת - - -‏ יֹ - שֹל - ה - הל
11. - לבֹ]‏- - - - - - - - - - -
12. - - - - חי יהוה אלה
13. יך ו]‏ ז - - - - א - קרא עב
14. דך א]‏ת[הספר - - - - -
15. ל -]‏- - - - - ור - - - - - (-)

---

[1] For fuller reconstruction and translation, *see page* 117.

NOTES

Although the last sentences in Letter VI establish a parallel to Letter III, by repeating the oath given there and thus showing its connexion with the same topic and its having been written in approximately the same situation and by the same person to the same man, it was nevertheless very difficult to read because of the many gaps in its legible text. Even the word-dividing dots used more often in the other letters appear but sparsely here and there, while in most places they seem to be forgotten, and no alternative indication—*i.e.* spaces between words—suggests where a new word begins.

The letter opens with the address "To my lord Ya'ush", given in an abbreviated form as in Letter III and without naming the sender.

The following greeting differs from the formula used in the other letters and calls for a special study. While the general meaning is quite clear from the parallel expressions, its proper interpretation is open to many different solutions. What we read in lines 1–2 is:

ירא יהוה א

ת . אדני אתהעתתהזה . שלם

Here ירא is parallel to יַשְׁמַע "may he let hear" in other letters; it seems to be יַרָא or יֵרֶא Hif'il imperf. of ראה "to see", "may he let see", and thus the whole sentence apparently says: "May Yhwh let see my lord ... peace". And even for the as yet unexplained letters (שלם) אתהעתתהזה[1] we have the parallel "(tidings of peace) *even now*", and as certainly no word for visions ("to see visions of peace", parallel to "to hear tidings of peace"), can be found in these letters, we have to look for an expression parallel to עת · כים "even now".

It may be mentioned that the verb ירא itself, while grammatically interpreted as above, *i.e.*, as 3. pers. imperf. jussive, Hif'il of ראה, could still be understood, not as "may he let see", but as "may he *saturate* my lord ... (with) peace (= well-being)". As has been to some extent recognized, forms of the root ראה (usually: to see) stand in many passages for רוה "to be satiated" (drinking), *e.g.*, in Job X, 15 שְׂבַע קָלוֹן וּרְאֵה עָנְיִי where we have to translate with many authorities in strict parallelism: "full (= satiated) of shame (not: confusion) and satiated with (not: therefore see) my affliction". Thus also in Hif'il one may have to interpret Job XXXIII, 26 וַיַּרְא פָּנָיו בִּתְרוּעָה not as "and he shall see his face with joy", but as "(he shall pray unto God, and he will be favourable unto him:) and he will fill (= satiate) his face with rejoicing". *Cf.* Job VIII, 21: "Till he fill thy mouth with laughing, and thy lips with rejoicing (תְּרוּעָה)".

However, in comparison with the usual formula "May Yhwh let hear" one would prefer the natural interpretation "May Yhwh let see".

Thus one is at first inclined to read את · העת . הזה "this time". However, this explanation is impossible for more than one reason:—

(*a*) The Hebrew word עֵת (for ענת, *cf.* the Aramaic כענת, כען "now") is feminine, marked as such by the ending, and could not be connected with the masculine pronoun הַזֶּה. But even this point needs some more specific proof. As is the case with other Biblical words used many times, there may be a few instances where, mostly through mistakes of the copyists, even this word seemed to be construed as masculine. These cases are בָּא הָעֵת קָרוֹב הַיּוֹם "the time is come, the day is near" (Ezekiel VII, 7) and בָּא הָעֵת הִגִּיעַ הַיּוֹם "the time is come, the day draws near" (Ezekiel VII, 12),

---

[1] For some time I considered the possibility that the doubtful ע could be כ; but this is not the case, nor can it lead to any plausible results.

where one ה (of בָּאה) has been left out before the following ה of העת (haplography); עֵת הַזָּמִיר הִגִּיעַ "the time of the vinegrowth[1] is come" (Song of Solomon II, 12), where the copyist has construed the verb after the masculine זמיר: "the time (when) the vinegrowth is come"; עֵת וָפֶגַע יִקְרֶה אֶת־כֻּלָּם "time and chance happeneth to them all" (Ecclesiastes IX, 11), where the verb follows the immediately preceding masculine פֶגַע, not עֵת; יוֹם עָנָן עֵת גּוֹים יִהְיֶה "a cloudy day, the time of the heathen shall it (the day) be" (Ezekiel XXX, 3) where the verb does not follow עֵת at all; כָּעֵת הָרִאשׁוֹן הֵקַל (Isaiah VIII, 23)[2] where we have to translate more correctly: "now[3] the first has lightly afflicted" not "at (the) first (time)"; וְקָרוֹב לָבוֹא עִתָּהּ (Isaiah XIII, 22) where the meaning is "and near is it, that her time will come," not and "near is her time to come"; and lastly לְעִתִּים מְזֻמָּנִים "at appointed times" (Ezra X, 14), where the copyist erroneously wrote מְזֻמָּנִים after the preceding עִתִּים[4] while he in the same book[5] (Nehemiah XIII, 31) correctly writes: בְּעִתִּים מְזֻמָּנוֹת.

This is all, except for some cases where the Massoretic manuscripts in the *Kethībh* erroneously showed הָעֵת הַהוּא but are corrected by the *Qerē* into the only possible reading הָעֵת הַהִיא; but הוּא instead of הִיא, i.e., a rather long downstroke of the י making it look like ו in the *Kethībh*, is such a regular and irrelevant occurrence that in the first chapters of the Bible we find cases such as "*she* (*the woman*; *Kethībh* הוּא 'he') gave me of the tree, and I did eat" (Genesis III, 12); "And Zillah, she (הוּא 'he') also bare Tubalcain" (IV, 22); "The Egyptians beheld the woman that she (הוּא) was very fair" (XII, 14); "that she (הוּא) is thy wife" (XII, 18); "She (הוּא) is my sister" (XII, 19; XX, 2, 5; XXVI, 7, 9) and many, many other examples. How could all these be considered as masculine? Opposed to these few unreliable testimonies stand all the many clear cases where בָּעֵת הַהִיא "at that time" is clearly written, or such constructions as בְּעֵת הַזֹּאת "at this time" and לָעֵת כָּזֹאת "for such a time" (Esther IV, 14); מָחָר כָּעֵת הַזֹּאת "to-morrow about this time" (Joshua XI, 6); וְעֵת־צָרָה הִיא לְיַעֲקֹב וּמִמֶּנָּה יִוָּשֵׁעַ "it (fem.) is even a time of trouble for Jacob; but he shall be saved out of it" (fem.) (Jeremiah XXX, 7); וּבָאָה עֵת־הַקָּצִיר לָהּ "and the time of her harvest shall come" (LI, 33); כִּי עֵת רָעָה הִיא "for it (fem.) is an evil (fem.) time" (Amos V, 13; Micah II, 3); וְהָיְתָה עֵת צָרָה "and there shall be (fem.) a time of trouble" (Daniel XII, 1); לְעִתִּים רְחוֹקוֹת "for times far off" (Ezekiel XII, 27); רַבּוֹת עִתִּים "many (fem.) times" (Nehemiah IX, 28) where unmistakable consonants prove the feminine use of עֵת. And if there might be such a crude grammatical mistake in sentences originally composed by the writer, this is impossible in a *formula* of greeting, given certainly in its correct and typical form.

(*b*) Even if the masculine הַזֶּה were correct, it would not be possible to say אֶת־הָעֵת הַזֶּה, אֵת designating only the accusative proper: "(I shall make) *this* (acc.) time (long or short)", not "*at* this time". Thus also אֶת־הַיּוֹם הַזֶּה "this (acc.) day", while occurring in the Bible, nowhere stands instead of הַיּוֹם "to-day".

(*c*) Also, "at this time" would not give the meaning, both expected and needed: "just now, very soon".

(*d*) There is, it is true, apparently some space between the ת of עת and the following ה, but not more than between this and the following ו; what may look like a dot after the ת is certainly no dot; on the other hand, the horizontal stroke of the ת in אתה is written right into the following ה, which also makes it unlikely that the words should be divided after את.

---

[1] This will be the best translation.

[2] In some Bibles: IX, 1.

[3] Probably to be read כָּ עֵתָּ.

[4] He even might have thought of עִתִּים מִזְמָנִים "hours from times".

[5] Ezra-Nehemiah was originally one book.

Now, עֵת being feminine, one would expect הזאת instead of הזה; this certainly could also be pronounced as the later Hebrew *fem.* זו(ה), but this would be hardly probable in the same letter where (in line 10) the regular form (כ)זאת is used. Even in those passages in the Bible where the feminine זו in this spelling is adopted by the Massoretic vocalization, as in

II Kings VI, 19,	וְלֹא־זֹה הָעִיר
Ezekiel XL, 45	זֹה הַלִּשְׁכָּה אֲשֶׁר
Ecclesiastes II, 2,	וּלְשִׂמְחָה מַה־זֹּה עֹשָׂה
„ II, 24,	גַּם־זֹה רָאִיתִי אָנִי
„ V, 15,	וְגַם־זֹה רָעָה חוֹלָה
„ V, 18,	זֹה מַתַּת אֱלֹהִים הִיא
„ VII, 23,	כָּל־זֹה נִסִּיתִי בַחָכְמָה
„ IX, 13,	גַּם־זֹה רָאִיתִי חָכְמָה

or כָּזֹה וְכָזֶה Judges XVIII, 4; II Samuel XI, 25; I Kings XIV, 5, there is no evidence to exclude definitely the simpler reading זֶה at least in pre-exilic records; for the pronoun is used in all these cases in an impersonal way for "it" or "that". Furthermore, we find זה (as זו) according to the Aramaic and Mishnaic syntax in correct texts always without the article ה; הַזּוּ would be a hybrid formation combining parts belonging to different periods of the language.

There is no need to add that the arguments given as (*b*), (*c*), (*d*) against the masculine את העת הזֶה are valid also against the feminine את העת הזֹה. As this attempt to explain the words contained in אתהעתהזה from their beginning seems unsuccessful, we may try the explanation from the other end. And here indeed we find the clear words עַתָּה זֶה "Now then, even now", occurring here, as in I Kings XVII, 24 עַתָּה זֶה יָדַעְתִּי כִּי אִישׁ אֱלֹהִים אָתָּה "Now then (just now)[1] I know that thou art a man of God"; II Kings V, 22 הִנֵּה עַתָּה זֶה בָּאוּ אֵלַי שְׁנֵי־נְעָרִים "Behold even now there be come to me two young men": and according to many scholars (*cf.* Gesenius-Buhl, *Handwörterbuch*, 17th edition, *page* 113 b), despite the Massoretic accents, also Ruth II, 7 וַתַּעֲמוֹד מֵאָז הַבֹּקֶר וְעַד־עַתָּה זֶה "and she has continued even from the morning until even now". And this must also be the correct reading in our letter, corresponding to עת · כים in the other ostraca.

From this we learn that עַתָּ or עַתָּה could, as in the Bible (*see* the note to ועת IV, 2), be written both ways, with or without the ה, as העירה is written in full IV, 7. The fuller form עתה may have been used particularly in connexion with the following short particle זה.

The three first letters אתה remain; but unfortunately these also can be read in different ways and with different meanings: (*a*) אֹתֹה "his sign, his token"; (*b*) אֹתֹה "him"; (*c*) אִתֹּה "with him"; (*d*) אַתָּה "thou". Which of these is meant here? At the same time we have to keep in mind that ירא may not necessarily be the Hif'il יַרְא or יְרֶא "may he let see" but could also be the simple conjugation (Qal) יֵרֶא "may he see".

(*a*) אֹתֹה "his token": "May Yhwh let see my lord his sign, even now: peace"? For this solution one can refer to such Biblical passages as Psalms LXXXVI, 17 עֲשֵׂה־עִמִּי אוֹת לְטוֹבָה "show me a token for good" and for the appositional use of שלם "peace": Numbers XXV, 12, הִנְנִי נֹתֵן לוֹ אֶת־בְּרִיתִי שָׁלוֹם "Behold, I give unto him my covenant[2] (of) peace", Malachi II, 5, בְּרִיתִי הָיְתָה אִתּוֹ הַחַיִּים וְהַשָּׁלוֹם "My covenant was with him (of) life and peace". However, as mentioned before (*see* notes to Letter IV, 13), אות "token" is nowhere in the Bible connected with a *genetivus possessivus*: "Yhwh's",

---

[1] Not "now *by* this". [2] "Covenant" and "token" are correlated ideas; *cf.* Genesis IX, 8–17.

or "my, thy token"; also, if this explanation be true, the letter must have said: "May Yhwh let see my lord even now a (or: his) token for peace (עתה זה את שלם)" not "his token even now (for) peace" (אתה עתה זה שלם).

(b) אתה "him": "May Yhwh let see my lord, *him* even now in peace"? But there would be no need to add this quite superfluous אתה "him" to the clear and simple "May Yhwh let see my lord even now peace". Neither would יֵרֶא "May Yhwh see" give here better sense.

(c) אתּה "with him", meaning either "with (near to) Yhwh" or "with my lord": "May Yhwh let see my lord with him ('With Yhwh' or 'about himself, in his home and surroundings') even now peace"? This, particularly in the second alternative, is not impossible, although rather improbable, as there is nothing gained by adding the word אתּה.

(d) אַתָּה "thou": "May Yhwh let see my lord: thou even now (in) peace" (or "May Yhwh see my lord: thou even now (in) peace")? Strange as it may appear at first, this seems to be the most likely reading, as it fits in with other formulas of greeting preserved in the Bible. In I Samuel XXV, 6, David sends a message to Nabal, saying: כֹּה לֶחָי וְאַתָּה שָׁלוֹם וּבֵיתְךָ שָׁלוֹם וְכֹל אֲשֶׁר־לְךָ שָׁלוֹם " (May it) so (please) to the one who lives[1] that *thou* shalt be (in) *peace* and thine house (in) peace, and all that thou hast (in) peace".

Here we have not only the construction אַתָּה שָׁלוֹם "thou peace" instead of "thou *in* peace" (= אַתָּה שָׁלֵם "thou safe"), as similarly אֲנִי־שָׁלוֹם "I am (for) peace" (Psalms CXX, 7); וְכָל־נְתִיבוֹתֶיהָ שָׁלוֹם "and all her paths are peace" (Proverbs III, 17); שָׁלוֹם אָהֳלֶךָ "thy tabernacle shall be (in) peace" (Job V, 24); בָּתֵּיהֶם שָׁלוֹם "their houses are (in) peace" (Job XXI, 9); but here we also have אתה שלום in the greeting at the beginning of a message, as in our ostracon. *Cf.* further passages as II Kings VIII, 13 הִרְאַנִי יהוה אֹתְךָ מֶלֶךְ עַל־אֲרָם "Yhwh hath shewed me thee (as) king over Aram", and Haggai II, 3, (מִי בָכֶם הַנִּשְׁאָר אֲשֶׁר רָאָה אֶת־הַבַּיִת הַזֶּה בִּכְבוֹדוֹ הָרִאשׁוֹן) וּמָה אַתֶּם רֹאִים אֹתוֹ עַתָּה ("Who is left among you that saw this house in her first glory?) And how (literally *what*) do ye see it now?"

From these passages, and from the fact that our sentence certainly gives no parallel to "tidings (of peace)" in the greeting-formula used in other letters, we may conclude that our sentence should not be understood as strictly parallel to that, but as similar to I Samuel XXV, 6. We have here not "May Yhwh (let) make see . . . (visions of peace)", just as "May Yhwh (let) make hear tidings of peace", with "my lord" and "(tidings of) peace" as the two accusative-objects of "let hear (or see)", but with the causative ירא "let see" = "show" as in many other cases and in the quoted passage II Kings VIII, 13, connected with the accusative(s) "my lord" (and the unspoken "me" or "us"), while שלם, as in the greeting of the message I Samuel XXV, 6 is predicate to אַתָּה "thou": "May Yhwh let see (=*show*) (us) my lord (*while*) thou art even now in peace"; *cf.* also Genesis XXVI, 29 אַתָּה עַתָּה בְּרוּךְ יהוה "thou art now the blessed of Yhwh". Here one could even take ירא as the simple יֵרֶא: "May Yhwh see my lord (while) thou art even now in peace", but the former explanation seems more likely.

Now, the greeting of our letter shows instead of עת כים of Letters II, IV and V, the clear parallel: עתה זה "even now". And this strengthens the suspicion, which I did not dare to suggest before: Is this כים, standing here after the simple עתה, as much, as כַּיּוֹם "as the day", "to-day", or is it another word, a particle, reinforcing simply the preceding עתה "now" as זֶה in עתה זה?

---

[1] As it seems: to God. The words כֹּה לֶחָי have found various interpretations which, however, make no difference to the question dealt with here, while this may help to throw light on the cryptic Biblical expression. The following translation is as literal as possible.

Already in the Bible there are a number of instances where the meaning "to-day"[1] for כיום or כהיום has been recognized as unacceptable. *Cf.*

Genesis XXV, 31:	וַיֹּאמֶר יַעֲקֹב מִכְרָה כַיּוֹם אֶת־בְּכֹרָתְךָ לִי
Genesis XXV, 33:	וַיֹּאמֶר יַעֲקֹב הִשָּׁבְעָה לִי כַּיּוֹם
I Samuel II, 16:	וַיֹּאמֶר אֵלָיו הָאִישׁ קַטֵּר יַקְטִירוּן כַּיּוֹם הַחֵלֶב וְקַח לְךָ כַּאֲשֶׁר תְּאַוֶּה נַפְשֶׁךָ
I Kings I, 51:	וְהִנֵּה אָחַז בְּקַרְנוֹת הַמִּזְבֵּחַ לֵאמֹר יִשָּׁבַע־לִי כַיּוֹם הַמֶּלֶךְ שְׁלֹמֹה אִם־יָמִית אֶת־עַבְדּוֹ בֶּחָרֶב
I Kings XXII, 5 = II Chronicles XVIII, 4:	וַיֹּאמֶר יְהוֹשָׁפָט אֶל־מֶלֶךְ יִשְׂרָאֵל דְּרָשׁ־נָא כַיּוֹם אֶת־דְּבַר יהוה
Nehemiah V, 11:	הָשִׁיבוּ נָא לָהֶם כְּהַיּוֹם שְׂדֹתֵיהֶם[2]

In these cases modern scholars (*cf.* Genesius-Buhl, 17th edition, *page* 294 a) assume for כַּיּוֹם the meaning "first, before": Genesis XXV, 31: "And Jacob said, Sell me first thy birthright"; Genesis XXV, 33: "And Jacob said, Swear to me first"; I Samuel II, 16: "And the man said unto him, Let them first burn the fat, and then take as much as thy soul desireth"; I Kings I, 51: "And lo, he hath caught hold on the horns of the altar, saying, Let King Solomon first swear unto me, that he will not slay his slave with the sword"; I Kings XXII, 5 = II Chronicles XVIII, 4: "And Jehoshaphat said unto the king of Israel, Enquire, I pray thee, first at the word of Yhwh"; Nehemiah V, 11: "Restore, I pray you, to them first their lands." However, this interpretation (*a*) does not make sense in Isaiah LVIII, 4: (הֵן לְרִיב וּמַצָּה תָּצוּמוּ וּלְהַכּוֹת בְּאֶגְרֹף רֶשַׁע) לֹא־תָצוּמוּ כַיּוֹם לְהַשְׁמִיעַ בַּמָּרוֹם קוֹלְכֶם "(Behold, ye fast for strife and debate, and smite with the fist of wickedness:) ye shall not fast . . . (first??)[3] to make your voice to be heard on high". And (*b*) how could this meaning "first" itself be explained? As a development of "to-day"? Certainly not. For the simple reason, that כיום or כהיום nowhere had this meaning and could not have had it.

כְּהַיּוֹם הַזֶּה, כַּיּוֹם הַזֶּה, כַּיּוֹם in the Bible means only (כַּיּוֹם) "*as* the day", (כַּיּוֹם הַזֶּה) "*as* this day is the case"[4] not "to-day", for which the Bible says הַיּוֹם or בַּיּוֹם הַזֶּה. Thus we shall have to look for another explanation.

Now, in the Accadic (= Assyrian and Babylonian) language, so closely related to Hebrew, a short particle, written *ki-a-am* or *ka-ia-am* and therefore pronounced *kiām*, similarly cognate with the Hebrew (and common Semitic) כֹּה, כֵּן, כַּךְ, כָּכָה, (כָּה in אֵיכָה, etc.), כְּנֵמָא in Aramaic, etc., "so, thus" likewise obtains in the developed sense of a strengthening complement to other frequent words, as in *shi kiām* "even *she*"; *shumma la kiām* "if not (so)"; *ashshum kiām* "therefore"; *annikiām* "here, now, even";[5] *ullikiām* "there".

Now this use of *kiām* in Accadic fully corresponds to that of similar "deictic elements" as *ka*, *fa*, *dha*, etc. in Semitic languages; *cf.* אֵיכָה "how?" אֵיפֹה "where?", Arabic *dhalika* (ذلك) "that", *kaifa* كَيْفَ "how?", to the use of כֵּן "so" in the modern Hebrew גַּם כֵּן "also", etc., of זֶה in מַה זֶּה "What then?" etc. We may more especially compare the use of the "enclitic" particle פוֹן in Aramaic, אֵפוֹא, אֵפוֹ in Hebrew[6] in examples as מִי אֵפוֹא "who then?" (Genesis XXVII, 33), לְכָה אֵפוֹא "to thee then" (Genesis XXVII, 37); אַיֵּה אֵיפוֹא "where then?" (Judges IX, 38), זֹאת אֵפוֹא "this

---

[1] For this suggested meaning, *see following.*

[2] For other examples, *see later.*

[3] For the translation "as ye do this day", *see following.*

[4] As to I Samuel IX, 13, *see following.* כַּיּוֹם without הַזֶּה has nowhere the meaning "as this day is the case".

[5] Many examples of this word are quoted and its meaning discussed by P. Krauss, in his instructive book, *Altbabylonische Briefe*, vol. II (1932), *pages* 13, 44, 124, etc. However, there is no reason to pronounce as he does *ki'ām* for what is regularly written *ki-a-am* (= *kiām*), not *ki'-a-am*.

[6] Not to be confused with the questioning אֵיפֹה "where?".

then" (Proverbs, VI, 3), אִם־לֹא־אֵפוֹ "if not (then)" (Job IX, 24; XXIV, 25 = Aram. אילוליפון, Accadic *shumma lā kiām*); *cf.* כִּזְעֵיר פּוֹן "a bit even", Targum of כִּמְעַט Genesis XXVI, 10, etc.

In all these cases one could use both the Accadic *kiām* as well as the Hebrew זה instead of Hebrew אֵפוֹא or Aramaic פּוֹן.

Now, the Accadic *kiām* or *kaiām* would correspond in Hebrew to a form *kayōm* or *kĕyōm* with the same "adverbial" ending "*ōm*" as in פִּתְאֹם "suddenly".[1]

Now this confirming particle *kĕyom* "thus, then", which in every instance could be replaced by זה or אפוא, is apparently our כיום, which in our letters in עת כים interchanges with זה עתה זה and which the Massorites did no longer distinguish from כַּיּוֹם "as the day". *Cf.* Genesis XXV, 31 "And Jacob said, Sell me then thy birthright"; Genesis XXV, 33: "And Jacob said, Swear then to me"; I Samuel II, 16: "And the man said unto him, Let them then burn the fat, and then take as much as thy soul desireth"; I Kings XXII, 5 = II Chronicles XVIII, 4: "And Jehoshaphat said unto the king of Israel, Enquire then, I pray thee, at the word of Yhwh"; Nehemiah V, 11: "Restore then, (read כיום for כהיום) I pray you, to them their lands . . ." but also Isaiah LVIII, 4: "Behold, ye fast for strife and debate, and to smite with the fist of wickedness: ye shall thus (then) not fast, to make your voice heard on high".

We now fully understand how sentences like "Sell me then", "Swear to me then" could in many instances have the sense of "Sell me first", "Swear to me first"; but *e.g.* in עת כים "now then, even now" this could not be so. And in such cases the copyists, who no longer knew this obsolete word and its proper use, may have even changed the text which they did not understand. This is undoubtedly the case in at least two instances, where עת כים or in fuller spelling עתה כיום actually was written in the Bible, but was not recognized by the copyists: In I Samuel IX, 12–13, in the story about Saul's visit to Samuel, the maidens whom Saul and his servant ask about the seer, answer: (וַתַּעֲנֶינָה אוֹתָם וַתֹּאמַרְנָה) יֵשׁ הִנֵּה לְפָנֶיךָ מַהֵר | עַתָּה כִּי הַיּוֹם בָּא לָעִיר כִּי זֶבַח הַיּוֹם לָעָם בַּבָּמָה : כְּבֹאֲכֶם הָעִיר כֵּן תִּמְצְאוּן אֹתוֹ בְּטֶרֶם יַעֲלֶה הַבָּמָתָה לֶאֱכֹל כִּי לֹא־יֹאכַל הָעָם עַד־בֹּאוֹ כִּי־הוּא יְבָרֵךְ הַזֶּבַח אַחֲרֵי־כֵן יֹאכְלוּ הַקְּרֻאִים וְעַתָּה עֲלוּ כִּי־אֹתוֹ כְהַיּוֹם תִּמְצְאוּן אֹתוֹ: "(And they answered them, and said:) He is; behold, he is before you; (literally:) *make haste now, for to-day he came* to the city; for there is a sacrifice of the people to-day in the 'Bamah'[2]: as soon as ye be come into the city, ye shall straightway find him, before he go up to the Bamah to eat: for the people will not eat until he come, because he doth bless the sacrifice; afterwards they eat that be bidden. Now therefore get you up, for (literally:) *him as to-day ye shall find him*".

Both "make haste now, for to-day he came"—adding a superfluous "now" to "make haste" and saying "to-day" where "now" is expected—and "him as to-day ye shall find *him*" are very puzzling.[3] But now that our letters show the lost formula, we recognize as the original text:

(*a*) מַהֵר עַתָּה כְיוֹם בָּא לָעִיר "make haste, *just now* he came to the city",

(*b*) אֹתוֹ כִּי עַתָּה כְיוֹם תִּמְצְאוּן אֹתוֹ "for *just now* you shall find him".

For the next sentence, lines 2–5, the proposed reading includes the restorations at the end of lines 3 and 4, which after repeated examination of the sherd seem to be sufficiently reliable and

[1] For these forms *cf.* my book *Die Entstehung des semitischen Sprachtypus*, vol. I (1916), particularly *pages* 1–64. Other developments of the same "element" *ka, kam, kiam*, are *e.g.* the Mishnaic כֵּיוָן and even כִּי אִם (*see* ibid., *page* 157), where the "ending" has been understood as an independent word.

[2] A kind of worship-house, not "high place", *see* the note on *page* 30.

[3] *See* the discussion of these difficulties by S. R. Driver, *Notes on the Hebrew Text and the Topography of the Books of Samuel*, 2nd edition (1913), *page* 72.

consistent; it is the logical continuation to "Thou hast sent me the king's letter with the letters of the officers" to say: "telling me: read and *see* what there is in them". Thus והנה "and behold" has the same sense as in Deuteronomy XIII, 15 (similar also XVII, 4; XIX, 18): "Then when thou inquirest and makest search, and askest diligently; and thou seest (וְהִנֵּה), it be truth . . .". ה in והנה has both times a different form than in זה עתה in line 2; particularly the second ה looks as if it were closed at the left by a vertically curved stroke. Still no reading other than והנה seems possible. ה is written differently. *Cf.* also the similar ה in הלא line 8. In line 3 certainly at the end [את ספ] has to be maintained.

In line 4 also [השר]ם לאמ] is as good as certain. The reading הַשָּׂרִם in the plural is the most probable; it is natural that with the king's letter should come those of his officers, and thus in Jeremiah XXVI, 21 we have "the king and all his valiant men and all the officers (הַשָּׂרִים)" who "heard of his (Uriah's) words". What he should find, when reading the letter of the king and his officers, is this: "The words of the . . . are not good, (liable) to loosen the hands".

Whose are the words that are "not good"? Certainly not the king's and his officers. As Letter V undoubtedly shows, and all the other letters tend to confirm, the writer of the letters (in this case there can be no doubt about it being Hosha'yahu, the writer of Letter III) is under Ya'ush's command and ordered to report to him about his conduct. There certainly is no room in this correspondence to judge the king's own words in a disrespectful way. We have here not the king's words, but the king's judgement on the words reported to him of another man.

Are they Hosha'yahu's words? Is *he* accused of having said "words liable to loosen the hands . . . of land and city", and is that why Ya'ush demands an explanation? This also appears impossible. Not only because there would be no room for such a long name as [וישעיהו]ה—six more letters after the visible ה at the end of line 5 (one would even expect עבדך "thy slave", not the name beginning with ה)—but mainly because this Hosha'yahu is a subordinate "slave" of Ya'ush, living in a small fortress and dependent upon his lord's goodwill; how could his words have such an influence that king and officers would consider them as liable to loosen the hands of city and country?

However, from the way the king speaks about these words, it is clear that they can be only words of a *preacher* or *prophet*. And the oath given in lines 12–16 of our letter is identical with that given in Letter III, where it is actually quoted as being written by Hosha'yahu to the open-eyed, the seer or prophet. Thus this letter must also be written by the same man, Hosha'yahu, and deals with the same incidents relating to the prophet as Letter III.

What word had been used for the prophet, whether הפקח, הנבא, or another word, is uncertain; the marks visible on the photograph are not traces of letters but deceptive scratches in the surface slip of the pottery. Still הַנָּבָא, the more usual word in the Bible, is found three times in our ostraca, and seems the most likely suggestion. (*See also* Letter XII.) לא טבם stands in place of the more usual אֵינָם טֹבִם "(the words) are not good". But לא־טוב "not good" occurs in the Bible rather as a compound expression, "not good, ungood", as *e.g.* in I Samuel XXIX, 6 וּבְעֵינֵי הַסְּרָנִים לֹא־טוֹב אָתָּה (literally) "but in the eyes of the lords art thou ungood"; or even Genesis II, 18 "(it is) not good (לֹא־טוֹב) that the man should be alone"; Exodus XVIII, 17: לֹא־טוֹב הַדָּבָר אֲשֶׁר אַתָּה עֹשֶׂה "Not good (is) the thing that thou doest"; I Kings XIX, 4 כִּי לֹא־טוֹב אָנֹכִי מֵאֲבֹתָי "for not better (am) I than my fathers".

But why send the king's damning judgement about the prophet to Hosha'yahu? This question is solved through the contents of Letter III, which can now form the basis for the explanation of

112

Letter VI: Hosha'yahu is accused of having spoken of the contents of confidential letters concerning the prophet. In order to refute this accusation, Hosha'yahu sent a letter to the seer, denying on oath that he had read such letters, a fact reported in Letters III, VI, and again in XII.

Thus through Hosha'yahu's alleged breach of confidence information about the prophet reached somebody for whom it was not intended.

To whom did this information come, which endangered the prophet? As line 4 of our letter shows, to the king and his officers whose indignation about the prophet's words caused Ya'ush to ask for explanations and to order Hosha'yahu to apologize in a letter to the prophet.

What could the information be, which reached the king through Hosha'yahu's or some one's indiscretion? It was probably not information about the prophet's *words*; these were preached publicly and only thus are they liable to demoralize city and land. But according to the information following Hosha'yahu's oath in Letter III (the general and the men with him going down to Egypt, the prophet's warning letter sent to Shallum) the *prophet's flight into Egypt* was betrayed by revealing the contents of his warning letter to some one, who reported it to the king. And therefore the letter had to be sent to Ya'ush; possibly its contents would offer some lead to show whether the king's information really had its source from this letter or not. And therefore Hosha'yahu speaks about the general and the prophet's letter in direct connexion with his oath and the accusation expressed against him. It is this letter which was responsible, perhaps, both for the accusation and the general's mission to Egypt, immediately after the king had heard of the prophet's flight.

All this proves further the results reached from our study of Letter III—that this prophet can be no other than Uriyahu of Qiryat-Ye'arim.

It is interesting to sum up the exact position of Ya'ush and his "slave" Hosha'yahu. Both are in the king's army, receiving the king's messages and acting according to them, and Ya'ush appears to be on the best of terms with the king. But still both men respect the prophet and believe in him, in spite of the king's attitude to him, and their hearts ache that they should be responsible for his destruction.

In the quotation of the king's damning judgement itself

5. דברי ה[נבא]

6. לא טבם לרפת ידי . . .

7. קט ידי הא[רץ . ו]העיר

רַפֹּת יָדַיִם "to loosen the hands" is a usual phrase in the Bible; *cf.* in the simple form רָפוּ יָדֵינוּ "our hands sank (= wax feeble)" Jeremiah VI, 24, and similarly II Samuel IV, 1; Isaiah XIII, 7; Jeremiah L, 43; Ezekiel VII, 17; XXI, 12; Zephaniah III, 16; Nehemiah VI, 9, and in the Pi'el (here causative) in the above quoted passage[1] Jeremiah XXXVIII, 4 about the prophet who "looseneth the hands of the man of war מְרַפֵּא אֶת־יְדֵי אַנְשֵׁי הַמִּלְחָמָה" and Ezra IV, 4 מְרַפִּים יְדֵי עַם־יְהוּדָה "they loosened the hands of the people of Judah".

קט at the beginning of line 7 is certainly not a complete word but only the end of it. Now, there are only a very few Hebrew words ending with קט; besides the here impossible vocables קי(ו)ט or נקט "to loath (something)", the unexplained יקוט Job VIII, 14 ("whose trust is יקוט") and לקט "to pick up, to glean" with the substantives לֶקֶט "gleaning" and יַלְקוּט "a bag (of the shepherd) in

---

[1] *See* the general remarks to Letter III, *page* 64.

which to put one's gleanings" (I Samuel XVII, 40: small stones), there is only the verb שקט "to be quiet, to rest". And this, in the Hif'il infinitive, לְהַשְׁקִט or וּלְהַשְׁקִט "(and) to make rest (stop) the hands of . . ." can be shown as the corrrect reading as a parallel to לרפת ידי "to loosen, to make sink (or: rest) the hands". While השקט ידים "to make rest the hands" from שקט "to rest" is a new phrase, not occurring in the Bible, we find from נוח "to rest", a verb synonymous with שקט and frequently used together with it, in Exodus XVII, 11, the report of Israel's fight with Amalek in Rephidim, the expression: "And it came to pass, when Moses held up his hand, that Israel prevailed: and *when he let down his hand* (וְכַאֲשֶׁר יָנִיחַ יָדוֹ), Amalek prevailed". Now, the intention of this story is also to explain the name of the place Rephidim (רְפִידִים) through *raphu yadaim,* רָפוּ יָדַיִם "the hands (of Moses) went down"[1] or וַיֶּרֶף יָדָיו "he let down his hands", and this expression certainly was used in the original version of the story and only later substituted by יָנִיחַ ידיו, thus showing הניח ידים as a parallel to רפת ידים. The same fact is shown by Ecclesiastes VII, 18 and XI 6, "It is good that thou shouldest take hold of this; yea, also from this *withdraw not* thine hand" (אַל־תַּנַּח אֶת־יָדֶךָ): "In the morning sow thy seed, and in the evening withhold not thine hand" (אַל־תַּנַּח יָדֶךָ). In both cases one could have said instead: "Slack אַל־תֶּרֶף יָדְךָ or אַל תְּרַפֶּה יָדֶךָ; *cf.* speaking of one's own hand Joshua X, 6 אַל־תֶּרֶף יָדֶיךָ מֵעֲבָדֶיךָ not thy hand from thy servants" or Ezekiel I, 24 and 25 בְּעָמְדָם תְּרַפֶּינָה כַנְפֵיהֶן "when they stood, they let down their wings". Also here הניח ידים "to make rest the hands" is the same as רפת ידים. And so we may safely conclude that also the synonymous שקט ידים "the hands come to rest" and השקט ידים "to make the hands rest" had the same meaning as רפת ידים "to loosen the hands"; and this all the more as שקט "to rest" originally, as Arabic *saqaṭa* (سقط), may have meant "to *fall* down, to *sink* down", and only out of such phrases as "the hands fall down" or "to sink down, to settle (wine) to its lees"[2] developed the new use for "to rest".

Now, if we thus have to fill up at the end of line 6 the letters להש or ולהש, it is impossible that any other word had stood between it and the preceding ידי. We shall simply have to read לְרִפֹּת יָדַיִם "to loosen the hands, to make sink the hands of the land and the city". The letter after ידי is therefore מ. The reading of ו[הער והאָ[רץ seems to be certain. From this passage we can also definitely deduce that העיר "the city" in our letters is Jerusalem, and not any other place. Following this sentence only one letter, apparently ע, is visible, then follow only uncertain traces at the end of line 7 and on through the first half of line 8. But in the second part of this line and lines 9–11 (*see* following) Hosha'yahu asks Ya'ush to write to the king and to ask them *not to do thus.* Before this and in continuation of "the words of the prophet are not good, demoralizing land and city" the missing words may have indicated what should be done to the prophet. Now the first letter after העיר seems to be ע which, if so, could be part of עת "now"; but the reading of this sign is not certain; some two letters may have stood after it. At the beginning of line 9, the traces of the three first letters could be those of יהו but other readings, בהו or פהו, are graphically possible, representing perhaps a verb with the pron. suff. 3. p. sg. masc. הו as "put him" or "send him" (singular or plural). But there is no indication whether the clear ו belongs to this "word" or to the letters which follow. Of these, the first shows a vertical stroke which could represent perhaps the remains of a נ, but above it something like an א is written, which might have been forgotten and inserted above the line. Could this mean נא "pray" (as in line 5), completing the preceding imperative

[1] *Cf.* H. Gressmann, *Mose und seine Zeit, page 55.*
[2] *Cf.* above the note to השמר III, 21, and my lecture *Research in Hebrew Lexicography,* Jerusalem, 1934, *page 9.*

"do him" or cohortative "let us . . . him"? The next letter may be ב followed by about five illegible letters. If this is so far correct, one would think that something like "put him, pray, *in* (ב) our hands" or "let us then[1] put him in jail" could be intended. In any case the continuation "my lord wilt thou not write . . . why do you do thus" necessitates that some evil intention is expressed here against the man who uttered the demoralising words. Possibly only here "now" עת or ועת "and now" opened the following sentence.

Lines 9–11 "my lord, wilt thou not write to them, saying (א]להם לאמ[ר) why (למ[ה], the most probable reading) should you do thus?". Details may be doubtful, but the main part of the sentence and its meaning is clear. Note that in הלא, line 8, as in והנה, line 5, the ה is almost closed at the left.

The fact that Hosha'yahu appeals to Ya'ush and asks him to use his influence with the king in order to save the prophet also suggests that Ya'ush is a man of high position, commanding the troops of Lachish as well as other garrisons, even north of Azeqah (*see* Letter IV).

In the beginning of lines 10 to 12 again only single letters and indefinite traces are left. Then the oath follows in lines 12–15, written, as in Letter III; the statement "and thy slave has sent (or written) a letter to the prophet and in it he has said", or something similar, seems to have preceded the oath, at least in the second half of line 11 and the first half of line 12. This statement is expressed in Letter III by the words (lines 4–8): "Thy slave has sent a letter to the seer and in it referred thy slave to the letter which my lord had yesterday sent to thy slave that thy slave's heart is sick since thou hast sent to thy slave and that he says: I do not know how to read a letter" (then follows the oath). Could anything like this have been expressed here in the letters at the end of line 10 and in the first half of line 11? Could the lines 10 to 11 be interpreted as הלא לב [עבדך דוה] "Is not thy slave's heart sick?" But if so, how can we explain the preceding and the following traces of letters? Many other ideas suggest themselves, but none are definite. Thus immediately before the signs הזהל at the end of line 10 one is very much tempted to read: ירשלם (or ירשלמה): "(to) Jerusalem". But could "Jerusalem" follow so soon, separated by only three letters from "why do you do thus?" Could it be אִישׁ, יֹשֵׁב, בְּנֵי, וְאֶל, בְּתֹךְ "within", "and to", "ye sons of", "dweller of", "man of" (Jerusalem)? But none of these restorations fits in with all the traces, and all of them would require a continuation, which could hardly be found in the last signs of the line.

Another, and perhaps the most plausible restoration, might be that the apparent traces of the letters שלם in line 10 belong to the proper name טבשלם Ṭobshillem (or Shallum?). Such a name is mentioned also in Letter XVIII, which fits on to the base of Letter VI, probably a postscript to our letter. It reads: "Until the evening [when Ṭob]shillem [returns] will thy slave send the letter which my lord has sent from here to the city". Is it not likely therefore that our letter here said that the same trusted messenger had gone (הלך, lines 10–11?) to carry the letter to the prophet (quoted later), or at least to a place whence it could be forwarded to the prophet himself? And this may well explain why Letter XVIII mentions that not "until the evening" will the trustworthy messenger return and be able to carry Ya'ush's letter to the city.

The following oath, lines 12–16, is mainly clear and its meaning sufficiently established by the comparison with the same oath in Letter III, divided as here in two parts: (*a*) I have not read the letter, (*b*) nobody has read it to me.

---

[1] For נא after the 1st person *cf.* Genesis XVIII, 21; XIX, 8, and 20; XXXIII, 15; L, 5; Exodus III, 3; IV, 18; Numbers XX,17, etc.

In the first part,
12. חי · יהוה אלה
13. יך ... א[ם] קרא עב
14. דך את הספר

"Yhwh lives, thy God, (to punish me) . . . if thy slave has read the letter . . ." is clear, and it is characteristic that instead of the simple חי יהוה (written חיהוה) of Letter III we here have חי יהוה אלהיך "Yhwh lives, *thy God*", a formula used in the Bible only twice instead of the frequent חי יהוה (I Kings XVII, 12, and XVIII, 10), in addressing the prophet Eliah, thus confirming that also this oath is addressed to a prophet.

After חי יהוה אלהיך, and before the contents of the oath proper, another word stands, which is partly obliterated, beginning, as it seems, with ו "and" (hardly כ [1]); such an addition of another guardian of the oath besides God in the Bible is only חַי יהוה וְחֵי נַפְשֶׁךָ [2] "Yhwh liveth and *thyself* (literally: thy soul) liveth (to punish)", invoking besides God the person one is addressing: I Samuel XX, 3 (David to Jonathan, son of King Saul); XXV, 26 (Abigail to David); II Kings II, 4 and 6 (Elijah to Elisha); IV, 30 (the woman from Shunem to Elisha), *i.e.* addressing kings, princes and prophets. Here, if we read the traces right, the same sense is expressed in a shorter form by (חי יהוה אלהיך) וא[ד]ני "(Yhwh, thy God, lives) *and my lord*".

The following signs are indistinct, but appear certain from the contents. Note also that there seems no room between הספר and the following ונסה for another letter, *e.g.* הַסֵּפָר(ם). Thus it is one letter which Hosha'yahu was supposed to have read and spoken about, apparently the warning letter mentioned in Letter III, 19–21.

The second half of the oath can also be tentatively reconstructed from the traces left with the help of Letter III:
14. ונסה [איש]
15. לקרא[ה לי] ודֹאת מֹנֹהֹ
16. [כל מאומה]

"and (if) [a man] has tried to read [it to me] and I have seen of it [anything]". *Cf.* the notes to Letters III and XII. לְקְרֹאֹה inf. c. suff. 3rd pers. sg. "to read it".

Thus I offer the following incomplete reconstruction and translation of Letter VI:

---

[1] While the reading כ is graphically possible, all my attempts to find a possible continuation after such a letter (starting from כי "that" or otherwise) proved unsatisfactory.

[2] The vocalization חֵי instead of חַי before other words than the names of God alone, is only a perpetual *Qerē* (prescription to pronounce another form than the one intended by the writing), to avoid an actual oath to somebody besides Yhwh. *Cf.* my article quoted above about חי יהוה, *Leshonenu*, vol. VI, *pages* 127–136. Also II Samuel XI, 11, we shall have to read חי יהוה וחי נפשך instead of חַיֶּיךָ וחי נפשך.

LETTER VI

RECONSTRUCTION

1. אל אדני יאוש · ירא · יהוה א
2. ת אדני אתה עתה זה · שלם מי
3. עבדך כלב כי · שלח · אדני א[ת ספ]
4. ר המלך ואת ספרי השר[ם לאמ]
5. ר קרא נא והנה · דברי · ה[נבא]
6. לא טבם לרפת · ידים · [להש]
7. קט ידי הא[רץ ו]העיר ע[–––]
8. – הו אב[–] [– – – –] אדני הלא תכ
   ב
9. תב א[ל]הם לאמר למ[ה] תעשו
10. כזאת – – – י – של – ה – הל
11. – – – – – – – – – – – לב
12. – – – – חי יהוה אלה
13. יך ו[אדני] א[ם] קרא עב
14. דך א[ת] הספר [ונס]ה [איש]
15. ל[קראה לי] ור[את מנהו]
16. [כל מאומה]

TRANSLATION

1. To my lord Ya'ush.   May Yhwh let see (us)
2. my lord, (while) thou (art) even now in peace.   Who is
3. thy slave, a dog, that my lord has sent the [lett]er
4. of the king and the letters of the offic[ers say-]
5. ing, Read, I pray thee, and (thou wilt) see: the words of the [prophet]
6. are not good, (liable) to loosen the hands, [to make]
7. sink the hands of the coun[try and] the city. . . .
8. . . . . My lord, wilt thou not
9. write to [them saying]: why should ye do
10. thus: . . . .
11. . . . .
12. . . . . .Yhwh lives, thy god
13. and my l[or]d lives (to punish) if thy sla-
14. ve has read the letter and [anybody has tri]ed
15. to rea[d it to him, or he has s]een [of it]
16. [anything].

117

GENERAL REMARKS

It is now clear that Letter VI is a recapitulation of Letter III, reiterating its main contents in another form, just as Letter V has its shorter counterpart in Letter IX. And, as will be seen later, Letter XII is another repetition of Letter VI rather than of Letter III directly. Even Letter II, giving the main part of Letter III in one short sentence, may have been sent about the same time as III and be meant as a duplicate of it, in case Letter III should get lost, or to follow it up as a reinforcing statement. So urgent and so painful was the matter dealt with in these letters that Hosha'yahu had to make doubly certain that his apologies should reach his lord before irreparable damage was done.

Practically all these repetitions of Letter III seem to be written by the same hand and some of them are on pieces of the same pot. The fact that in the case of Letters III and VI not less than four "duplicates" have been preserved, again emphasizes that we have here an almost intact correspondence, and not just the remains of many letters incoming during the last days of the fortress. These duplicate letters are of immense value for the elucidation of our story, and not only for the reading of their texts. As one can see, they have not been copied from one another, although in V and IX they are almost alike; according to the size of the sherd used, the writer gives a longer or shorter version of his message, and thus he selects different details of his subject. By comparing and summing up the points given in the different versions we are now able to fill in the picture of the incidents behind Letter III, that is to say, of the Biblical story about the prophet Uriyah, with some new illuminating details.

The king had written to Ya'ush about the prophet's demoralizing words and had ordered him to find Uriyah. This is the reason for Ya'ush's accusation or suspicion that Hosha'yahu has betrayed the direction of Uriyah's flight, made known to him through the prophet's warning letter. In order to examine this possibility Ya'ush wanted to see this letter personally and ordered Hosha'yahu to send it to him.

Again, Ya'ush's high position becomes clearer; he is the commander of Lachish, if not in fact of the whole western defences. The king appeals to him in everything concerning this part of the country; therefore Hosha'yahu's correspondence to him was not originally left scattered upon the floor of the gate-room, but had been brought there later. Until then, perhaps, it had been filed in the archives where Ya'ush also kept the letters of the king and other officials, which, even if sent to Hosha'yahu or another subordinate, were returned to him for safe keeping.

But why should this one-man correspondence, this whole dossier of Hosha'yahu, be brought to this open room at the city-gate? Mr. Starkey suggests a simple and ingenious explanation: The city-gate suggests the court of judgement; not only in ancient Israel, but throughout the Orient, the city-gate is the place of judgement, and thus particularly in the Bible the word שער "gate" is in many instances the word for "Court of Justice". And it is possible that Hosha'yahu, who appears in the letters about the prophet as a man suspected of some kind of treachery, had perhaps been summoned to Lachish by his lord Ya'ush and had there stood his examination. For this his dossier, which may have also contained many documents written on papyrus, now burnt and destroyed, was brought forth from the archives. Hosha'yahu's trial, during the last days of Lachish, may have been the *last case* dealt with at the city-gate; thus his dossier was found there, enabling a later generation to hold the final historical judgement about Hosha'yahu and his alleged treachery.

Mr. Starkey's suggestion may well give the probable explanation of the surprising fact that Hosha'yahu's messages on potsherds have been found almost complete. There is one feature common to all Hosha'yahu's letters: in each one he is accused or suspected of some kind of treachery, and in all of them he tries to exculpate himself.

There are three very definite occasions when Hosha'yahu seems to have betrayed his lord's trust: (a) in the events connected with the prophet, whose hiding-place he may have betrayed (Letters II, III, VI, VII, VIII, XII, etc.); (b) in the case of Semakhyahu, who may have heard him curse the king (Letter V); (c) in his military duty, including the attentive observation of the signals given from Azeqah and Lachish (Letters IV and XIII). In all of them Hosha'yahu pleads his innocence, but he has to give proof: he has to send the prophet's warning letter (III, 19–21), and he certainly has to name witnesses; therefore the list of names in Ostracon I may well be a list of witnesses whom Hosha'yahu sends to vouch for the truth of his letter.

It is peculiar that all the letters we are able to read deal with accusations raised against Hosha'yahu. Certainly this man had written other letters, containing reports and questions, which would in no way concern his personal attitude. So apparently not all his letters were produced to the court, but only those relevant to the establishment of Hosha'yahu's guilt or innocence.

Thus the Lachish Letters seem to be the remains of the documents used in the trial of Hosha'yahu's alleged treachery, suspected in at least three instances.

These three events did not happen at one and the same time. The one with the prophet possibly months or years before, the cursing of the king perhaps some time later; but the last event as told in Letter IV shows all the characteristics of the last tragic weeks, if not days, of Lachish. And when at last Hosha'yahu was examined, and his dossier brought forward from the archives, the enemy may have interrupted the proceedings and thus the documents became scattered at the place of judgement. There may even be no need to assume that Hosha'yahu was called for examination to Lachish. There is the other possibility that Hosha'yahu's place, probably Qiryat-Ye'arim, was conquered by the Babylonians before the fall of Lachish, and that Hosha'yahu fled to this, the last stronghold of Judah. But here he may have been suspected of complicity in the conquest of the fortress with whose defence he was entrusted, and brought to trial before a military court.

Thus the fact that the Lachish ostraca have been found between the two burnt layers—perhaps of 597 and 588 B.C.—only proves that the letters were not written later than 588, though in all probability some of them may be earlier. And this disposes of the chronological arguments against the identity of the prophet and "open-eyed one" of our letters with Uriyah from Qiryat-Ye'arim.

The writing of Letter VI differs from that of Letters I–V only in so far as even less word-dividing dots are visible. The writing is cramped and narrow, as though to save space; nevertheless, it must have been very beautiful and the hand closely resembles that of Letter III, which may have been written by the same scribe. And this is not surprising, as Letter VI is only a repetition of that letter.

LETTER VII

Photo: S. W. Michieli

LETTER VII

TENTATIVE RECONSTRUCTION OF THE FIRST LINES

1. [וישמע יה]וֹה [את אד]
2. [ני שמעת שלם] עת כ]ים מ]ַי עֹבֹדֹך כֹלֹב כֹ
3. [י זכר]ת אֹת עבדֹך [- - - - -]
4. [- - - - -] ערב [-] [- - - - -]
5. [ט - - - עב]דֹך [- - - - - -]
6. בשלם את הסֹפֹר מזה]
7. [העי]רה [- - - -]

TRANSLATION

1. [May Yh]wh [let hear my lord]
2. [tidings of peace,[1] even] now: [Who is] thy slave, a dog, that
3. [thou hast remember]ed thy slave [and sent to him]
4. [thy letter? . . .] evening [. . .]
5. [. . . thy] slave [. . . To-]
6. bshillem the lett[er from here]
7. [unto the c]ity . . .

---

[1] Or "good".

NOTES

Letter VII is only partially preserved. On the obverse are traces of about ten lines, and on the reverse about four lines are visible. At the top, to the left, two fragments are missing which would originally have completed the rounded upper edge. A larger portion is missing from the middle than from the top left-hand corner, where it appears that only a very narrow fragment has been broken off.

Reading and explanation of this letter as a whole seem hopeless. Traces here and there suggest words such as "slave" or "letter" and probably show that this message also, written on a sherd from the same pot used for Letters II, VI, VIII and XVIII, belonged to the same correspondence and contained statements of the same nature as these documents; but a complete reconstruction is impossible.

However, after recognizing the fact that in this letter and in the fragmentary Letter XVIII from the same pot [Tob]-shillem (?) is mentioned in connexion with a letter, presumably as the messenger who had to bring it to the city, it seems possible that in the beginning of Letter VII the same or a similar statement is made. On this basis a tentative reconstruction of part of Letter VII is attempted, showing that the suggestion offered is not unlikely, though many details remain very doubtful.

For the general contents, and for the words used *cf.* the notes on Letter XVIII, *page* 183.

Here are a few additional remarks:—

The reconstruction of lines 1–3 is based upon the traces visible after a comparison with Letter II. The phrase "that thou hast (or: my lord has) remembered thy slave" means, as shown in the notes on Letter II, only "that thou hast sent thy letters", and this may have been added in lines 3–4.

The reading of the first part of line 5 is very doubtful. In spite of the size and apparent distinctness of the signs, many readings are possible, but none probable. However, lines 5–6 seem to correspond very closely with Letter XVIII: "thy slave shall send, when [To]bshillem arrives, the letter from here unto the city".

LETTER VIII

Photo: S. W. Michieli

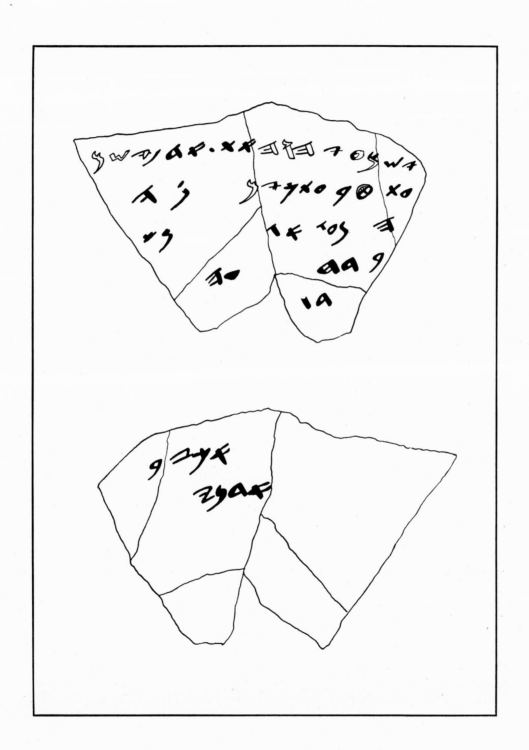

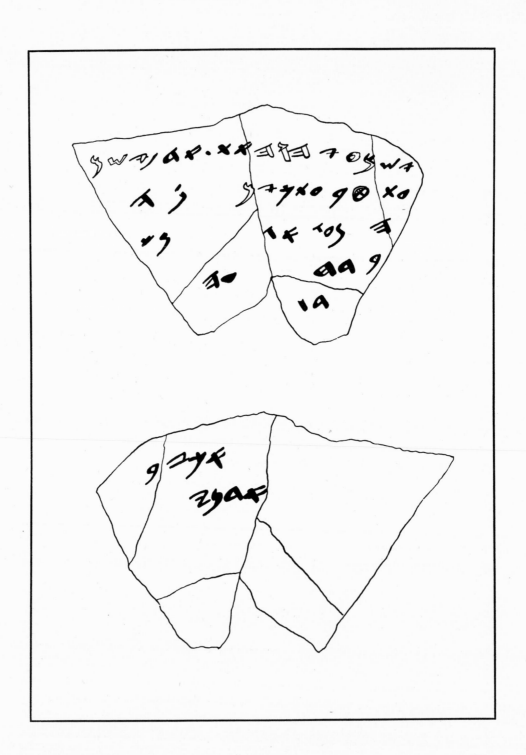

128

LETTER VIII

TRANSLITERATION

OBVERSE

1. ‫ישמע יהוה את · אדני ש]מ[‬
2. ‫עת טב עָת כֹים – – נֹ – ה –‬
3. ‫ה – נב – א – – – – נֹ‬
4. ‫ב – רח – – –ּיה‬
5. ‫אֹ – ר –‬

REVERSE

1. ‫אכזב‬
2. ‫אדני‬
3.

No translation of this fragmentary letter can be given. On a sherd from the same pot as Letters II, VI, VII and XVIII the same writer, after the greeting "May Yhwh let hear my lord tidings of good, even now", certainly reports about the same subject. The prophet may even be referred to in ‫נבא‬ (?) on the obverse in line 3. However, this and the reading of the single letters in lines 4–5, may be wrong. The word which on the reverse line 1 looks like ‫אֲכַזֵּב‬ "I have lied", may rather be ‫אֶכְתֹּב‬ "I shall write".

The writing of Letter VIII resembles that of Ostracon I and possibly the list of names may have accompanied this letter, perhaps as a list of witnesses supporting the truth of Hosha'yahu's messages.

129

LETTER IX

Photo: S. W. Michieli

132

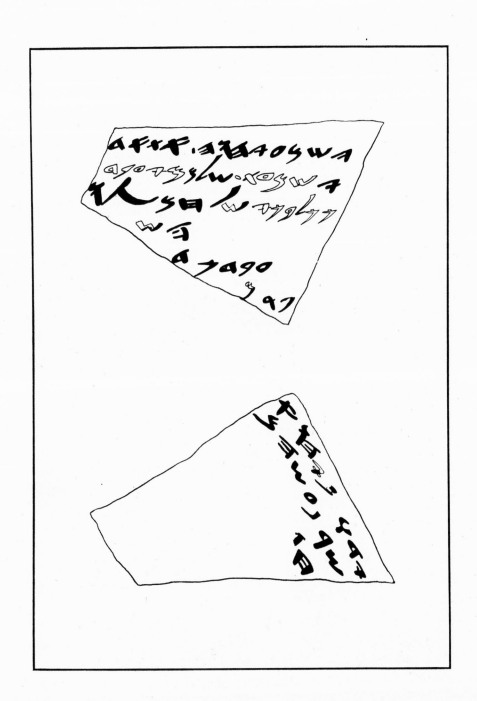

LETTER IX

PRELIMINARY TRANSLITERATION [1]

OBVERSE

1. ‏ישמע יהוה · את [א]ד
2. ‏נִי שמעת שלם מן[י ע]בד
3. ‏[ךָ · כלב] כי שלח – – – –
4. ‏[ספר   [הֹשֵׁ
5. ‏ב עבדך –
6. ‏פר –

REVERSE

7. ‏ידע-כיהוא
8. ‏שר נעשה מ
9. ‏ה

NOTES

Letter IX is only partly readable. What is left makes it clear that our ostracon is only a shortened, though similar, repetition of Letter V (*see* the notes on Letter V). After the greeting, the first subject mentioned must be letters which the lord has sent to his slave (3–4) and, as in Letter V, the traces of הֹשֵׁב עבדך in lines 4–5 and פר in line 6 are complementary to lines 3–4 (the acknowledgement of letters received): "thy slave has returned the letters": השב עבדך הספרם. The ה of הספרם is faintly visible at the end of line 5. The remaining ספרם had to be put into the narrow lower corner of the sherd and was therefore written in a curve. The partly visible סם rises up almost into line 5, and what is left of the ם necessarily stands above line 6. According to this the word in line 4 should be (ס]פרי) "the letters of", not the singular ספר "the letter". However, a reading of the signs at the end of line 3, after שלח or שלחת is impossible. None of the signs visible point definitely to a certain letter.

On the reverse I was at first inclined to read:

Reverse 1.	‏ידע · טֹבֹיהו א	7.
,, 2.	‏שר · נעשה מ	8.
,, 3.	‏[ח]ר]	9.

"Ṭobiyahu knows what we shall do to-morrow". However, in the broad and bold writing of our letter there is no room between ע[2] and כ or ב in line 7 for a dividing dot or a space, necessary between the words, and such a large letter as ט; also there is no ר really visible after the ה or ח in line 9. Furthermore, it is most unnatural and certainly not in keeping with our other letters to

---

[1] For fuller reconstruction and translation *see* the following. Mr. Harding's hand copy, given above, shows what he sees on the sherd and differs in some points from what I recognize on it.

[2] The sign itself could graphically be also an incomplete ק.

However, a form of ידע "to know" is postulated by the following "what has been done", while no verb beginning with ידק or ירק is possible. No down stroke of a ק is visible on the sherd.

say: "Ṭobiyahu knows what we shall do to-morrow" and nothing else. *All* the other letters sent to "the lord" are exculpating letters, and most of them invoke Yhwh as judge and witness for the writer's innocence.

Then we see that as lines 1–6 correspond to the first part of Letter V, so also the signs of the reverse are almost the same as those of V, 7–9:

V, 7–9.   ידע[נ]ך יהוה – – – – – ה · מה
IX, 7–9.   ידע[-]ך יהו אשר נעשה מה

Should these not, therefore, be essentially the same words?

Still there seemed to be some difficulties. There was a letter between ידע and the following ך, and thus the word could not be simply יֹדֲעֶךָ; but as shown in the notes of Letter V, we have to expect here the ancient fuller form יֹדִעֶנְךָ "may he let thee know". Another difficulty is יהו, where we should expect יהוה; but again in Letter V the scribe, probably the same as in this letter, writes in line 10 ביהו instead of ביהוה using the shorter form יהו as in the proper names, and as in Elephantine, where the descendants of the same Jews, showing so many features in common with the men of Lachish, exclusively use this form. Thus we shall have to translate: "May Yhw let thee know what had been done".

The following מה also seemed to correspond to the beginning of the last sentence in Letter V, lines 9–10: "What (מה) aileth thy slave that he should curse in (the name of) Yhwh seed to the king". However, it is very doubtful whether this same sentence was written here. There are no certain traces visible on the sherd, and the other examples of repetition in our correspondence (*cf.* particularly Letters II, III, VI, XII) show that such doubles were not necessarily literal copies. Thus one could assume that the writer, realizing that it might not be necessary to repeat in this short duplicate the last sentence, did not continue this after he had already started to write its first word מה; he might even have blotted out this word by a stroke, which now is no longer visible. But it is more probable that he closed the preceding sentence in that way: "May Yhwh let thee know (the thing) which happened (telling thee), *what it was*" (מה הוא—but *see* following), *cf.* Biblical passages as Numbers XIII, 18 וּרְאִיתֶם אֶת־הָאָרֶץ מַה־הִוא "And see the land (to know) what it is" and the parallel of Letter IV, 7–8: ועבדך אדני ישלח שמה איהו "and thy slave, my lord, will send thither (asking) where he is". Thus the writer, while remembering his longer message, gives it a final twist, saying: "(the thing) that happened, what it was", just as he closes one topic in Letter IV, 8: "will send thither (asking) where he is".

Instead of "(the thing) that happened, what it was" he could have said simply "(may Yhwh let thee know) what it is that happened", just as in Numbers XIII, 18 one could have said: "see what the land is" instead of "see the land, what it is". In our letter one may even understand: "may Yhwh tell thee about the thing that happened, what it really was". The addition of מה הוא "what it is" is not strictly necessary; but the same is the case in Numbers XIII, 18, and also *e.g.* in Psalms XXXIX, 5, where we even find the same verb and subject as in our letter: הוֹדִיעֵנִי יהוה קִצִּי וּמִדַּת יָמַי מַה־הִיא "Yhwh, make me know mine end, and the measure of my days, what it is", parallel to ידענך יהו אשר נעשה מה הוא "May Yhwh make thee to know (the thing) that happened, what it is".

Now "what it is", originally מה הוא, could probably also be written in a contracted form as one word מהו as is usual later in Mishnaic Hebrew (*cf.* Ben-Yehouda, *Thesaurus VI, page* 2827 f.), just

136

as Letter III, 12 (and Job IV, 12) show the contracted מנהו (and thus in connexion with other prepositions), where Isaiah XVIII, 2 and 7 gives the full form מן־הוא in two words. So מהו apparently might have stood here. And as shown above, *page 95*, we may have to recognize the same מהו "what it is" also at the end of the parallel sentence in Letter IX, lines 8–9.

Thus we reach the following reconstruction of Letter IX.

RECONSTRUCTION OF LETTER IX

OBVERSE

1. ד[א] את יהוה ישמע
2. בד[ע] . י[מ . שלם שמעת נ
3. — — — שלחת כי [. כלב . ך
4. שֹה [— — — — ספרי]
5. ה עבדך . ב̄
6. ספרם̄

REVERSE

7. א . יהו ך[נ]ידע
8. מ . נעשה . ער
9. הו̄

TRANSLATION

1. May Yhwh let hear my lord
2. tidings of peace. Who is thy slave
3. a dog that thou hast sent
4. the letters of . . . . . thy
5. slave has returned the
6. letters

7. May Yhwh let thee know, (the thing)
8. that happened
9. What it is!

For the meaning of this Letter, *cf.* the notes on Letter V.

LETTER X

Photo: R. Richmond Brown

140

LETTER X

Only very indefinite traces of this letter containing about thirteen lines are preserved; here and there one can make out distinct letters—particularly ל stands out clearly—and many seductive possibilities suggest themselves, but no word can be read with certainty.

LETTER XI

Photo: S. W. Michieli

144

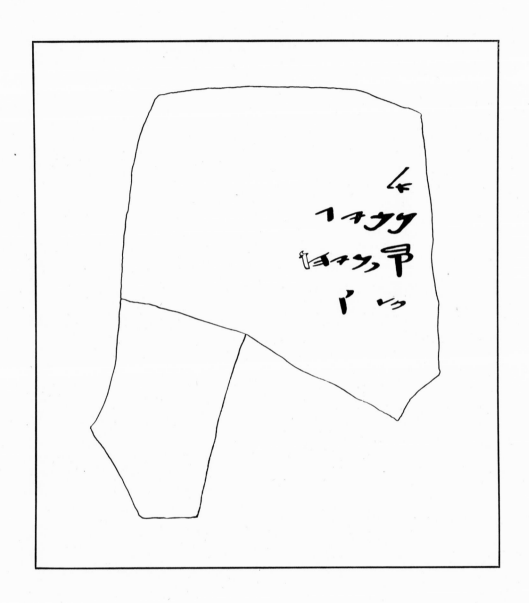

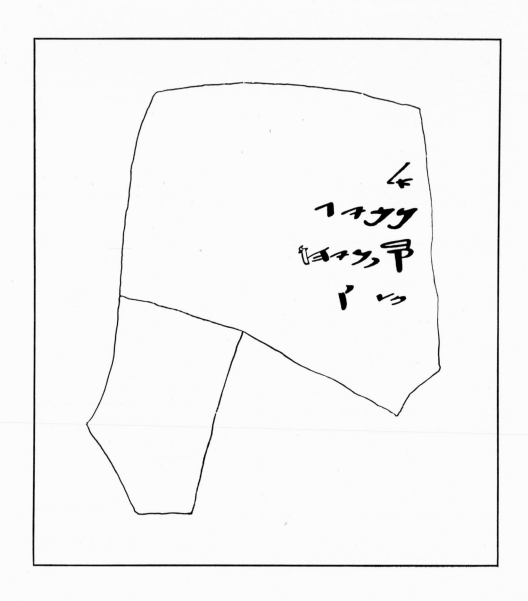

LETTER XI

Traces of about thirteen lines can be seen on the sherd; one recognizes at the beginning of lines 2–5 and at the end of line 4:—

	כֹּלֹב	.2
	אֹלֹן	.3
אֹל	[? מֹכיהו]ה	.4
	סמכיהו	.5

Here only the name סמכיהו Semakhyahu in line 5 is certain; it may be assumed that this is the same man as mentioned in Letter IV, and possibly in Letter V, as a high officer who should have inspected Hoshaʿyahu's place, but went up to the city, and who also, according to Letter V, had accused Hoshaʿyahu of cursing the king. Our letter may be connected with one or both of the events (*cf.* also the notes on Letter XIII).

In line 4 מכ with the following יהו will hardly be the main part of the name [ס]מכיהו as in line 5, although this is not impossible; there seems to be too much room and possibly even a word-dividing dot between כ and י. What shows on the photograph before the doubtful מ is not a letter, but a mark on the sherd.

147

LETTER XII

Photo: R. Richmond Brown

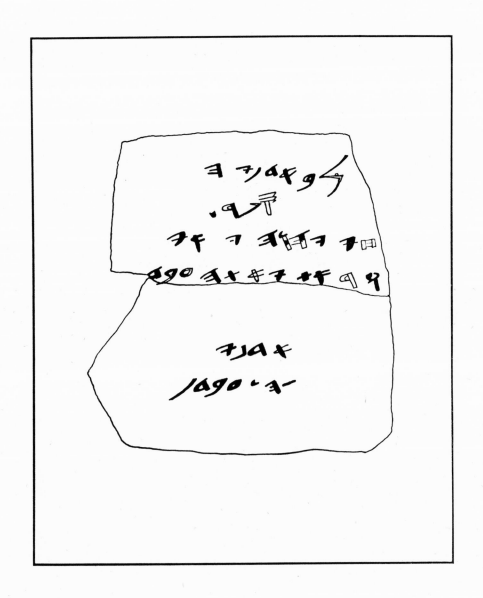

LETTER XII

TRANSLITERATION[1]

1. ‏‏·· כֹלב · אדני · ה‏
2. ‏[ס]פר‏
3. ‏(ח)י יהוה ¯¯י‏
4. ‏[קר]אתי [א]תה עבד‏
5.
6. ‏אדני‏
7. ‏ה · עבדך‏
8.

NOTES

This letter showed very faint traces of writing, most of them now unfortunately lost in the unavoidable cleaning. Thus there was only the first photograph, taken while the sherd was still partly covered with mud, as a basis for its reading. From the traces such fragments as "my lord", "letter", "Yhwh lives", "I have read it", etc., could be recognized, and from them one could safely conclude that this letter, as Nos. II, III, VI, etc., dealt with the events concerning the prophet and the letter Hosha'yahu was supposed to have read.

While a real reconstruction of this letter, or letter-fragment, must remain conjectural, it is clear even from the few words left that Letter XII, like Letters II and VI, repeats the same statement as given in Letter III, although it probably resembles more closely Letter VI than Letter III.

The writing of Letter XII also strongly resembles that of Letters II, III and VI.

---

[1] The lines of this possibly incomplete letter are numbered as visible on the sherd.

LETTER XIII

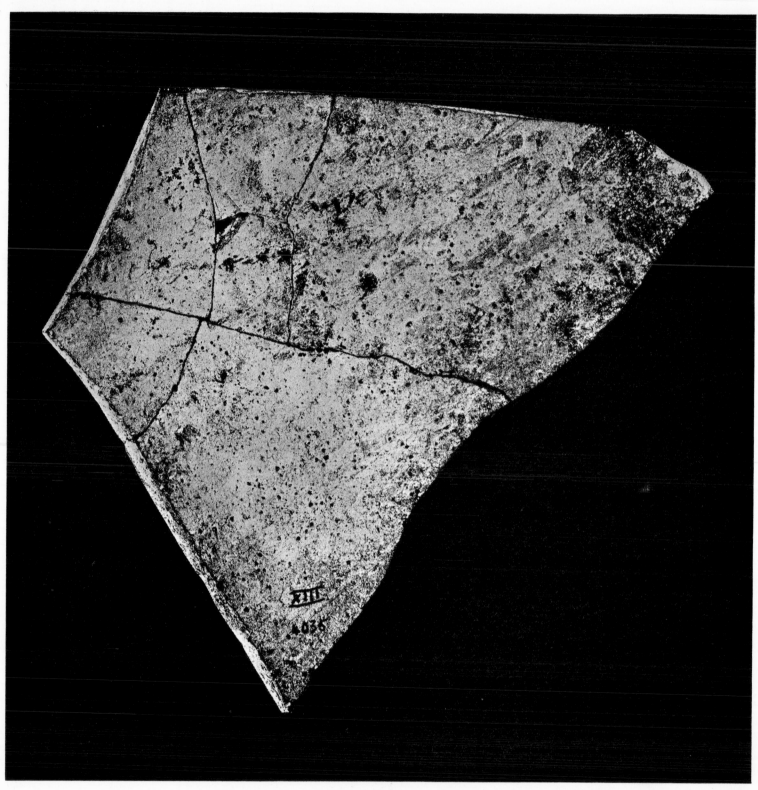

Photo : S. W. Michieli

156

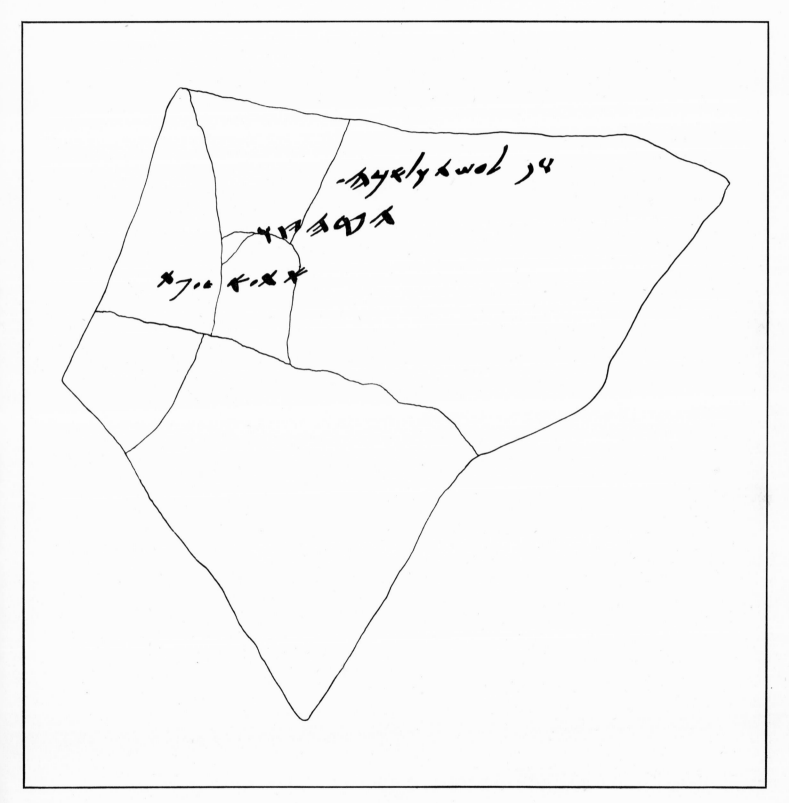

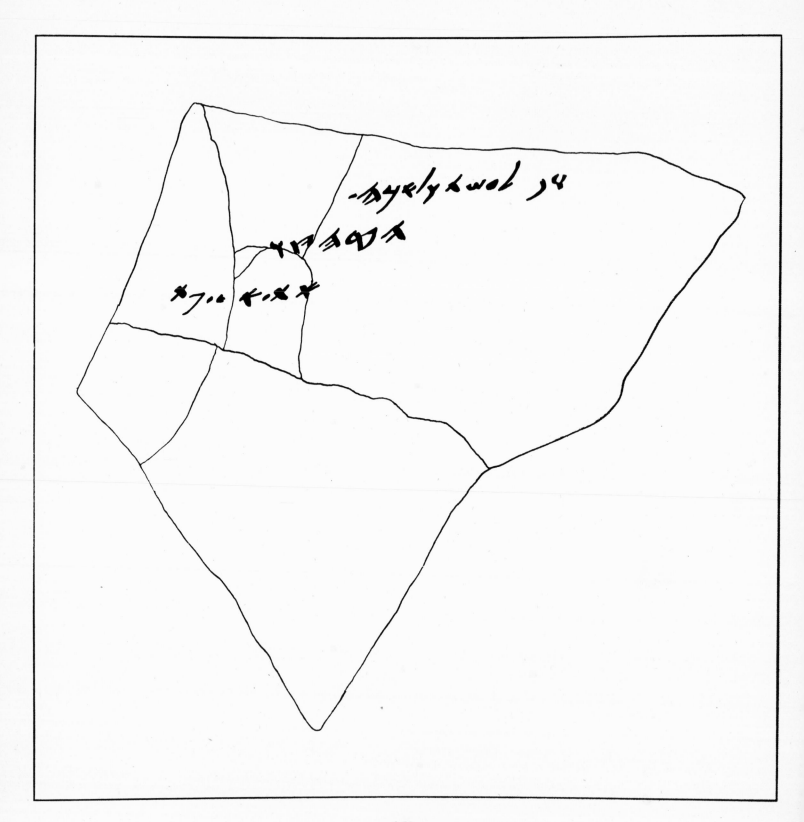

158

LETTER XIII

REVERSE

1. קם לעשת מלאכה‍ן
2. וסמכיהו יחפרה‍ה‍ן
3. – – – – ו – – את . אשפת‍ן

TRANSLATION

1. **Stand up to do work**
2. **and Semakhyahu shall dig it out**
3.   **quivers**

NOTES

This most interesting ostracon is entirely different from all the other potsherds found at the gate-room of Lachish. While most of the writing has vanished, still the last part, written on the inside of the potsherd, shows that it is probably not an incoming letter, written by Hosha‘yahu to his lord Ya'ush, but a military order, sent possibly by Ya'ush to Hosha‘yahu. This order probably mentions Semakhyahu, who at this time (*cf.* Letter IV) should be at Hosha‘yahu's post. The sentence might have read: "Stand up to do work [and prepare a trench for the defence]; Semakhyahu shall take care of the digging work, [while other men shall make ready or bring in bows and arrows and] quivers ". That קם is to be understood as an imperative depends on the reading of the following יחפרהו, which seems most likely.

This letter may not be the original order sent to Hosha‘yahu, but the copy of it brought from the archives together with Hosha‘yahu's letters. And it can easily be seen how this would also fit in well with the supposition that the documents found at Lachish formed part of the dossier of Hosha‘yahu, brought from the archives to the court-room for use in the examination of this officer. Also in the case of this message he was perhaps suspected of having disobeyed his lord's orders. And as Semakhyahu is mentioned here, this order may be more directly connected with the matters spoken of in Letters IV and V.

Semakhyahu should perhaps have taken the leading part in the defence-work ordered in our ostracon. But Hosha‘yahu, not on good terms with this officer, may not have obeyed this order.

And thus in Letter IV we find him denying that Semakhyahu had visited his post; he is not, or is no longer, there. Hosha'yahu writes that he is ready to send letters and to inquire about Semakhyahu's whereabouts. But by this he only may hide the fact that his behaviour has driven Semakhyahu away. Thus we may have to vocalize the legible words.

1. . . . . קָם לַעֲשׂת מְלָאכָה
2. . . . . וּסְמַכְיָהוּ יַחְפְּרֵהוּ
3. . . . . אֶת אַשְׁפֹּת

Taken by itself the word אשפת could also mean "dunghill", and חפר "to spy out, to explore", but this seems unlikely here.

LETTER XIV

Photo: S. W. Michieli

162

LETTER XIV

Many traces of single letters are visible, some of them are quite clear. However, as so many signs resemble each other, what looks like כ may also be ב or even מ, etc. About the left centre of the potsherd יהוה ‧ א seems to stand out distinctly, which may be the remains of "may Yhwh ... my lord" [אדני א]ת יהוה or "Yhwh lives ... if" [א]ם יהוה חי.

LETTER XV

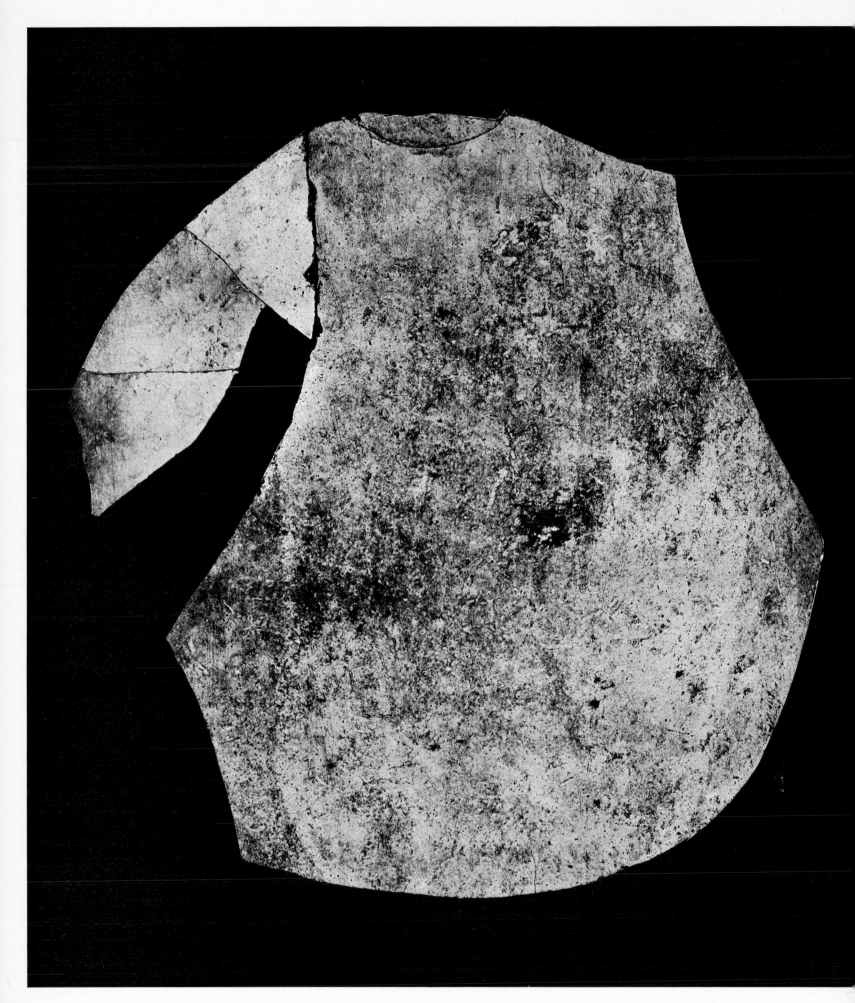

Photo: S. W. Michieli

166

LETTER XV

This is the largest ostracon; unfortunately the writing upon it is no longer legible. The traces remaining in line 3 at the left-hand upper corner suggest single words as שלח עבדך, but these readings are very doubtful.

LETTER XVI

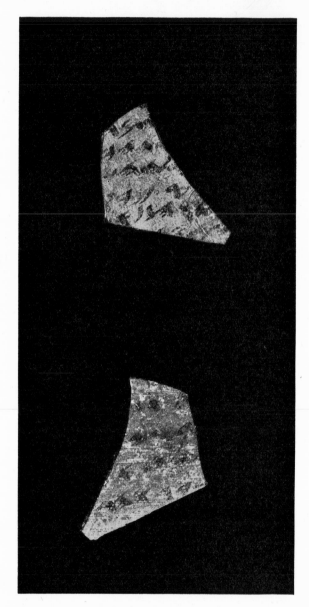

Photo: R. Richmond Brown

170

172

LETTER XVI

TRANSLITERATION

OBVERSE

1. ‏[חמתֹ‏]
2. ‏[הין ה‏ · ‏]
3. ‏ש‏[‏ל‏חה ע‏]נבדך
4. ‏ס‏[‏פר בני־‏]
5. ‏[הו הנבא־‏]‏ · ·
6. ‏[‏ - - - ‏]

REVERSE

1. ‏[‏ - א -‏]
2. ‏[ע - - -‏]
3. ‏[שלח א‏]
4. ‏[‏דבר וח -‏]

This tiny fragment out of the middle of a letter most probably dealt with the events concerning the prophet Urijah (‏הנבא‏, ‏[ארי‏]הו obv. line 5), as did Letters II, III, VI and XII, but the scattered signs—some quite well preserved—are not sufficient to make any interpretation reliable.

In line 1 the letters ‏חמה‏, if the last incomplete letter is correctly identified and belongs to the same word, could mean ‏חֲמַת‏ (st. cstr.) "anger, wrath", ‏חֹמֹת‏ or ‏חֹמַת‏ "wall(s)", ‏נֶחָמֹת‏, ‏נֶחָמַת‏ "consolation(s)" or ‏נִחַמְתָּ‏ "thou hast comforted" (Pi'el) or "regretted" (Nif'al), etc.

From the following scattered words, "he was (‏היה‏?)" . . . "sent it (‏שְׁלָחֹה ע‏]נבדך) thy slave" . . . "letter of Benay[ahu]" or "letter of my son (or, the sons of) . . . [Uriy]ahu the prophet", "he sent", only the general subject of the letter can be established. On the reverse, line 4, ‏דבר וח‏ could be [‏דֶּבֶר וָחֶ‏]רֶב or [‏דֶּבֶר וְחַ‏]יָּה (‏רָעָה‏) "pestilence and sword" or "pestilence and (noisome) beast" (as threatened punishment for the evil done to the prophet?). *Cf.* Ezekiel XIV, 21: "the sword and the famine and the noisome beast and the pestilence" (‏חֶרֶב וְרָעָב וְחַיָּה רָעָה וְדָבֶר‏); however, even the simple reading [‏דָּבָר אֶחָ‏]ד "one word" might be intended.

LETTER XVII

Photo   S. W. Michieli

176

LETTER XVII

‎1. עבדֹן
‎2. אדנין
‎3. רמיהֹן

This fragment gives only the words "(thy or his) slave . . . my lord" and what apparently was the name ‎ירמיהו Yirmeyahu (Jeremiah), the same name as in Letter I, 4.

LETTER XVIII

Photo : R. Richmond Brown

180

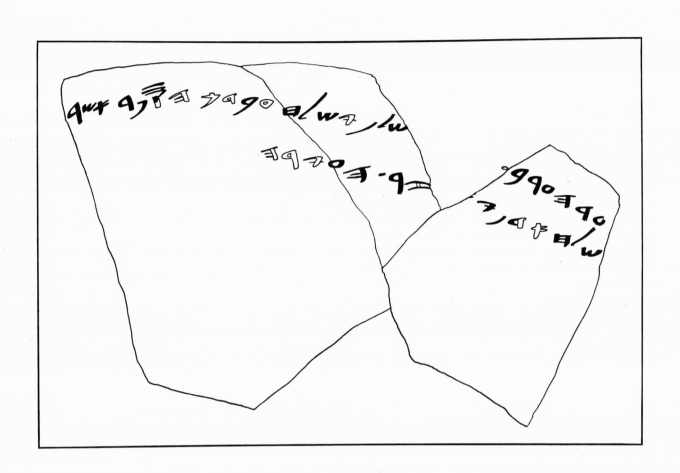

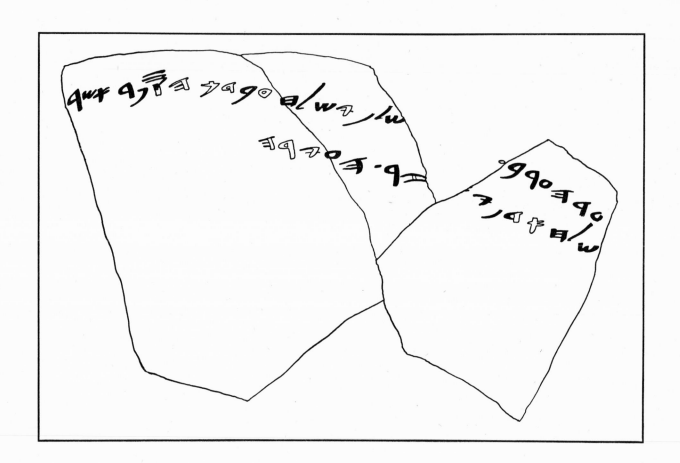

LETTER XVIII

TRANSLITERATION

1. עד הערב [בבא טב]שלם ישלח עֲבְדְּךָ הספר אשר ·
2. שלח אדני [מ]זה · העירֹה

TRANSLATION

1. Until the evening [when comes Ṭob]shillem shall send thy slave the letter which
2. my lord has sent, from here unto the city.

182

NOTES

LINE 1. בְּבֹא טב[שלם] "when Ṭobshillem[1] comes", or perhaps בשוב טבשלם "when Ṭobshillem returns". Such a restoration seems most likely; there must be some reason why the letter will be sent only "until the evening", and as Ṭobshillem is a name occurring certainly in Letter I, line 2, such a name, and such a reason for keeping the message until the evening, would be probable enough. Ṭobshillem may be a trustworthy messenger, and it would be worth while to wait for his coming. *See also* the notes to Letter VI, 10, *page* 115, and to Letter VII, *page* 124.

Far less plausible would it be to read instead of the missing letters אל יר[שלם] "Until the evening [*unto Jeru*]salem", as this would offer an unnatural order of the words in the sentence and make העירה "unto the city" at the end of the message an unnecessary tautology. For עַד הָעֶרֶב, "until the evening", *cf.* Leviticus XI, 24.

In line 2 also the reconstruction מִ[זֶּה] "from here", the same expression as in Letter III, 18, seems almost certain. There is no room for more than one missing letter; thus no name of an addressee with the preceding אל "to" could have stood here. The traces of the last sign look, it is true, more like ר, with a dot after it. However, no such reading seems possible. The receiver of the letter in "the city" is probably the king himself.

This short message is written upon a sherd taken from the same pot as Letters II, VI, VII and VIII, and actually joins on to the bottom of Letter VI. Thus it is also written by Hosha'yahu, and in all probability sent the same day as Letter VI, perhaps together with it. Thus the informality of the message will be explained by its character as a postscript to Letter VI. (*See* the notes to VI, 10–11.) Also the word-dividing dots, scarce in Letter VI, seem to be missing entirely in its postscript, Letter XVIII.

In Letter VI Hosha'yahu—before his defence—mentions the king's letter and the letters of his officers, which had come to Ya'ush and cause this officer to ask for the writer's explanations. And, while acting upon the facts learned from the king's letter, Ya'ush would have to acknowledge receipt, and send his preliminary report—if nothing else—to the king. And this letter to the king, which Ya'ush may have sent together with his letter to Hosha'yahu (mentioned as having arrived "yesterday" in Letter III), he wants to be forwarded "from here" to "the city", as shown on *page* 114, the city of the king, Jerusalem. Thus the regular route from Lachish to the "city" passes the accused's post. This supports the opinion expressed in the notes on Letter IV that Hosha'yahu's post, probably the prophet Urijah's home-town Qiryat-Ye'arim, was a middle station between the main fortresses of the western frontier and Jerusalem. The fact that Ya'ush sends one of the king's letters, which he had already received and read, to Hosha'yahu saying "read, please" (Letter VI, 5) certainly does not contradict this suggestion; the letters "coming to" (Letter III) Hosha'yahu, but not intended for him, were, as he himself declares, not read by him or to him; the king's official letters were probably under seal; the finding of the seal impression "of Gedalyahu, who is over the house (of the king)" and other clay sealings in Lachish shows that sealed correspondence written on papyrus was quite usual.

The writing of Letter XVIII resembles that of Letters VI and XII as well as of II and III.

---

[1] Hardly "Shallum" or Shillem alone; *cf.* also בשלם[in Letter VII, 6, and the notes on Letter VI, line 10, *page* 115.

DESCRIPTION OF THE POTSHERDS

Letter No.	Size		Thickness		Description of Pottery
	Cms.	In.	Mm.	In.	
I	10·5×8	4×3	7	$\frac{1}{4}$	Hard fire. Rough surface. Buff wash outside. Dark core, pink edges. Contains crushed limestone.
II	10×9	$3\frac{3}{4}×3\frac{1}{2}$	5	$\frac{3}{16}$	Hard fire. Rough surface. Buff wash outside. Inner half red, outer half brown. Contains fine crushed limestone. Same pot as Nos. VI, VII, VIII and XVIII.
III	15×10·6	5×4	6	$\frac{1}{4}$	Medium fire. Rough surface partially burnished. Buff wash outside, pink inside. Dark brown core, red edges. Contains crushed limestone.
IV	13×8	5×3	4	$\frac{1}{8}$	Soft fire. Rough surface. Red wash outside. Brown core, red edges. Contains much crushed limestone.
V	10·5×7	$4\frac{1}{4}×2\frac{3}{4}$	5	$\frac{3}{16}$	Soft fire. Rough surface. Red wash outside. Brown core, red edges. Contains much crushed limestone.
VI	16×10·7	$6\frac{1}{4}×4$	6	$\frac{1}{4}$	Hard fire. Rough surface. Buff wash outside. Inner half red, outer half brown. Contains fine crushed limestone. Same pot as Nos. II, VII, VIII and XVIII.
VII	12·8×13·5	5×3	4	$\frac{1}{8}$	Medium fire. Rough burnish outside. Inner half dark grey, outer half red. Contains fine crushed limestone. Near base of pot. Same pot as Nos. II, VI, VIII and XVIII.
VIII	9·8×6·9	4×2	3–5	$\frac{1}{8}$–$\frac{1}{4}$	Hard fire. Pink wash changing to white in corner. Red through except in corner, where it is inner half grey, outer half red. Contains fine crushed limestone. Same pot as Nos. II, VI, VII and XVIII.
IX	8·8×5·7	3×2	7	$\frac{1}{4}$	Hard fire. Brownish wash outside. Black core, dark brown edges. Contains crushed limestone.
X	14·8×14	$5\frac{7}{8}×5\frac{1}{2}$	6	$\frac{1}{4}$	Hard fire. Smooth surface outside, rough inside. Buff wash outside. Black core, red edges. Contains much crushed limestone.
XI	12·5×8·5	$4\frac{3}{4}×3\frac{1}{4}$	4	$\frac{3}{16}$	Medium fire. Buff wash outside. Brown core, pink at outer edge. Contains some crushed limestone.
XII	8·3×8·2	3×3	6	$\frac{1}{4}$	Soft fire. Pink slip outside. Black core, red edges.
XIII	18×12·7	7×5	6	$\frac{1}{4}$	Hard fire. Rough surface. Buff wash outside. Outer half red. Inner half brown. Has contained crushed limestone: inner surface pelted.
XIV	18·5×14·2	7×6	5	$\frac{3}{16}$	Medium fire. Brown wash outside. Black core, red edges. Contains little crushed limestone.
XV	20×17·3	$8×6\frac{3}{4}$	5	$\frac{1}{4}$	Hard fire. Smoothed surface. Buff wash outside. Brown core.
XVI	3·4×3·4	1×1	4	$\frac{1}{8}$	Hard fire. Buff wash outside. Black core, red edges. Contains crushed limestone.
XVII	3·7×3	$1\frac{1}{2}×1\frac{1}{4}$	5	$\frac{3}{16}$	Hard fire. Red wash outside. Black core, red edges. Contains crushed limestone.
XVIII	16·5×10·5	$6\frac{1}{2}×4\frac{1}{2}$	4	$\frac{1}{8}$	As Nos. II, VI, VII and VIII.

The potsherds bearing Letters III, IV and VI are the property of the Government of Palestine.
The potsherds bearing Letters I, II, V, VII to XVIII are the property of the Wellcome Archaeological Research Expedition to the Near East.

NOTES ON THE CHART OF ALPHABETS

THE comparative table of alphabets, *facing page* 220, was compiled as follows:

The Lachish Letters from the originals.

The Samaria ostraca from *Harvard Excavations at Samaria*, vol. II, *page* 55 (excepting the ס, פ, and the second ק which are taken from the hand copies in vol. I, *pages* 239–243).

The Ophel ostracon from a photograph kindly supplied by the Department of Antiquities, Jerusalem.

The Siloam inscription from a cast.

The Gezer calendar from a cast.

The Moabite Stone from a cast.

The Tell ed Duweir scarab and seal impressions from the originals.

The Maccabean and Samaritan from the *Encyclopaedia Judaica*, vol. II, *page* 407.

The writing of the Lachish Letters appears to have been done with a reed or wood pen, the nib part being broad but not thick; *see* ר II, 5, reverse of III, etc. The evidence is insufficient to show whether the nib was split, but from the general appearance of the writing it does not appear to have been. Letters I to VI give good examples of all letters of the alphabet, from which the other Letters VII to XVIII do not vary in any marked degree.

א The *aleph* maintains the same form throughout.

ב The *beth* with the angular tail in I is not repeated in any of the other letters, but seems to be the common form in the Samaria ostraca, and is usual in all cut inscriptions. The other example given from I is curiously malformed and is not repeated. The most usual form is the first example in III, but the loop is not always joined to the head of the downstroke; this form occurs in the Ophel ostracon.

ג The *gimel* shares with the *tsade* the honour of being the rarest letter.

ד *Daleth* is fairly consistent in form, sometimes with and sometimes without a top tail. Some examples might be mistaken for an *'ayin* (III, ex. 1) or a *resh* (VI, ex. 2), but generally the downstroke is too definite for confusion with *'ayin* and too short for *resh*. The cut form becomes more triangular.

ה *Hē* has no variations, except in Letter VI, lines 5 and 8, where it may be smeared.

ו *Waw* also does not vary much except in its cut forms: the Siloam inscription has the same form as our letters, whereas the Gezer calendar and Moabite Stone examples are forked only at the top.

ז *Zayin* presents several variations: III and VI have the central stroke: in III and V the bottom line is straight, whereas both lines in I and II curve back at the ends. In this they resemble the Samaria characters, while the Ophel example most closely resembles IV. The curve back at the ends of the horizontal strokes in the Siloam example shows that a written script was being copied, as these curves are natural to quick handwriting but would not normally occur in carving. (*See also* the tail of the *waw* and the curve back at the end of the *tsade* in this inscription.)

ח *Ḥeth* is consistent throughout, the apparent two strokes of VI, ex. 2 being due to the merging of the second and third strokes.

185

ט _Ṭeth_ occurs here for the first time in its written form; there having been previously only two specimens on the Moabite stone (not visible on the cast) and a probable example on the Gezer calendar, in which the central cross is upright and not on its side as in the letters.

י _Yodh_ presents two variations, with and without a tail. The former type occurs in I and VIII, and in the Samaria ostraca: the latter in all other letters and in the Ophel ostracon. The tailed variety is common in all cut inscriptions.

כ _Kaph_ has many varieties in the letters, all of them different from the examples from Samaria, Siloam and the Moabite Stone. The commonest form seems to consist of a curved downstroke to which a slanting stroke is joined either at or just below the head; this in turn has a short vertical stroke attached to the middle of it. Sometimes this vertical stroke connects the slanting with the downstroke.

ל _Lamed_ is consistent throughout, and has an angular base, in contradistinction to the round base of the Samaria ostraca. The Gezer example also has an angular base. Can we see in this a distinction between northern and southern conventions of writing?

מ _Mem_ is sometimes angular and sometimes curved, but appears to be always made in the same way, _i.e._ two small ticks, the second of which is prolonged into the downstroke. The same form occurs both in Samaria and Ophel, but it is very different in the cut inscriptions, of which the Gezer form seems to be the most archaic.

נ _Nun_ is written either with or without a top tick: the latter form is usually curved but occasionally angular. The Ophel example has no tick, but it is present in the Samaria ostraca and in the cut inscriptions.

ס _Samek_ shows well the return stroke at the end of the horizontal lines, that of the lowest line being extended to join the vertical stroke. The return strokes are omitted in the cut examples, where the otherwise superfluous stroke branching from the upright may be intended to represent this.

ע, פ _ʿAyin_ is consistent in every case, as is the _fē_, except for the Gezer calendar, where the _fē_ is almost vertical.

צ _Tsade_ shows no variations except in the Moabite Stone, where the form is nearer to that of the later Aramaic.

ק _Qoph_ shows two main variations which occur both in the Samaria and Ophel ostraca. The cut forms differ from either of these.

ר _Resh_ has only one variation, in II, which is not repeated in any other examples.

ש, ת _Shin_ and _taw_ are both consistent throughout, except the Gezer _taw_, which is more upright than other examples, again suggesting the archaic script, and the _taw_ in Letter I, where the thin cross strokes seem to have been made independently.

Variations in the form of a sign can occur within the same letter, such as _kaph_ in IV, _nun_ in III, etc., so that difference in form does not necessarily mean difference in date. The Ophel ostracon most closely resembles the Lachish Letters in the forms of the signs, particularly the _yodh_. (This is only visible in the photograph kindly supplied by the Department of Antiquities, not in the published photographs or in the hand copies.)

In making the facsimile copies of these letters I adopted the system of placing a piece of transparent celluloid, ruled in $\frac{1}{8}$ in. numbered squares, over a natural size photograph of the letter, and transferring from it to tracing linen placed over paper ruled and similarly numbered in $\frac{1}{4}$ in.

squares, thus effecting a twice natural size enlargement. These drawings have been reduced again to natural size for publication. Comparison with the original document was also made at the same time. It will be noticed that in the case of Letter V, lines 5, 8, 10, and Letter VI, line 10, some of the signs in the drawing do not agree with Prof. Torczyner's transliteration. These signs are admittedly rather vague on the originals, and scarcely appear at all in the photograph, but after very careful study of both, I have reproduced what I consider I can see, though Prof. Torczyner reads the traces differently. For these and any other variations and inaccuracies in the drawings I must take the blame, and while it may seem strange to have two different readings in the same book, I console myself with the thought that there must be at least ten other possible combinations of the same faint signs. No doubt they will eventually all see the light of day.

In other cases there were traces of signs which Prof. Torczyner could reconstruct with certainty: this has been done in open outline. The copies have been made as accurately as hand and eye permit, but neither is infallible. No doubt there are many with better claims to the title הפקח (the open-eyed) than I have, and we look to them to provide us with fresh food for thought.

L. H.

REPORT ON THE LACHISH LETTERS WITH
REMARKS UPON THE USE OF IRON
INKS IN ANTIQUITY

CONCERNING my work in connexion with the writing upon the Lachish sherds I have made two series of experiments: one to determine the nature of the ink and the other for the purpose of intensifying the inscriptions on the unreadable sherds. These are given in greater detail on *pages* 194–197. At present I am engaged in an examination of early inscriptions, primarily those of the British Museum, for the purpose of correlating materials with period.

A survey of the literature indicated that the inks of antiquity were basically carbon, quotations from Dioscorides, Vitruvius and Pliny being usually given in support of this view.

The chemical work is not very extensive. Blagden [1] in 1787 found the ink on vellum documents of the ninth to fifteenth centuries to be iron free of carbon, and Wiesner [2] in 1887 showed both carbon and iron inks on paper of the ninth to thirteenth centuries from the Fayum. Mitchell [3], writing more recently on the ageing of inks, states that "the writing of the Greeks and Romans . . . was a mixture of fine lamp black or other form of carbon with a dilute solution of gum or glue. It is not possible to state the exact period when carbon inks of this type were replaced by iron-gall inks. The earliest reference made to the latter by the monk Theophilus is in an encyclopædia of Christian art of the eleventh century." Lucas, in a recent chemical examination of early inks [4], obtained carbon without iron for the earlier writing. The later documents, ranging to the twelfth century A.D. "in all instances . . . gave the reactions for iron. . . . If the date of the earliest specimen tested, which is given as the seventh or eighth century A.D., be accepted, then iron ink was known and used at that time, which is several centuries earlier than is generally supposed." Mitchell, in the discussion that followed, stated "that the iron was probably originally in combination with tannin, and the examples to which Mr. Lucas had referred were, probably, the first instances of the use of an iron tannin ink". Mitchell [5] a few years later in his book on inks again referred to this example as "the earliest known instance of the occurrence of an iron ink".

Thorpe [6] says: "Iron-gall inks have been known since the eleventh century", and most other references, including the *Encyclopaedia Britannica*, agree generally with these statements. Some contrary evidence comes from Gardthausen [17], who writes that about the fifth century A.D. a brownish metallic ink came into use, and that oak galls were selected on account of their iron content! Another doubtful reference [21] states that the earliest accounts of the use of galls for the preparation of iron inks come from the ancient Egyptians. Of more importance is a section in the paper by Davy in 1821 [22], later confirmed by Graux [23], in which he writes: "the earliest MSS probably in existence on parchment are those codices . . . of Cicero . . . (of) the 2nd or 3rd century. . . . The vegetable matter which rendered the oxide of iron black is entirely destroyed, but the peroxide of iron remains; Monsignore Mai uses a solution of galls for reviving the blackness." However, in view of the present consensus of opinion that iron inks displaced carbon inks some time during the Middle Ages, it was presumed that the ink on the Lachish Letters would almost certainly be carbon.

For the chemical examination, using the Letter XVIII which had been returned from earlier experiments, spot tests were first used. Eventually a microscope technique was devised which permitted tests on portions of material a few hundredths of a millimetre in size. However small the fragment detached from the surface, it was always composed almost entirely of siliceous or earthy matter, the ink, even under the microscope, appearing at best as a slight stain.

The possible components of this ink included carbon, ferric iron, sepia and the various black pigments of the Egyptians; bitumen was excluded by the insolubility of the writing in organic solvents. These substances are not essentially clear cut in properties and appearance, but can exist in various shades of brown to black, and in varying states of inertness. In this connexion must be considered the problem of the colour of carbon.

Underwood [7] had doubted the assertion that certain early inks of brownish tinge were carbon, because carbon was black and supposedly unchangeable. Lucas dealt with this point at some length [4], after finding that certain Roman papyri, with ink ranging from black to brown, gave no reaction with various reagents. Of these inscriptions, presumably pre-iron in date, and carbon by virtue of chemical inertness, he asserts that, as "... in a few instances the ink has been tested and proved not to be an iron compound, it must be accepted that what has been originally a black ink of the carbon type does sometimes become brown". This is because "the ink has contained very little free carbon in the first place, but has contained compounds...which have turned brown . . . (and that these have) masked any small amount of carbon present. In some cases the carbon of the ink may have been rubbed off the paper, leaving a brown stain due to a small proportion of some ingredient other than carbon that was present." Thus it is suggested that when carbon, as indicated by the chemical evidence, is brown, it is not carbon but various impurities. Or if an inert brown stain is free of carbon, it must have been originally a black ink of the carbon type. Yet there still remains a possibility of a brown carbon, for colloidal forms are sometimes brown, and certain soots reported as carbon, for example the water colour "bistre", are brown. Therefore a brownish tint of the writing on the Lachish Letters would not definitely exclude a purely carbon ink.

At first the results of the tests tallied with those in a report on the Letter XVIII received previously,[1] and also with those obtained by Lucas [4] when working on ostraca; heat destroyed the stain, and reagents of all kinds had little apparent effect, which is what would be expected for carbon. Under the microscope it was observed, however, that the stain at high temperatures did not burn away; but it formed a colourless glass with the surrounding material, thus presenting the possibility of a metallic ink. The negative chemical results were eventually found to be due to the inertness of the material, and partly to the swamping by the reagent of the small amount of

---

[1] These tests were reported as follows:—

(1) Heating in a Bunsen flame to about 600° C. caused the writing to disappear, indicating carbon.

(2) Ammonium sulphide, tannic acid, and thiocyanate all had no effect, indicating absence of iron.

(3) The writing was insoluble in chloroform, indicating that it is not uncarbonised bitumen.

(4) No improvement of legibility on dusting with lamp-black.

colouring produced. The tests, under the microscope, were made effective by applying the reagents in vapour form, the thiocyanate test for iron being then sufficiently delicate.

The problem was further complicated by the abundant presence of iron both in the body of the pot and over the whole surface of the sherd, the stain being markedly visible on the surface of the buff slip. It was noticed, however, that the reaction for iron responded roughly in proportion to the original intensity of the stain. For the writing this gave an intensity several times that for the remainder of the surface. Now following some of the tests, a small quantity of microscopic particles had been observed among the disintegrated siliceous residues, and as these had survived the most drastic reagents, they were presumed to be carbon. An inspection of the Letter XVIII under the microscope showed the writing for the most part as a brownish stain almost transparent in parts. Thus the writing on this letter, although containing carbon, is primarily an iron stain. Some imitation sherds, prepared with various carbon inks for the experiments on intensification, were in striking contrast with this, for, viewed under the microscope, the remaining traces of the pigment stood out as a jet-black material on the pottery surface. These were very similar in appearance to the ostraca viewed later in the British Museum, which are, without doubt, of carbon ink.

An inspection of the other Lachish Letters showed Letter II as in the case of XVIII to be primarily a brownish stain. The Letters I, III, VI and VIII had the appearance of a mixture of iron and carbon, while the more eroded Letters IV, V, IX, XI, XVI and XVII were mainly carbon. In general, the better preserved the characters, the browner was the stain of the ink mark. Thus the Lachish Letters differ considerably from all other ostraca examined in London.

It is possible, but unlikely, that the iron has been deposited preferentially where once was a simple carbon ink. It is more reasonable to suppose that this iron was an original constituent of the ink.

Now the Middle Ages were essentially uninventive, and the primary struggle was to conserve the remnants of classical culture. No clear case of an important invention during the dark ages comes to mind, and it is, therefore, unlikely that iron inks were the product of the medieval world. The classical world, though receptive of new ideas, was also uninventive; it had little need to be inventive, for it was perpetually busy importing new ways and methods, as its realm spread outwards. If the use of iron ink was an importation by the classical world, then the ink of the Lachish Letters need not be regarded as a solitary and exceptional case. In that event, this medium would have persisted throughout the medieval and classical periods, and we would look to the East, whence writing came in the first place, for its origin.

With this possibility in mind it seemed worth while to search the literature a stage further. The lack of adhesion of carbon ink to skins would have induced the people who used them to search for a more permanent ink, and it is among such people that iron is likely to have come into use. Now there is considerable evidence of the very early use of skins as material for writing. "In Egypt there is mention of documents written on skins in the time of the Fourth Dynasty" [8] and we have the mathematical manuscript in the British Museum, assigned to the seventeenth century B.C., as an example. "Diodorus Siculus says (Lib. ii) that the ancient Persians wrote their records on skins" [9], and Kenyon [10], following Astle, states "that the Ionians . . . had formerly used skins as writing material", as indicated by Herodotus v. 58. "The usual word for a written document . . . in the (Hebrew) Bible . . . designates the skin

190

of an animal,[1] the writing material anciently employed by the Orientals, and not papyrus" [11]. The passage in Jeremiah XXXVI, 23, suggests the use of skins, and "the Talmudists were no doubt only confirming the existing and traditional practice" in requiring all copies of the Law to be written on skins [8].

The ancient world was well acquainted with oak-galls. "Theophrastus (372–286 B.C.) referred to the gall-nuts as an article of trade and to the superior quality of those from Syria" [12], and Pliny [13] gave details of their use in medicine and in tanning. Copperas or ferrous sulphate was also well known, although, no doubt, in an impure condition, copper sulphate being a probable contamination. The chemical evidence indicates that the "atramentum sutorium" and one of the varieties of "alumen" described by Pliny were both ferrous sulphate.

Not only were these substances familiar to antiquity, but they were known to produce a black coloration, and were utilized for that purpose. The name "atramentum sutorium" for copperas indicates its use on leather [14], where it would react with the tan. The statement [15] that Pliny "was acquainted with the blackening of paper containing green vitriol by immersion in an infusion of nut-galls" may refer to the test for adulteration of verdigris by copperas, in which papyrus previously steeped in extract of gall-nuts became black. Pliny was also aware that copperas was turned black by pomegranate juice or by an extract of nut-galls [16].

Earlier indications of this knowledge come, as was expected, from the Eastern Mediterranean; and here the substances are referred to specifically as materials for writing fluids. As stated by Gardthausen [17], Philo of Byzantium in the second century B.C. knew of an ink of galls developed by a metallic solution, for sending secret messages. Another reference to a mineral ink, used in early Palestine, states [11] that "as the ancient world had mixed copper sulphate (? presumably copperas) with the ink of gall-nuts, Rabbi Meir (A.D. 100 approximately) . . . did the same with *deyo*, the national ink of the Jews", to make the writing more permanent. Smith [18] mentions that for ritual purposes "the ink, *deyo* . . . was to be of lamp-black dissolved in gall juice, though sometimes a mixture of gall juice and vitriol was allowable". The Mishnah, although completed in the second century A.D., was a compilation of already ancient tradition. There copperas is repeatedly mentioned as a writing material [19]; for example, "it may be written with anything— ink, caustic, red dye, gum, copperas, or with whatsoever is lasting, but it may not be written with liquids or fruit juice or with whatsoever is not lasting" and also ". . . he may not write with gum or copperas or aught that leaves a lasting trace, but only with (carbon) ink . . . (which) can be blotted out".

It might be mentioned here that the ink (*deyo*) used for ritual purposes was a carbon ink, for "only black, effaceable ink, which was renewed when necessary, might be used for Biblical works" [11]; a precaution presumably to prevent improperly erased errors from being confused with a worn-down text. An example of this usage is the ninth century Hebrew Pentateuch (B.M. Oriental MS. 4445) in which those parts of the dead black writing which have flaked off have left the vellum clean and uninjured.

---

[1] This, however, has been recognized as incorrect, since this Hebrew word (סָפַר) is no original Hebrew derivation of the verb סֵפֶר which (later!) also means "to shave off," but a loanword from *Accadian* (*i.e.* Babylonian) *šipru* "message, letter".—[TORCZYNER.]

As this evidence clearly pointed to the use of iron inks in antiquity, an examination was made of the material available in the British Museum. An inspection of the earliest manuscripts gave support to this view. Most of the writing on vellum of the early Christian period was a red-brown tint, and the vellum in many cases was heavily corroded by the ink. Under the microscope the lettering was often of a transparent gelatinous appearance, varying from yellow through a reddish hue to a very dark rust verging on black. The more transparent examples were completely free from particles of pigment so that the absence of carbon in such cases is evident. The earliest of these was the second-century leaf from a codex, concerning which Kenyon [8] says, "The earliest extant examples (of vellum) are probably two leaves, one in the British Museum containing part of Demosthenes' *De Falsa Legatione* (B.M. Additional MS. 34473 i) . . .". A minute fragment of this taken from a broken edge of a paragraphing line, after subdivision into portions of about 0·02 millimetre in size, was tested under the microscope. This gave quite emphatically, as was expected, the reaction for iron, the ink being entirely soluble and leaving no residue of carbon. Of the third- and fourth-century vellum documents or fragments, only three out of twelve were carbon. Among the nine of iron type is the Codex Sinaiticus, which affords a good example of this gelatinous brown ink.

The few pre-Christian vellum or skin documents are in carbon, two of the first century B.C. (B.M. Additional MS. 38895 A and B) and the Egyptian mathematical sheet of the seventeenth century B.C.

All the papyri from Egypt—including the Hieroglyphic, and those of the Ptolemaic and Roman periods—had the appearance of carbon. It is to be remarked, however, that in many of these the gum has turned a reddish yellow, which gives at first sight the impression of a ferric iron constituent of the carbon ink. Of 49 early Byzantine papyri only one had the appearance of iron, but of 126 late Byzantine papyri, 72 were of the carbon type, 26 of a brownish iron type, and the remainder doubtful. Of the ostraca, mostly late Coptic, all were of the black carbon type. Specimens of these have yet to be tested chemically.

It is thus quite clear that iron inks were in use in antiquity. Carbon inks were used with papyri until a comparatively late period, whereas iron was used on all but few of the earliest vellum manuscripts. The question remains as to the original nature of these yellow-brown iron inks. The view that the early iron-gall inks gave a permanently black or nearly black writing is not quite in accordance with the chemical evidence. Mitchell [5] mentions that ink prepared from "iron green tannins" after six months' exposure left only "rust-like" stains. Some recent chemical work, by Zetzsche and others [20], on the ageing of ink salts, showed parallel series of changes for the various representative preparations tried. From these experiments it is reported that ". . . neutralization of the acid first occurs (and) blue-violet insoluble primary ink salts are formed. By the further action . . . (these) are oxidized, . . . brown, secondary ink salts resulting. . . . The black shade of written characters (*i.e.* after the ink has been exposed for a week or so) is due to a mixture of primary and secondary salts, and . . . possibly ferric hydroxide. After 20–30 years no primary ink salts remain. The brown secondary salts constitute the written characters. After 100 years or more, ferric oxide and hydroxide alone will remain." That some early iron-gall inks are still well preserved may be due occasionally to an admixture of carbon as supposed by Underwood [7], but is more likely due to the presence of inhibitors or protectors; gum, for example, would exclude the atmosphere. However, in the case of the classical vellum manuscripts, the writing is iron in its final rust-brown state of oxidation, forming an almost transparent gel with the substance of the vellum. It can hardly be doubted that these early writers insisted upon an ink of good appearance when fresh, and carbon being absent, the iron must have been in combination with a gall or tannin extract. It thus appears that the correct knowledge possessed by Davy more than a century ago has since given place to the present erroneous view.

In conclusion, it may be affirmed that the ancient world was very well acquainted with iron inks and with the various combinations that could be made with carbon, copperas, oak galls, and gum; and it was with such an iron and carbon mixture that the Lachish Letters were written.

Special thanks are due to Mr. H. Idris Bell, Keeper, and Mr. T. C. Skeat, Assistant Keeper of the Department of Manuscripts, British Museum, London.

A. L.

TESTS UPON THE INK OF THE LETTERS

THE primary facts of the chemical examination have already been stated. A delicate micro-technique later replaced the rougher preliminary tests. These were performed on the Letter XVIII and are given here below.

1. The action of heat was determined using a miniature flame, approximately one millimetre in length. This caused at first a darkening of the ink followed by blackening of the buff surface slip, then the disappearance of the ink, and finally the removal of the surface blackening, during which the slip swelled unevenly. This test was taken to indicate that the ink was carbon or sepia and not metallic in nature.

2. A small borax bead gave a very faint yellow coloration, indicating a possibility of iron.

3. The flame coloration test showed the presence of sodium and calcium.

4. A drop of dilute sulphuric acid had little action on the writing, but a slight effervescence indicated carbonates.

5. No marked action on the ink was observed on applying drops of the following concentrated reagents: sulphuric acid, nitric acid, sodium hydroxide, ammonium hydroxide and solution of iodine.

6. Solutions of potassium thiocyanate, sodium hypochlorite, potassium dichromate, hydrogen peroxide and various other reagents were without clearly defined effect.

These tests indicated that the characters were of an inert material but destructible by heat. The calcium, sodium, and carbonate present would constitute together with chloride, sulphate, and magnesium, the usual incrustation of long buried pottery. Therefore, in accordance with the general view, the ink was presumed to be of the carbon type.

The micro-technique developed consisted in observing the reaction of reagents on particles of the material under a magnification ranging from 50 to 250 fold. The smallest possible portion was detached from the surface of the sherd by means of a sharp glass edge. A fragment of this, about 0·01 to 0·05 millimetre in size was placed on a cover-slip, and viewed preferably under direct illumination. The addition of the reagent provided a difficulty, for the smallest applicable drop would sweep the particle out of the field of view. Also, its comparatively enormous bulk would swamp any coloration produced, and very slight colorations became invisible under the microscope. This difficulty was overcome eventually by the use of reagents in vapour form, and where this was not possible, by the following device. The particle was placed at the end of a deep groove cut in a glass plate and then moved into the field of view; a drop of the reagent was then added near the other end of the cut which acted as a channel for a small amount of the reagent. The reaction could then be observed between comparatively equivalent quantities, without the usual troublesome and often ineffective manipulation.

Using the first method, the particle was exposed to the vapour from a glass rod moistened with a solution of potassium thiocyanate and hydrochloric acid. Where iron was present, this soon gave to the small quantity of liquid condensing round the particle a deep ruby coloration; and the depth and amount of the coloration gave an indication of the quantity of iron. The second method was used for the ferrocyanide test and for the application of other reagents.

194

With this technique, it was found that the material under examination behaved unevenly. A test applied to successive fragments would give varying responses, and different parts of apparently similar material would react differently. For example, dilute hydrochloric acid would dissolve certain points of the brown stain, while neighbouring parts would be quite inert. This may be due in part to protection of the stain within fissures of the siliceous material, but it can also be due to varying degrees of inertness of the ferric iron. For freshly formed ferric hydroxide, such as results from the decomposition of iron compounds, is usually active and soluble, but becomes progressively inert with time, the final product being a comparatively insoluble form of ferric oxide. This general inertness of the iron may account for the earlier negative results.

A large number of experiments were performed and a summary of these follows below:—

EXPERIMENTS PERFORMED UPON FRAGMENTS FROM THE SURFACE OF THE SHERD WITH THE AID OF THE MICROSCOPE

1. As previously mentioned, some of the browner points of the stain commenced to shrink at a high temperature, and at a dull red heat the brown coloration was generally discharged, these more fusible points becoming sharply defined colourless glass spheres. Hence the decolorization is not necessarily a combustion as with carbon, or a volatilization as with sepia, and the simultaneous fusion permits the possible inference of a metallic ink.

2. Dilute hydrochloric acid had a limited solvent action on the stain, the resulting pale yellow solution reacting with thiocyanate or ferrocyanide to show the presence of iron. This action could also be obtained for most parts of the sherd surface, but was always more marked for the material of the stain.

3. A dilute solution of acid thiocyanate, in addition to the above reaction, would often convert the insoluble stain from brown to red, indicating that this also was iron.

4. Sulphuric and nitric acids both dilute and concentrated and also concentrated hydrochloric acid, had only a slight action.

5. Caustic soda and ammonia both weak and strong had little visible action.

6. Many other reagents were tried with negative or doubtful results.

The acids always decomposed the carbonate present with a brisk initial effervescence, and then followed a slower disintegration of the fragment. In the resultant whitish siliceous residue were observed the black carbon particles standing out clearly.

An inspection of the letters under the microscope showed that the writing varied from a brownish stain in the best preserved specimens to a carbon residue in the more eroded examples. The intensity of the brown stain corresponded approximately with the response of the chemical test for iron.

The writing is therefore a mixed iron and carbon ink, the latter constituent being the more permanent.

A. L.

EXPERIMENTS FOR INTENSIFYING THE WRITING

THE experiments were devised on the assumption that any remaining trace of the inscription upon the most eroded sherds would be in carbon. This view is in accordance with the results of the examination of the letters, the iron being the more perishable constituent. The intensification of any remaining trace of the latter in any event would be rendered impossible by the general abundance of iron on the pottery surface.

The experiments were performed partly on Letter XVIII and partly on imitation ostraca. These were prepared on pieces of pottery contemporary with, and found in the vicinity of the letters. The inks: (i) a lamp-black in a solution of gum acacia; (ii) a Chinese ink tablet; (iii) a lamp-black water-colour, after drying on the pottery, were washed off, leaving, however, a faint trace of the lettering.

The experiments are described below:—

1. Several of the original letters were inspected under various colour filters, using the mercury arc and sunlight as sources, and also in the light of a monochromatic illuminator, but no certain improvement was observed.

2. After preliminary tests to ensure the inertness of the writing to various solvents, several specimens were completely immersed, on the supposition that a liquid with refractive index approximately that of the sherd surface might reveal deep lying carbon. The liquids used included benzene, carbon tetrachloride, toluene, chloroform, ether, carbon disulphide, aniline, oil of cedar, Canada balsam in xylene, camphor in toluene and many mixtures of these. The effect of immersion in general was to produce an immediate darkening of the inscription followed by a slower darkening of the pottery background. The refractive index of the liquid appeared to be immaterial and the effect did not differ greatly with the liquid used; even ether vapour behaved in a similar fashion.

Photographs taken, using various colour filters, of the Letters IV and VI immersed in ether, gave no improvement, however.

The following more drastic experiments were performed on the imitation ostraca:

3. Specimens of these were exposed to the following vapours without visible result:

(*a*) Iodine vapour;
(*b*) Iodine vapour followed by carbon tetrachloride and also by camphor vapour;
(*c*) Iodine vapour followed by the application of starch solution;
(*d*) Dilute benzene vapour followed by iodine vapour;
(*e*) Turpentine followed by chlorine.

4. Imitation sherds were exposed to sublimation of iodine, anthracene and camphor, but no preferential deposition took place.

5. Adsorption of dyes from solution gave no visible improvement. Eosin and fluorescein were taken up by the carbon, and methylene blue unlike these acidic dyes was strongly adsorbed by the pottery.

6. Preferential catalysis of the hydrogen peroxide decomposition did not occur on the imitation sherds, the coating of fine bubbles forming evenly over the surface.

7. Deposition of silver from several solutions of ammoniacal silver nitrate with formalin took place evenly over the potsherd.

8. Various silver solutions in presence of zinc dust did not give a preferential local action on the carbon particles.

As the experiments were generally negative the question of applying these methods to the original letters did not arise.

[1] BLAGDEN, *Trans. Roy. Soc.* (1787), **77**, (2), 451
[2] WIESNER, *Mittheilungen aus der Sammlung der Papyrus Erzherzog Rainer* (1887), **2–3**, 239–240
[3] MITCHELL, *The Analyst* (1920), **45**, 248
[4] LUCAS, *The Analyst* (1922), **47**, 9–14
[5] MITCHELL AND HEPWORTH, *Inks* (Griffin, London), (1924), 10, 57
[6] THORPE, *Dictionary of Applied Chemistry*, **3**, 628
[7] UNDERWOOD, *J. Soc. Arts* (1857), 67
[8] KENYON, *Books and Readers in Greece and Rome* (1932), 42, 92
[9] ASTLE, *On the Origin and Progress of Writing* (1803), 203
[10] KENYON, *The Palaeography of Greek Papyri* (1899), 14
[11] *Jewish Encyclopaedia*, under Manuscript, Ink
[12] *Encyclopaedia Britannica*, ed. 14, under Galls
[13] *Pliny*, BOSTOCK AND RILEY (1855), **16**, 9, 10; **24**, 5; **36**, 32
[14] MELLOR, *Treatise on Inorganic Chemistry*, **14**, 242
[15] *Encyclopaedia Britannica*, ed. 11, under Ink
[16] *Pliny on Chemical Subjects*, BAILEY (1929), **1**, 206; (1932) **2**, 179
[17] GARDTHAUSEN, *Griechische Palaeographie*, **1**, 202–205
[18] SMITH, *Dictionary of the Bible*, 3576
[19] *The Mishnah*, Danby, (1933), Gitt. 2, 3; Sot. 2, 4
[20] ZETZSCHE, *J.S.C.I.* (1924), B 224
[21] WIESNER, *Die Rohstoffe des Pflanzenreichs*, **1**, 946
[22] DAVY, *Phil. Trans. Roy. Soc.* (1821), 205
[23] GRAUX, *Revue de philol.* (1880), 82–84

A. L.

THE PERSONAL NAMES MENTIONED IN THE LACHISH LETTERS

The name	Pronounced	Meaning	Occurs in Lachish Letters	Seal Inscriptions	THE BIBLE Before Jeremiah	In Jeremiah's time	After Jeremiah	Elephantine	New Babylonian records	Remarks
1. אחיהו	Ahiyahu	My brother is Yhwh	III, 17.	+	+	–	+	(אחיו)	+	f. of Hodawyahu
2. אלנתן	Elnatan	El (God) has given	III, 15; cf. XI, 3.	(אלנתן)	–	+	+	–	+	f. of Yikhbaryahu
3. אור[יה]	Uriyahu	My light is Yhwh	XVI, obv. 5.	?	+	+	+	+	+	The prophet
4.(?)[?] בניה[ו?]	Benayahu (?)	Yhwh builds	XVI, 4 (?).	+	+	+	–	+	+	?
5. גמריהו	Gemaryahu	Yhwh fulfills	I, 1.	–	–	+	–	+	–	s. of Ḥiṣṣilyahu
6. הודויהו	Hodawyahu	Acknowledge Yhwh	III, 17.	–	–	+	–	+	–	s. of Aḥiyahu
7. הושעיהו	Hosha'yahu	Yhwh helps	III, 1.	–	–	+	+	+	–	The writer of the letters, officer in Qiryat-Ye'arim
8. הצליהו	Ḥiṣṣilyahu	Yhwh saves	I, 1.	–	–	–	(–)	–	–	f. of Gemaryahu
9. חגב	Ḥagab	Locust	I, 3.	–	–	+	[+]	–	–	s. of Ya'zanyahu (a)
10. טבשלם	Ṭobshillem	Good he has repaid	(a) I, 2; (b) VII, [5-6]; XVIII, [1].	–	–	–	–	–	–	(a) f. of Ya'zanyahu (a); (b) a messenger
11. יאוש	Ya'ush	He is strong	II, 1; III, 2; VI, 1; XII, 1.	–	–	+	–	+	–	The receiver of the letters, Governor of Lachish
12. יאזניהו	Ya'zanyahu	Yhwh listens	(a) I, 2; (b) I, 3.	+	–	+	–	+	–	(a) s. of Ṭobshillem; (b) f. of Ḥagab
13. ידע	Yaddua'	(Yhwh is) the knowing one	III, 20.	–	+	–	+	–	–	f. of Shallum
14. יכבריה[?]	Yikhbaryahu[?]	Great is Yhwh	III, 15.	–	–	(אכבר)	–	–	–	s. of Elnatan, commander of the army
15. ירמיהו	Yirmeyahu	Yhwh shoots	I, 4; [XVII, 3].	+	+	+	+	–	–	f. of Mibṭaḥyahu
16. מבטחיהו	Mibṭaḥyahu	Trust in Yhwh	I, 4.	–	–	–	–	+	–	s. of Yirmeyahu
17. מתניהו	Mattanyahu	Gift of Yhwh	I, 5.	–	–	++	–	–	++	s. of Neriyahu
18. נדביהו	Nedabyahu	Generous is Yhwh	III, 19.	(נדביה)	–	–	–	–	++	grandson or grand-nephew of the king
19. נריהו	Neriyahu	My light is Yhwh	I, 5.	+	+	+	–	+	+	f. of Mattanyahu
20. סמכיהו	Semakhyahu	Yhwh supports	IV, 6; [V, 5; IX, 4]; XI, 5; XIII, 2.	–	+	–	–	+	–	high officer, inspecting the army
21. שלם	Shallum	(Yhwh is) Repaying	III, 20.	+	+	+	+	+	–	s. of Yaddua'
22. שמעיהו	Shema'yahu	Yhwh hears	IV, 6.	+	+	+	+	+	–	f. of Uriyahu?

198

GLOSSARY OF HEBREW WORDS

The Hebrew words are arranged in their usual order as given in Biblical dictionaries following the Massoretic spelling, while the actual spelling (but vocalised) in the Lachish Letters, when different, is given afterwards. Where the word referred to is not fully visible the reference number is put in angular brackets.

א

אָדוֹן   *lord*; c. suff. 1. p. sg. אֲדֹנִי *my lord* II, 1. 2. 4. [5/6?]; III, 3. [6.] 8. 21; IV, 1. 2. 4. 4/5. 7/8. 12; V, 1. 4. 7; VI, 1. 2. 3. [8.] 12; [VII, 1/2.]; VIII, 1; rev. 2; IX, 1/2; XII, 1. 6; XVII, 2; XVIII, 2; וַאדֹנִי *and my lord* [VI, 13]; לַאדֹנִי *to my lord* III, 2.

אָדָם   *human being, somebody* IV, 5/6.

אוֹ   *or, see* אַף.

אָז   *then*, in מֵאָז *since* III, 7.

אזן   Hif'il, *to listen*, in p. n. יאזניהו *Yhwh listens*.

אָח   *brother*, in אחיהו *my brother is Yhwh*.

אַיֵּה   *where?*, c. suff. 3. p. sg. masc. אַיֵּהוּ *where is he?* IV, 8.

אַיִן (שָׁם)   *(there) is not* IV, 5.

אִישׁ   *man*, III, 9/10; [VI, 14]; pl. c. suff. 3. p. sg. masc. וַאֲנָשָׁו *and his men* III, 17/18.

איש   *to be a man, to be strong*, in p. n. יאוש *He is strong*.

אֶל   *to* II, 1; III, 4. 6. 7. 20. 21; IV, 10; V, 4. 7; VI, 1; XI, 3 (?); c. suff. 1. p. sg. אֵלַי *to me* III, 11; IV, 4; c. suff. 3. p. pl. masc. אלהֹם *to them* VI, 9; *see* the notes to III, 10.

אֵל   *God*, in p. n. אלנתן *El (God) has given*.

אֱלֹהַּ   pl. אֱלֹהִים *God*; c. suff. 2. p. sg. masc. אֱלֹהֶיךָ *thy God* VI, 12/13.

אִם   *if, though* IV, 9 (כִּי אִם *for though*); (in a negative oath: Yhwh lives to punish) *if* III, 9. 11; [VI, 13].

אמר   *to say*; 3. p. sg. masc. perf. אָמַר *he has said* VI, 12; 3. p. sg. masc. imperf. יֹאמַר *he says* III, 8; inf. cstr. with ל: לֵאמֹר *saying* III, 14. 20/21; [VI, 4/5. 9]; c. suff. 1. p. sg. אָ[מְר]ִי *my saying* II, 5/6 (?).

אֶמֶשׁ   *yesterday* III, 6.

אַף   *even* (or אוֹ *or*) [III, 12].

אֶרֶץ   *country, land*, c. art. [הָאָ]רֶץ VI, 7.

ארר   *to curse* 3. p. sg. masc. imperf. יָאֹר *he should curse* V, 9/10.

אַשְׁפָּה   *quiver*, pl. אַשְׁפֹּת *quivers* XIII, 3.

אֲשֶׁר   *which* II, 6; III, 5. 11; IV, 2. 4. 11; [V, 8?]; IX, 7/8; XVIII, 1.

אֵת־, אֶת   nota accusativi II, 2. 4. 5; [III, 3]; IV, [1.] 12; V, [1.] 5; VI, [3.] 14; VII, [1.] 3. 6; VIII, 1; IX, 1. 3; XIII, 3; וְאֵת *and* III, 16; VI, 4; c. suff. 3. p. sg. masc. אֹתה *(him,) it* III, 12; XII, 4.

אֵת   *with*, with prep. מִן: מֵאֵת־ *from* III, 20.

אַתָּה   *thou* VI, 2.

ב

ב   *in, on*, cf. תסבה, תוך, יהוה, בוא.

בוא   *to come*, 3. p. sg. masc. imperf. יָבֹא *it comes, came* III, 11; inf. cstr. c. ב: [בְּבֹא?] *when comes* (?) XVIII, 1; c. ל: לָבֹא *to come* III, 15; Hif'il, 3. p. sg. masc. perf. הֵבָא *he had brought* III, 19.

בטח   *see* מבטח.

בַּיִת   *house, room*, in בֵּית הָרֶפֶד *sleeping-house, sleeping-room* IV, 5.

בקר=בכר   Pi'el, *to investigate* (?) 3. p. sg. masc. imperf., jussive: יְבַקֵּר *may he investigate* (?) II, 5.

בֵּן   *son*, st. cstr. בֶּן *son of* I, 1–5; III, 15. 17. 20; pl. st. cstr. בְּנֵי (?) *children* (but rather n. p. [בני]הו) XVI, 4.

בנה   *to build*, probably in n. p. [בני]הו *Yhwh builds* XVI, 4 (?).

בקר   Pi'el, *to look over*, to inspect; 3. p. sg. masc. perf. בִּקֵּר *he had inspected* IV, 9; see בכר.

ג

גַם   *also*; וְגַם *and also* III, 10.

גמר   *to fulfil*, in n. p. גמריהו *Yhwh fulfils*.

ד

דָּבָר   *word, thing, something* II, 6; XVI, rev. 4 (?), *see* דֶּבֶר; st. cstr. עַל דְּבַר *about* IV, 5; pl. st. cstr. דִּבְרֵי, *the words of* VI, 5.

דֶּבֶר (?)   *pestilence* (?) XVI, rev. 4, *see* דָּבָר.

דָּוֶה   *sick, faint* III, 7.

דֶּלֶת   (*door-board*, then): *sheet* (of papyrus), c. art. הַדֶּלֶת IV, 3.

ה

ה   def. article, *see* נביא, מלך, דלת, ארץ, אות, שר, רפד, פקח, ערב, עיר, ספר.

הֲ   interrogativum in הֲלֹא *not?* VI, 8.

היה (?)   *to be*; 3. p. sg. (pl.?), masc. perf. הָיָ[ה] (?) *he was* XVI, 2.

הִנֵּה   *behold*, in וְהִנֵּה *and behold* VI, 5.

ו

ו   *and, see* הנה, גם, את, אמר, אל, איש, אדון, עיר, עבד, ספר, נסה, מות, כי, ידע, טוב, חטא, ראה, עת, תוך, *and before proper names*; waw consecutivum in ויעלהו IV, 7; וידע IV, 10.

ז

זֶה   *this, here*, in עַתָּה זֶה *even now* VI, 2; c. praep. מִן: מִזֶּה *from here* III, 18; [VII, 6?]; XVIII, [2]; fem. כָּזֹאת in זאת *thus* VI, 10.

זכר   *to remember*, 3. p. sg. masc. זָכַר *he has remembered* II, 4; 2. p. sg. masc. [זכר]ת (?) VII, 3.

זרע   *seed, offspring* V, 10.

ח

חָגָב   *locust* in n. p. חגב.

חיה   *to live*, (חי יהוה written:) חיהוה *Yhwh lives* III, 9; XII 8; חי יהוה אלהיך *Yhwh thy god lives* VI, 12/13.

חמת?   XVI, 1.

חפר   *to dig*, 3. p. sg. masc. imperf. c. suff. יַחְפְּרֵהוּ (?) *he shall dig it out* XIII, 2.

ט

טוב   *good* in שְׁמֻעָת טֹב *tidings of good* IV, 2; [VII, 2?]; VIII, 2; וְטֹב *and good* V, 2, and in the n. p. טֹבְשַׁלֵם *Good he has repaid*; pl. m. טֹבִים VI, 5.

י

יָד   *hand*, plur.-dual יָדַיִם *hands* VI, 6; st. cstr. יְדֵי *the hands of* VI, 7.

ידה   Hif'il, *to acknowledge* in n. p. הודויהו Hodawyahu or Hoduyahu, *Acknowledge Yhwh!*

ידע   *to know*; 3. p. sg. masc. perf. with waw consecutivum וְיָדַע *then he would know* IV, 10; 1. p. sg. c. suff. or emphatically pronounced לֹא יְדַעְתָּה *or* לֹא יָדַעְתָּה *I do not know* (it) II, 6; III, 8; *see* the notes to this passage; Hif'il 3. p. sg. masc. c. suff. 2. p. sg. with nun energicum יֹדִעֶ[נְ]ךָ *may he let thee know* V, 7; IX, 7; יָדָע n. p. (God is) *the knowing one*.

יהוה   *Yhwh* II, 2. 5; III, 3; IV, 1; V, 1. 7/8; VI, 1; [VII, 1]; VIII, 1; IX, 1; XI, 4; XII, 1; XIV middle, and in חי יהוה (חיהוה) III, 9; VI, 12; XII, 3, *see* חי; In 15 or 16 proper names and IX, 1 יהו; with ב: V, 10 ביהו *in Yhwh*; *cf.* the notes on Letter I and Letter V.

(יום)   *see* to כיום.

ירד   *to go down* 3. p. sg. masc. perf. יָרַד *he went down* III, 14.

ישע   Hif'il, *to help, to deliver*, in n. p. הושעיהו *Yhwh helps*.

כ   *as, according to, cf.* זה, כל; *see* כי, .כיום

כבר   *to be great, to be mighty,* in n. p. יכבריהו *Great is Yhwh.*

כזב (?)   Pi'el, *to lie;* perhaps 1. p. sg. imperf. אֲכַזֵּב *I do* [*not*] *lie,* but more probably אכתב, *see* כתב VIII, rev. 1.

כִּי   *that* (stating) III, 6; IV, 10; (consecutive) II, 4; V, 4; VI, 3; [VII, 2]; IX, 3; with waw: וכ (=וְכִי) *and that* (stating) III, 8; וְכִי *and when* IV, 4.

כיום   *hardly* כ־יום *as to-day,* but enclitic particle: כִּם *thus, then* (*see* the notes on VI, 1–2), in עַתָּ·כִם *even now* II, 3 (twice); IV, 1; V, 2. 3; [VII, 2]; VIII, 2.

כָּל־, כָּל־   (st. cstr.) *all, every;* כָּל III, 11; כָּל מְאוּמָה *everything* III, 13; with כ *according to all* IV, 11; כְּכָל אֲשֶׁר *according to whatever* IV, 2, 3/4.

כֶּלֶב   *dog* II, 4; V, 4; VI, 3; VII, 2; [IX, 3]; cf. XI, 2.

כֵּן   *so, thus* IV, 3.

כתב   *to write,* 1. p. sg. perf. כָּתַבְתִּי *I have written* IV, 3; 1. p. sg. imperf. אֶכְתֹּב *I shall write* (?) VIII, rev. 1, *see* כזב; 2. p. sg. imperf. תִּכְתֹּב *thou wilt write* VI, 8/9.

ל

ל   *to, cf.* נגד, מלך, מה, לקח, בוא, אמר, אדון, שקט, רפה, קרא, עשה, עבד, ספר, נצח; c. suff. 1. p. sg. לִי *to me* III, 10; [VI, 15].

לא   *not* (before a verb) II, 6; III, 8; IV, 12; (before an adjective) לא טבם *ungood* VI, 6; with ה interrogativum הֲלֹא *not?* VI, 8.

לאך   *see* מלאכה.

לֵב   *heart* III, 6.

לכש   in n. l. לָכִשׁ, Lachish.

לקח   *to take,* 3. p. sg. masc. perf. c. suff. לְקָחֹה *he has taken him* IV, 6; infinitive cstr. with ל: לָקַחַת *to take* III, 18.

מְאוּמָה   *anything,* (after the denying oath-particle אִם) enforced by כל: כָּל מְאוּמָה *anything at all* III, 13.

מִבְטָח   *trust,* in n. p. מבטחיהו *Trust is Yhwh.*

מָה   *what?* V, 9; with ל: לָמָה *why?* [VI, 9]; c. suff. מַהוּ *what it is* IX, 8/9, perhaps also V, 8/9.

מִי   *who?* II, 3; V, 3; VI, 2; [VII, 2; IX, 2].

מְלָאכָה   (√לאך) *work* XIII, 1.

מֶלֶךְ   *king,* with def. article הַמֶּלֶךְ *the king* III, 19; VI, 4; לַמֶּלֶךְ *to the king* V, 10.

מִן   *from,* c. suff. 3. p. sg. masc. מֶנְהוּ III, 12; *see* זה, את, אז.

מַשְׂאֵת   *beacon, signal-station;* pl. משאת (read מַשֻּׂאֹת or מַשְּׂאֹת) IV, 10.

מתן   √נתן *gift* in n. p. מתניהו *Gift of Yhwh.*

נ

נא   *pray, do,* in קְרָא נָא *read, I pray thee* VI, 5.

נבא   *see* נביא.

נביא   (the) *inspired, prophet;* c. art. הַנָּבָא *the prophet* III, 20; [VI, 5]; [VIII, 3?]; XVI, 5.

נגד   Hif'il, *to show, to tell;* infinitive cstr. with ל: לְהַגִּד *to tell* III, 1/2; Hof'al, 3. p. sg. masc. perf. הֻגַּד *it has been told* III, 13.

נדב   *to be generous,* in n. p. נדביהו *Yhwh was* (*is*) *generous.*

נַחְנוּ   *we* IV, 10/11.

נֶכֶד   *grandson, grand-nephew* III, 19.

נסה   Pi'el, *to try,* 3. p. sg. masc. perf. נִסָּה *he has tried;* with waw: וְנִסָּה *and has tried* [VI, 14].

נֶצַח   with ל: לָנֶצַח *ever, absolutely* (for the past).

נצל   Hif'il *to save,* in n. p. הצליהו *Yhwh has saved, Yhwh saves.*

נֵר   *light,* in n. p. נריהו *My light is Yhwh.*

נתן   *to give,* part. praes. נֹתֵן *giving* IV, 11; and in n. p. אלנתן *El* (*God*) *has given, see* מתן.

סבב see תסבה.

סמך to support in n. p. סמכיהו Yhwh supports.

סֵפֶר letter [III, 4.] 9. 10. 11; VI, [3/4.] 11; XII, 2; [XVI, 4]; וְסֵפֶר and the letter (st. cstr. before a relative clause) III, 19; הַסֵּפֶר the letter VI, 14; VII, 6; XVIII, 1; לַסֵּפֶר to the letter III, 5; pl. הַסְּפָרִם the letters V, 6/7; IX, 6; st. cstr. סִפְרֵי the letters of [V, 5]; VI, 4; [IX, 4].

עֶבֶד slave, servant; c. suff. 2. p. sg. masc. עַבְדְּךָ, עַבְדֶּךָ (but cf. the notes on II, 3/4) thy slave II, 3/4; III, 1. 4. 5. 7. 7/8; IV, 3; V, 3. 4/5. 6; VI, 3. 13/14; VII, 2. 3. [5]; IX, [2/3.] 5; XII, 2. 7; XV, 3 (?); [XVI, 3 (?); XVII, 1]; XVIII, 1; misspelt עבך III, 21; וְעַבְדְּךָ and thy slave IV, 7; לְעַבְדְּךָ to thy slave V, 9; וּלְעַבְדְּךָ and to thy slave III, 13; c. suff. 3. p. sg. masc. עַבְדֹּה his slave II, 4/5.

עד until, till XVIII, 1.

עזק in n. l. עזקה, Azeqah.

עיר city, in וְהָעִיר and the city, i.e. Jerusalem VI, 7; הָעִירָה unto the city IV, 7; [VII, 7?]; XVIII, 2.

על upon IV, 3; עַל דְּבַר about IV, 5.

עלה Hif'il, to bring up, 3. p. sg. masc. imperf. c. waw consecutivum and c. suff. 3. p. sg. m. וַיַּעֲלֵהוּ and he brought him up IV, 6/7.

עֶרֶב evening, הָעֶרֶב the evening XVIII, 1, see VII, 4.

עשה to do, 3. p. sg. masc. perf. עָשָׂה he has done IV, 3; 2. p. pl. masc. imperf. תַּעֲשׂוּ you should do VI, 9; XII, 7; infinitive cstr. with ל: לַעֲשׂת to do XIII, 1. Nif'al 3. p. sg. masc. perf. נַעֲשָׂה it has been done, it happened [V, 8?]; IX, 7/8.

עַתָּה (ענה√) now עַתָּ II, 3; IV, 1; V, [2.] 3. [6]; [VI, 7?]; VII, 2; VIII, 2; עַתָּה VI, 2; וְעַתָּ and now [III, 4]; IV, 2; see כים, זה.

פִּקֵּחַ open-eyed, c. art. הַפִּקֵּחַ the open-eyed, the seer III, 4.

צָבָא army, c. art. הַצָּבָא (שַׂר) (the commander of) the army III, 14.

קום to rise, to stand up, imperative sg. masc. קֻם stand up! XIII, 1.

קרא to read, 3. p. sg. masc. perf. קָרָא he has read VI, 13; 1. p. sg. perf. קָרָאתִי I have read III, 12; XII, 4; imperative sg. masc. קְרָא read! VI, 5; infinitive cstr. קְרֹא to read III, 9; with ל: לִקְרֹא; with ל and c. suff. 3. p. sg. masc. [לְ]קְרֹאֹה to read it (?) [VI, 15].

ראה to see; 3. p. sg. masc. perf. with ו: 1. p. sg. רָאִתָ I have seen III, 12; [VI, 15]; 1. p. pl. imperf. נִרְאֶה we see IV, 12; Hif'il, to let see, 3. p. sg. masc. imperf. jussive יֵרַא or יַרְא may he let see VI, 1.

רזם to hint, to refer to (ל); 3. p. sg. masc. perf. רָזַם he has referred (to) III, 5.

רמה to shoot, in n. p. ירמיהו Yhwh shoots (?).

רֶפֶד (or רָפָד) in בֵּית הָרֶפֶד sleepinghouse, sleeping-room IV, 5.

רפה Pi'el, to loosen, to weaken (the hands), infinitive cstr. with ל: לְרַפֹּת to loosen.

שַׂר (high) officer, st. cstr. שַׂר הַצָּבָא the commander of the army III, 14; pl. c. art. [הַשָּׂרִ[ם the officers VI, 4.

שוב Hif'il, to return, to send back, 3. p. sg masc. perf. הֵשִׁב he has returned V, 6; IX, 5/6; see the notes on XVIII, 1.

שלח to send, 3. p. sg. masc. perf. שָׁלַח *he has sent* III, 1. 4. 6. 18; IV, 2. 4 (twice); VI, 3; IX, 3; XV, 3 (?); XVI, rev. 3; XVIII, 2; 3. p. sg. masc. perf. c. suff. שְׁלָחֹה *he has sent it* III, 21; XVI, 3; 2. p. sg. masc. perf. שָׁלַחְתָּ (?) V, 4; IX, 3; 3. p. sg. masc. imperf. יִשְׁלַח *he will send* IV, 8; XVIII, 1; infinitive cstr. c. suff. 2. p. sg. masc. שָׁלְחֲךָ *thy sending*.

שָׁלוֹם *peace, welfare*, spelt שלם II, 2/3; III, 3; [V, 2]; VI, 2; [VII, 2?]; IX, 2.

שלם Pi'el *to repay*, in n. p. טבשלם Ṭobshillem, *Good he has repaid*, and שלם Shallum (*God is*) *Repaying*.

שָׁם *there*, with the locative ending *ā(h)*: שָׁמָּה *thither* IV, 8.

שְׁמוּעָה *report, tiding*; pl. st. cstr. שִׁמְעֹת II, 2; III, 3; IV, 2; [V, 2; VII, 2]; VIII, 1/2; IX, 2.

שמע *to hear*, in n. p. שמעיהו Shemaʿyahu, *Yhwh has heard*; Hif'il, *to let hear*, 3. p. sg. masc. imperf. jussive יַשְׁמַע *may he let hear* II, 1; III, 2; IV, 1; V, 1; [VII, 1]; VIII, 1; IX, 1.

שמר *to watch* (*for* אל), *to look out* (*for*), part. praes. pl. masc. שֹׁמְרִם (נַחְנוּ) (*we are*) *watching* IV, 11; Nif'al, *to beware*, imperative sg. masc. הִשָּׁמֶר *beware!* III, 21.

שקט *to be quiet*, Hif'il השקט *to make rest* (or: *sink*), infinitive cstr. with ל: לְהַשְׁקֵט יְדֵי *to make rest* (*sink*) *the hands of* VI, 7.

ת

תוך *middle*, with ב and ו: [וּבְתֹכֹה] *and in it* [III, 5].

תְּסִבָּה *turning* (√סבב), c. suff. 3. p. sg. masc. and ב: בְּתִסְבָּתֹה *in his turning* IV, 9.

NAMES OF COUNTRIES AND CITIES

ירשלם (?) Jerusalem, hardly VI, 10.

לָכִיש spelt לכש Lachish IV, 10.

מִצְרַיִם with the locative ending *ā(h)*: מִצְרַיְמָה *unto Egypt* III, 16.

עֲזֵקָה Azeqah IV, 12/13.

SUMMARY

THE DATING OF THE OSTRACA

Archaeological evidence.—The eighteen inscribed potsherds, now known as the Lachish Letters, were found in the ruins of a small room under the eastern outer gate tower which formed part of the main defences of Tell ed Duweir. The deposit of ash and charcoal, in which they lay, is now shown to represent the latter of two destructions of the city, which are separated by only a few years. It is assumed that both are the results of the two Babylonian attacks against Judah.

Literary evidence.—From the personal names, both those listed on ostracon No. 1 and those occurring in the other ostraca, it is obvious that the documents belong to Jeremiah's age and to the last phase before the Babylonian invasion. Thus the dating between the two Babylonian attacks against Judah (597 and 588 B.C.) is suggested by literary evidence as well as by archaeological facts. A more exact dating seems indicated by Letter IV. The contents of this ostracon appear to show that it was written in the last weeks of Judah's struggle: ". . . we are watching for the signal-stations of Lachish according to all the signs which my lord gives, because we do not see (the signals of) Azeqah". Thus we are led to believe that it was no longer possible to maintain communication by fire-signals, and perhaps Azeqah was already in enemy hands.

However, examination of the other ostraca makes it probable that not all of them were written within this same short period of a few days or weeks. One group of potsherds—five of them distinguished by the fact that they are all written on fragments of the same pot (II, VI, VII, VIII and XVIII) and at least three others (III, XII and XVI) reflecting the same situation and dealing with the same subject (the tragic facts concerning the fate of "the prophet")—seem to be written a few years before 588–587 B.C. Other letters, while clearly belonging to the same correspondence, give no further indication of their date.

GRAPHIC AND LITERARY CHARACTER OF THE DOCUMENTS

The Lachish ostraca, with one exception, are original letters received in Lachish. Ostracon I, a list of names, may have accompanied a letter and thus formed a part of the information sent in it. Letters that required sealing may usually have been written on papyrus, though less private messages could be written on potsherds—a handy substitute when papyrus was scarce. As in other countries where potsherds were used for messages, the writer begins his letter on the outside of the sherd and continues only where necessary on the less smooth inner surface. The scribes of the Lachish Letters used a reed pen, and wrote in an iron-carbon ink, as the chemical analysis has shown.

The texts were written in pre-exilic Phoenician-Hebrew script, and all the letters of the alphabet are represented. The writing is careful and beautiful, and shows the characteristics of a literary tradition of centuries. The writer of the letters could not read (Letter III), and when he stated that "he has written upon the page" (Letter IV), the actual writing was not his. However, different handwritings show that several men were literate at Hoshaiah's small post, and the many "letters" mentioned within the Lachish ostraca as written, received, read, returned, or forwarded

204

by writer, addressee, or other persons show a regular coming and going of written messages. The literary tradition is apparent also in the method of address and greeting of the letters which follow conventional formulae throughout.

THE CORRESPONDENTS AND THEIR METHODS OF COMMUNICATION

The Lachish Letters were sent by one Hoshaiah (Hosha'yahu), stationed north of Lachish and Azeqah. They were addressed to his commanding officer "lord Jaush (Ya'ush)", a person unknown from other sources. According to the facts mentioned in the documents he was probably governor of Lachish and controlled the defences along the western frontier of the Judaean kingdom at the time of the Babylonian invasion. Jaush received the king's instructions concerning the smaller forts, and the officers in charge sent him their reports, while he acted as intermediary for them with the authorities in Jerusalem.

Hoshaiah's station was midway between Jerusalem and the fortresses of the western frontier, and was in touch with the spurs which commanded the view southwards over the line of forts in the foothills. Orders received by Hoshaiah from Jaush were usually relayed through Azeqah, eleven miles north-east of Lachish—a sister fort. Therefore his post was nearer to it than to Lachish. It is presumed that the king's letters from Jerusalem to Lachish and Jaush's replies passed through Hoshaiah's post and were forwarded by him through trusted messengers. According to Letter III, he had no authority to read these despatches.

Jaush's orders were normally sent by letter, and Letter XIII may be such an order; but in urgent cases they were transmitted by fire-signals relayed from hill to hill, and observed from a high point near the appropriate fort. The fact that letters sent to Hoshaiah for inspection had to be returned to Jaush indicates that these and other documents were kept at Lachish in archives.

MAIN THEME OF THE CORRESPONDENCE

The ostraca are all part of one dossier dealing with charges against Hoshaiah, which he denies in his letters. Thus, in Letter V, he refutes such an accusation (a) by invocation of God: "May Yhwh make you know what really happened"; and (b) by logical argumentation in question form: "What reason had I to curse the king?" It is interesting to see how similar twofold argumentation seems to be contracted into one sentence in Letter II: (a) May Yhwh investigate whether I have said anything (b) which I did not know, i.e. How could I have said this, which I did not even know? In other letters (III, VI and XII) he expresses his denials in a formal oath: Yhwh lives to punish me, if ever I have read any letter not intended for me.

The gate-room, where the correspondence was found, was possibly used on occasions as a court-room, where these and other documents were produced as evidence from the governor's archives, and submitted to a court-martial, which may have examined Hoshaiah after he had withdrawn to Lachish. Thus the letters would have been messages written some time before the inquiry, some a few days, others perhaps months or even years, before the final fall of the city.

TOPOGRAPHY

The last sentence in Letter IV establishes that the residence of "my lord", the recipient of the correspondence, was at Lachish. Thus the site of Tell ed Duweir, where the sherds were found, must now be identified with that great Judaean stronghold.

The contents of the letters and their probable connexion with events recorded in the Bible seem to indicate the ancient Qiryat-Ye'arim as the place whence Hoshaiah sent his letters to Jaush.

CULTURE AND RELIGION

Many facts concerning the language, the knowledge and method of writing, the use of fire-beacons for military signals, the mentioning of a village rest-house[1] at Hoshaiah's post, and other details throw light on the cultural conditions in ancient Judah.

As the formation of the personal names in the letters shows, the men mentioned by the writer were all faithful worshippers of Yhwh. This is surprising, for the prophets directed unceasing recrimination against Judah's treachery to Yhwh. Perhaps special religious conditions existed west of Jerusalem at that time, owing, as it seems, both to the lasting effect of Josiah's reformation (II Kings XXII, XXIII), and to the fact that the people of the district may have formed a religious party following the prophet Urijah of Kirjath-Jearim.

THE LACHISH LETTERS AND THE BIBLE

Letter III mentions a "prophet" or "open-eyed", *i.e.* seer. His name apparently occurred in Letter XVI, but the crucial part is missing. In the twenty-sixth chapter of Jeremiah the story of Urijah (Uriyah) of Kirjath-Jearim is recorded. Like Jeremiah, he spoke against the government; king Jehoiakim wanted to put him to death, but he fled to Egypt and was brought back to Jerusalem by the commander of the army, Elnatan the son of Achbor, and killed there.

Parallel facts in the letters strongly suggest that the "prophet" is to be identified with this Biblical character. In Letter VI, the writer states that the king accuses the prophet of demoralizing words which "loosen the hands, weaken the hands of country and city" (*cf.* Jeremiah XXXVIII, 4). He implores Jaush to write to the king and his officers asking them not "to do thus". In Letter III it is stated that the commander of the army, Achbor the son of Elnatan, has gone down to Egypt with some men.

If Urijah's destructive activity commenced at the beginning of Jehoiakim's reign, it is possible that it was not until Judah's alliance with Egypt against Babylon, that the king could arrange for the extradition of his enemy. Perhaps the arrangements were not completed until the reign of Zedekiah. In Letter III, Nedabiah, a relation (the word used is equivalent to the Latin *nepos*) of the king is mentioned. If he is to be identified with Nedabiah, son of king Jeconiah (I Chronicles III, 18), his youth would not preclude a date in Zedekiah's reign. It was also Zedekiah's policy to rely on Egypt for support, and he suppressed the advocates of peace with Babylonia.

Urijah's death and Hoshaiah's letters about him, may be dated only a few years before Nebuchadnezzar's second campaign against Judah in 588–587 B.C., and his destruction of Lachish, Azeqah and Jerusalem recorded in Jeremiah XXXIV, 7.

Further study may reveal new points which may tend to clarify the doubtful passages, and it is hoped that this full presentation of the texts may stimulate research and discussion of these invaluable documents by other scholars.

---

[1] For a modern parallel *cf.* the following extract from *The Palestine Post*, June 22nd, 1937:

"SACRED HOSPITALITY
ARAB WOUNDED IN GUEST HOUSE
A crime looked upon as a violation of the sacred rules of Arab hospitality was committed on Saturday night in Kalkilieh village.

Ibrahim Hussein Nassar was shot and wounded while sleeping in the guest house (*madaffa*) of the village. He was removed to hospital and two persons have been arrested on suspicion."

FREE TRANSLATIONS OF THE LACHISH LETTERS

LETTER I

> Gemariah son of Hissiliah,
> Jaazaniah son of Tobshillem,
> Hagab son of Jaazaniah,
> Mibtahiah son of Jeremiah,
> Mattaniah son of Neriah.

LETTER II

To my lord Jaush: May Yhwh soon let my lord hear pleasant tidings! Who am I, your slave, a dog, that you have remembered me? May Yhwh investigate (and punish me) if I have spoken about a thing, of which I did not even know.

LETTER III

Your slave Hoshaiah writes to inform his lord Jaush. May Yhwh give you prosperous tidings! And now: I have written to the seer, referring to the letter which you sent to me yesterday, and have told him that my heart is sick since I had your letter and that I declare: "My lord, I cannot read a letter. Yhwh lives (to punish me) if any one has ever tried to read me a letter. I have not read any letter which came to me, nor seen anything of it."
And I have been told that the commander of the army, Achbor, the son of Elnathan, has gone down to Egypt, and he has sent an order to take Hodaviah, the son of Ahijah and his men from here. And the letter which Nedabiah, the king's grandchild (or grand-nephew) has brought from the prophet to Shallum, the son of Jaddua, saying: "Beware!", have I sent to you.

LETTER IV

May Yhwh soon let my lord hear good tidings!
I have carried out all the instructions you have sent me, and have recorded on the page all that you ordered me. You instructed me also about the rest-house, but there is nobody there. And Shemaiah has taken Semachiah and brought him up to the city (Jerusalem), and I will write and find out where he is. Because if on his rounds (turnings) he had inspected, he would have known that we are watching for the signal-stations of Lachish, according to all the signals you are giving, because we cannot see the signals of Azeqah.

LETTER V

May Yhwh soon let my lord hear good and pleasant tidings! Who am I, your slave, a dog, that you have sent me . . . iah's letter? And now I have returned the letters to you.
May Yhwh tell you what has happened! Who am I, that I should curse the king's seed in Yhwh's name?

LETTER VI

To my lord Jaush. May Yhwh let us see you in prosperity! Who am I, your slave, a dog, that you should send me the letter of the king and the letters of the officers, saying: "Read, and you will see that the words of the (prophet) are not good, and are lowering the morale of the whole country and the city". . . . My lord, will you not write to them saying: "Why should you do thus?" Yhwh your God lives and you live to punish me if I have read the letter or got any one to read the letter to me or seen anything of it.

LETTER IX

May Yhwh give my lord pleasant tidings!
Who am I, your slave, a dog, that you should send me the letters of . . . I have returned them to you.
May Yhwh tell you exactly what has happened!

LETTER XVIII

This evening, when Tobshillem arrives, I shall send your letter up to the city (Jerusalem). . . .

INDEX OF BIBLICAL REFERENCES

PERSONAL NAMES

THIS index contains only those personal names mentioned individually, and excludes those mentioned solely as examples for linguistical rules. For general observations on personal names and for terms compounded with personal names (as Mesha-stone, etc.), *see* General Index, *pages* 216 ff. For personal names occurring in the Lachish Letters, *see* the table of "Personal Names Mentioned in the Lachish Letters", *page* 198. The asterisk (*) in this index denotes main passages in which the names so marked are discussed. The Biblical personal names are given in this index in their usual English spelling, and only where this seems necessary an approximate[1] transcription of their Hebrew pronunciation is added in brackets.

[1] According to recent studies, now partly published in *Monatsschrift für Geschichte und Wissenschaft des Judentums*, 1937, *pages* 340–351, and in the Hebrew Quarterly *Leshonenu*, VIII, *pages* 297–306, the Greek and Latin transcriptions of Hebrew represent a later pronunciation, based decisively upon Babylonian phonetics acquired by the Jews in the Babylonian exile, while pre-exilic Hebrew differed from it in main points, pronouncing *e.g.* also כ, פ, ת throughout as k, p, t, not as ch, ph, th (Akbor, Shapan, Elnatan, not Akhbor, Shaphan, Elnathan). However, in this publication, the transcription adopted in 1935 has not been changed.

GENERAL INDEX

For place-names occurring in the Lachish Letters, *see also* the Glossary of
Hebrew Words, *page* 203

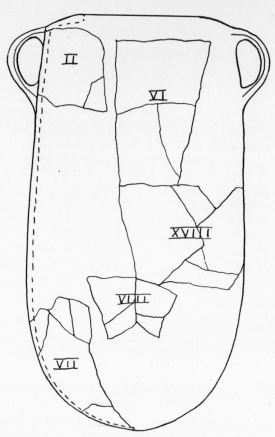

Reconstruction of pottery vessel, showing the positions of sherds which form part of a single pot.

(c)	(b)	(a)
		בראשית ברא
		אלהים את
		השמים ואת
		הארץ והארץ
		היתה תהו
		ובהו וחשך
		על פני תהום
		ורוח אלהים
		מרחפת על
		פני המים
		ויאמר אלהים
		יהי אור
		ויהי אור
		וירא אלהום
		את האור כי
		טוב ויבדל
		אלהים בין

The first verses of Genesis I, in (a) "Assyrian" Hebrew script; (b) modern Samaritan script; and (c) VIth century B.C. Judaean script

INNER GATEWAY WITHIN SOUTH-WEST BASTION

showing rising cobbled approach running up to original threshold with upper and later
stone sill of Persian gateway left *in situ*. Drain from city passing below lower sill.

COURT OR GUARD ROOM (F. 18 C) IN EASTERN TOWER ADJOINING OUTER GATE.

Late Judaean period.   Discovered after removal of later Persian ruin.   Hasan Awad (Hanajreh Bedawy) clearing burnt deposit in which "The Lachish Letters" were found.   Inner city gate left, with ruin of flanking tower.   City wall against skyline.

Photograph by R. Richmond Brown

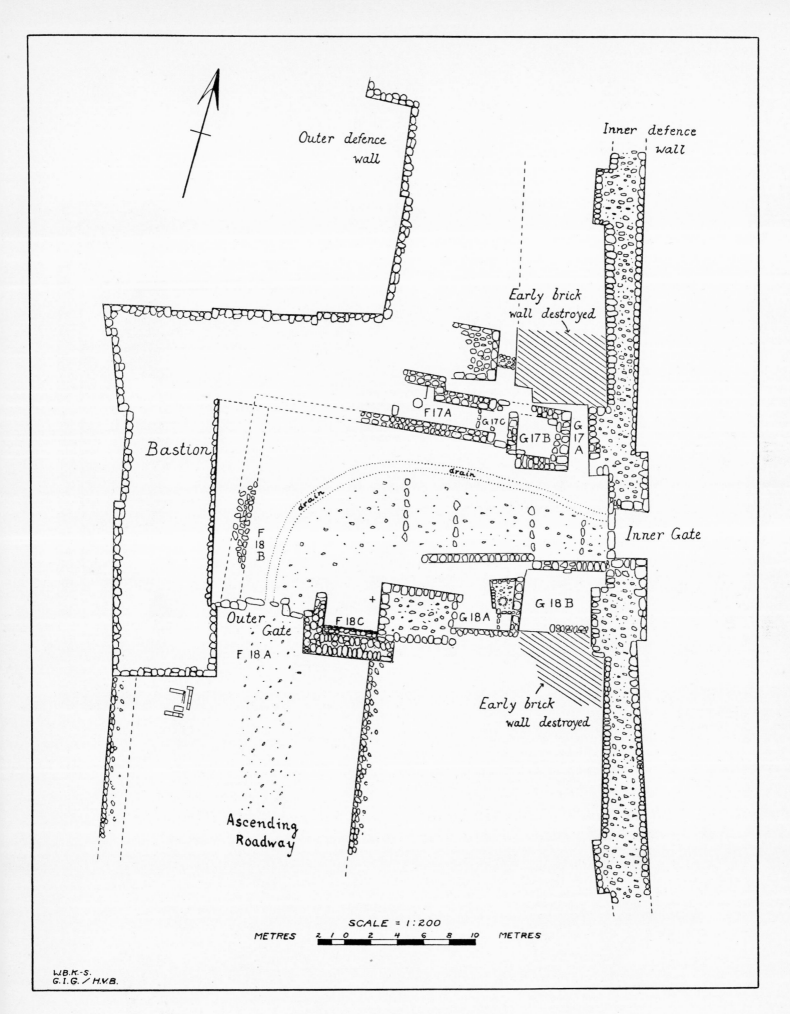

Outer defence
wall

Inner defence
wall

Early brick
wall destroyed

Bastion

F 17 A

G 17 C

G 17 B

G
17
A

drain

drain

F
18
B

Inner Gate

F 18 C

G 18 A

G 18 B

Outer
Gate

F 18 A

+

Early brick
wall destroyed

Ascending
Roadway

SCALE = 1:200

METRES   2 1 0 2   4   6   8   10   METRES

W.B.K.-S.
G.I.G. / H.V.B.

PLAN OF BASTION AND GATEWAYS.